SIGMUND FREUD:
ESSAYS AND PAPERS

ESSAYS AND PAPERS

Sigmund Freud

Authorized Translation from the
German under the supervision of
Joan Riviere

Selected, with a preface by
Lisa Appignanesi

riverrun

The texts in this selection are sourced from *A General Introduction To Psychoanalysis: The Classic Work On the Subject, A Complete explanation in clear, simple language by Freud Himself*, 1962, by Washington Square Press, *Collected Papers Volume I*, 1946, by Hogarth Press, *Collected Papers Volume II*, 1950, by Hogarth Press and *Collected Papers Volume IV*, 1957, by Hogarth Press.

This edition published in Great Britain in 2020 by

riverrun

An imprint of

Quercus Editions Ltd
Carmelite House
50 Victoria Embankment
London EC4Y oDZ

An Hachette UK company

A CIP catalogue record for this book is available
from the British Library

PB ISBN 978 1 78747 932 6
EBOOK ISBN 978 1 78747 931 9

Every effort has been made to contact copyright holders. However, the publishers
will be glad to rectify in future editions any inadvertent omissions brought to their attention.

Quercus Editions Ltd hereby exclude all liability to the extent permitted by law for any errors
or omissions in this book and for any loss, damage or expense (whether direct or indirect)
suffered by a third party relying on any information contained in this book.

10 9 8 7 6 5 4 3 2 1

Typeset by CC Book Production

Printed and bound in Great Britain by Clays Ltd, Elcograf S.p.A.

Papers used by Quercus are from well-managed forests and other responsible sources.

Contents

Preface   *vii*

The Aetiology of Hysteria (1896)   3

Clinical Papers

The Sexual Enlightenment of Children (1907)   47

A Case of Paranoia Running Counter to the
    Psycho-Analytical Theory of Disease (1915)   58

The Psychogenesis of a Case of Homosexuality
    in a Woman (1920)   72

The Economic Problem in Masochism (1924)   109

Papers on Technique

Observations on 'Wild' Psycho-Analysis (1910)   129

The Dynamics of the Transference (1912)   139

On Beginning the Treatment: The Question of the First
    Communications. The Dynamics of the Cure (1913)   151

Recollection, Repetition, and Working Through (1914)   180

Observations on Transference-Love (1915)   193

Papers on Metapsychology

Formulations regarding the Two Principles in
Mental Functioning (1911)   213

On Narcissism: An Introduction (1914)   223

Instincts and their Vicissitudes (1915)   261

Repression (1915)   291

Mourning and Melancholia (1917)   308

Papers on Applied Psycho-Analysis

The Most Prevalent Form of
Degradation in Erotic Life (1912)   333

Some Character-Types Met with
in Psycho-Analytic Work (1915)   351

One of the Difficulties of Psycho-Analysis (1917)   382

The 'Uncanny' (1919)   394

Endnotes   439

Preface

SIGMUND FREUD ARRIVED IN the English language abetted by a remarkable and talented midwife – Joan Riviere. Her wit, her lucidity and leaps of metaphoric imagination, as well as her background, mark her out as close kin of the Bloomsbury Group, even if she doesn't often feature in its annals. Freud's own language had been shaped in that hothouse of the modern which was turn-of-the-nineteenth-century Vienna. His style distinguished him from the German scientists and academics of his day: it largely lacked their pedantry and convoluted long-windedness. Instead, Freud addresses his readers and listeners directly, collars us, argues, ironizes, and often enough engrosses as readily as a novelist. Riviere's fluent German, her 'ear', was attuned to Freud's both from his writings and her year on his couch. Translation, after all, may be another form of transference.

Though she was not Freud's earliest translator into English, nor his last, Joan Riviere was the first to give his work – his *writing* itself – the place it warrants in the literary canon.

Unsurprisingly perhaps, she did so under the aegis of the Hogarth Press, the publishing house run by Leonard and Virginia Woolf. Alongside Woolf's own works, this crucible of modernism published the vanguard of Britain in the wake of the Great War: from T. S. Eliot, Gertrude Stein and E. M. Forster on the literary front to thinkers like the economist John Maynard Keynes and Sigmund Freud – who was something of an honorary Englishman by the time four volumes of his *Collected Papers*, in an 'authorized translation under the supervision of Joan Riviere' appeared.

Riviere was a remarkable woman. Born in 1883 to Hugh John Verrall, a solicitor from an old county family in Lewes with literary connections dating back to Tom Paine, and Anna Hodgson, a vicar's daughter who had been a governess before she married, Joan was sent to Wycombe Abbey, a leading boarding school for girls. The stillbirth of a brother had preceded her arrival by a year and her relations with her mother remained difficult. She idolized her father. At seventeen, for reasons that remain unclear, but may have had something to do with rebelliousness, she was sent to Gotha to learn German and complete her studies. On her return, in line with her marked talent for design and drawing, she took up an apprenticeship with the firm of Nettleship, the court dressmaker. An eye for beauty stayed with her throughout her life and was manifest in her home and personal, as well as her writing, style.

Riviere's more academic bent was honed in Cambridge where

her uncle, the illustrious classicist A. W. Verrall, lectured. A pioneering spirit, Verrall was renowned for his ability to 'cut through conventional attitudes and superficial shams'.[1] His wife, Margaret Merrifield, was attached to Newnham College and her feminist agenda influenced Riviere. Verrall was a prominent figure in the Society for Psychical Research, a group instrumental in fostering interest in Freud and psychoanalysis in the early part of the century. Indeed Freud contributed 'A Note on the Unconscious and Psychoanalysis' to its proceedings in 1912.

For over half a century, the meetings and social gatherings of the Verrall circle stayed fresh for James Strachey, Lytton's younger brother, who eventually became a psychoanalyst and translator of the *Standard Edition* of Freud's work in English. Strachey first met Joan Riviere at the Verralls' salon as an undergraduate. In his 1962 obituary of her, he wrote: 'I still have a vivid visual picture of her standing by the fireplace at an evening party, tall, strikingly handsome, distinguished-looking, and somehow impressive.'[2]

The combination of class and beauty affected and somewhat frightened Ernest Jones, the central figure in the founding of psychoanalysis in Britain, and the son of a Welsh mining clerk. Joan Riviere went to see him in 1916. By then, she had already been married for some ten years to Evelyn Riviere, a Chancery barrister and the son of a Royal Academician. The couple's daughter was born in 1908 and soon afterwards Joan's beloved father died. She plunged into a breakdown and received the same conventional,

Edwardian, treatment for 'nerves' as had Virginia Woolf, a mixture of rest and sedation in the confinement of a clinic. For a while the two women shared a doctor, but Riviere, perhaps under the influence of her uncle's circle, went on to engage in psychoanalytic treatment, first with Ernest Jones whom she saw – with the break of a year when tuberculosis struck – until June 1921.

Jones recognized how formidably intelligent she was and recruited her into the fold. By war's end in 1918, she was already seeing patients of her own and was amongst Britain's first lay analysts, a member of the newly formed British Psycho-Analytical Society. But along the way, Riviere fell in love with the mercurial Jones. When he referred her for further analysis to Freud in a letter of 21 January 1922, he confessed that her case was 'the worst failure I have ever had'. Desperate at what she experienced as the 'hardness' of Jones's rejection of her, Riviere had grown suicidal.

Freud had already provided something of an extricating analysis for an earlier follower, C. G. Jung, who had sent Sabina Spielrein to the Professor when a transference had gone astray and patient and practitioner had become overly entangled – not only, in Jung's case, in fantasy alone. To give Jones his due, it was a particularly difficult and emotional time for him. During the period that he saw Joan Riviere, he broke up one relationship, entered into a quick marriage with someone else and tragically lost his new wife after little more than a single year. A year later, he was married again, this time for life.

The fact that Jones saw Riviere outside analytic hours acted as a spur to their messy entanglement. He encouraged her into the profession and into translating Freud's Introductory Lectures, something she did so brilliantly that she set a 'new standard', one which made it 'possible for the first time for readers of English to realize that Freud was not only a man of science but a master of prose writing', as James Strachey later put it. Early in the analysis, Jones also let Riviere stay in his country house, which as he openly stated to Freud was a mistake, though with an attempt at self-exoneration, he emphasized Riviere's 'strong complex of being a well-born lady' and having the 'most colossal narcissism imaginable':

> I underestimated the uncontrollability of her emotional reactions and in the first year made the serious error of lending her my country cottage for a week when I was not there, she having nowhere to go for a holiday. This led to a declaration of love and to the broken-hearted cry that she had never been rejected before (she has been the mistress of a number of men). From that time on she devoted herself to torturing me without any intermission and with considerable success and ingenuity, being a fiendish sadist . . . The treatment finally broke down over my inability to master this negative transference, though I tried all means in my power.[3]

When Freud, perhaps misreading the meaning of Jones's report of Riviere's 'declaration of love', and ever quick to take the patient's side in such matters since it was essential to a 'corrective' analysis, rebuked Jones, the latter protested that Riviere was not 'the type that attracts me erotically, though I certainly have the admiration for her intelligence that I would have with a man'.[4]

Riviere's analysis with Freud lasted almost nine months, brief by later standards, though she came back for top-ups, and Freud indicated he wished he could have her for another six months. But the experience enabled her to return to her family and carry on working, from all accounts in an improved manner, with colleagues and importantly with Ernest Jones. If her wit remained acerbic and her tongue sharp, Jones claimed early in 1924 that 'she has proved a most valuable and loyal co-operator, has given not the slightest trouble to anyone and is on the best of terms with myself'.

Freud's analysis of Riviere helped to shape the thinking he was doing in the early 1920s about the ego ideal and his second topography of the mind: the id, ego, and superego. He had a 'kind feeling towards her, partly based on her intellectual capacity and practical efficiency'. He confided to Jones:

> She cannot tolerate praise, triumph or success, not any better than failure, blame and repudiation . . . You know what that means, it is an infallible sign of a deep sense

of guilt, of a conflict between Ego and Ideal. So the interest in her case is turned to the narcissistic problem, it is a case of a character-analysis superadded to that of the neurosis. To be sure this conflict which is the cause of her continuous dissatisfaction, is not known to her consciousness; whenever it is revived she projects her self-criticism to other people, turns her pangs of conscience into sadistic behaviour, tries to render other people unhappy because she feels so herself. Our theory has not yet mastered the mechanism of these cases. It seems likely that the formation of a high and severe ideal took place with her at a very early age, but this ideal became superseded, 'repressed' with the onset of sexual maturity and ever since worked in the dark. Her sexual freedom may be an appearance, the keeping up of which required those conspicuous compensatory attitudes as haughtiness, majestic behaviour etc.[5]

Freud persuaded Jones to make Riviere the Translations Editor of the *International Journal*, which then published his close circle as well as many of his own articles. Alongside James Strachey, for a period contemporaneously in analysis with Freud, she was also part of the important Glossary Committee, responsible for turning Freud's key technical concepts into their English equivalents. Riviere thus became a key player in the way in which psychoanalysis was disseminated in English. She remained translations editor of the *Journal* until 1937, when she turned more of her attentions to her clinical practice: amongst her famous trainee patients were D. W. Winnicott, Hanna Segal, John Bowlby and Herbert Rosenfeld.

Riviere wrote a number of papers of her own which have become classics. She was one of the women who bridled at Freud's first ideas on femininity. 'Womanliness as a Masquerade' (1929) is an essay that has leapt across generations and influenced Judith Butler's own thinking on 'gender trouble'. As Freud's letter about Riviere already suggests, for Riviere there is no line of demarcation between genuine womanliness and its mask: 'whether radical or superficial, they are the same thing.' The case through which she elaborates her thinking may not be all that far from her own. The woman in question, she stresses, is of a generation more modern than Freud's. She is a professional, an intellectual who like so many of her kind fulfils the duties of her profession at least as well as the average man, all the while being an excellent wife and mother, interested in personal appearance, friends and family – in other words a woman who is both masculine and feminine. Yet despite her success and ability, she needs male reassurance and compulsively seeks both sexual and professional compliments after any public engagement, in order 'both to hide the possession of masculinity and to avert the reprisals expected if she was found to possess it'.[6] However, for her there is no genuine womanliness. The mask rules over the feminine, whether homo- or heterosexual.

Riviere's gifts as a translator extended to her translation of Melanie Klein, turning Klein's often murky German prose into powerful English renditions. In the eventual battles that took place within the British Society between Klein and Anna Freud, Riviere, despite incurring Freud's displeasure (or perhaps, given her fierce and prickly independence, abetted by this very fact), sided with Klein and helped to shape the long-time Kleinian persuasion of British psychoanalysis.

Nonetheless, her great understanding of Freud and his work, coupled with admiration, is ever evident. They shared a love of literature, which is perhaps what also made her so attuned to the translation enterprise. In 'A Last Word about Freud', something of an obituary piece, she notes:

> the aim of impressing himself on people seemed to be lacking or minimal in him. Yet he had developed this special capacity for presenting his conclusions as if he were bent on enabling the reader to take them in — so much so that it colours his whole style and gives the presentation a simplicity and lucidity . . . that is peculiar to him and most rare in such work . . . I came more and more to realize the underlying importance in him of the creative side of his work.[7]

Freud the writer is what Joan Riviere so elegantly presents to the English language reader. This volume focuses in on the

Collected Papers – the set of supervised translations that made up the first library of Freud in English. It does not include Riviere's longer translations – *A General Introduction to Psychoanalysis* (later known as the *Introductory Lectures*) or the felicitously named *Civilization and its Discontents*, Riviere's title for *Das Unbehagen in der Kultur*, a title in English which became a catchphrase all of its own. Nor does it include the famous case histories translated by James and Alix Strachey, which are readily available in any number of imprints.

Instead, the focus here is on Freud the essayist. It is in the essays that so many of Freud's most fertile ideas and insights occur. Too often, we only know these at second or third hand, purveyed by other writers, sometimes cited, at others simply assimilated into received culture without reference to their originary source.

From the Collected Papers, whose sequence Riviere carefully organized – at first with Ernest Jones (and by the time of Volume 4 with the analyst Masud Khan), and whose translations she either oversaw, edited or undertook herself – I have chosen only one paper from the earliest writings in order to draw the reader's attention to Freud's thinking: namely 'The Aetiology of Hysteria', written in 1896, a moment when he was leaving behind neurological models to concentrate on nascent psychoanalytical ones. Thereafter the classification of these papers – in some cases truly kin to Montaigne in their *essai* or attempt to arrive at the understanding of a problem – I have kept the classification of the original volumes. Clinical papers, whatever their date, are grouped together, as are the Papers on Technique, on Metapsychology and on Applied Psychoanalysis.

These are amongst my favourite of Freud's writings. 'The Psychogenesis of a Case of Homosexuality in a Woman' bears some of the elements of 'Dora' but presented by a master story-teller of post-World War One Vienna, and one open to the vagaries of his patients. The Papers on Technique illuminate the many imponderables of psychoanalytic practice, while the more theoretical and speculative Papers on Metapsychology bring to the fore a Freud whom we cannot seem to get round or beyond, even in our new century. For the literary and the social historians, there is no better Freud than the Papers on Applied Psychoanalysis.

It is a rich brew and I hope it is one that may both stimulate and prove useful to readers of Freud, new and old.

I am grateful to Paul Keegan, the editor of this series, for all his help in sifting a volume of Riviere's Freud. No less than the man she translated is she a figure to be hidden from history. The papers collected in this volume were either translated by Joan Riviere or overseen by her with her usual rigour.

Lisa Appignanesi

Sigmund Freud:
Essays and Papers

The Aetiology of Hysteria

(1896)

I

WHEN WE ENDEAVOUR to form some opinion about the causation of a morbid condition such as that of hysteria we first of all adopt the method of anamnestic inquiry, examining the patient or his friends about the harmful influences to which they themselves trace the appearance of the particular neurotic symptoms. The value of what we discover in this way is, of course, impaired by all the various circumstances which commonly conceal from a patient the knowledge of his own condition – his lack of scientific understanding of aetiological influences, the fallacy *post hoc, ergo propter hoc*, the distress it causes him to think or speak of certain noxiae and traumas. Hence, in making any such inquiry we adhere to the principle of not adopting the patients' belief without a thorough critical examination and not allowing them to lay down for us our scientific opinion upon the aetiology of the neurosis. Although on the one hand we acknowledge certain constantly recurring statements, as that the hysterical condition is a long-persisting effect of an emotional disturbance which once took place, we have on the other hand introduced into the aetiology of hysteria a factor which the patient himself never cites and only reluctantly admits – namely, the disposition inherited from his parents. You know that in the opinion of the influential school of Charcot heredity alone is to be recognized as the real cause of hysteria, whilst all other harmful influences of the most varying kind and intensity only play the part of exciting causes, of '*agents provocateurs*'.

You will readily admit that it would be desirable to find another way of arriving at the aetiology of hysteria, one in which we should feel less dependent on the statements of the patients themselves. The dermatologist, for instance, is able to recognize the luetic character of a sore from the nature of its edges, of the crust upon it and from its shape, without being misled by the protestation of the patient who denies any source of infection. In forensic medicine, the physician can explain how an injury has been caused, even without any information from the injured person. Now in hysteria there exists a similar possibility of penetrating from the symptoms to knowledge of their causes. As for what concerns the relation which the method to be employed bears to the older method of anamnestic inquiry, I will put before you a simile taken from an advance which has in fact been made in another field of work.

Imagine that an explorer comes in his travels to a region of which but little is known and that there his interest is aroused by ruins showing remains of walls, fragments of pillars and of tablets with obliterated and illegible inscriptions. He may content himself with inspecting what lies there on the surface and with questioning the people who live near by, perhaps semi-barbaric natives, about what tradition tells of the history and meaning of these monumental remains, and taking notes of their statements – and then go his way. But he may proceed differently; he may have come equipped with picks, shovels and spades, and may press the inhabitants into his service and arm them with these tools, make an onslaught on the ruins, clear away the rubbish and, starting from the visible remains, may bring to light what is buried. If his work is crowned with success, the discoveries explain themselves; the ruined walls are part of the ramparts of a palace or a treasure-house, from the ruined pillars a temple can be constructed, the many inscriptions, which by good luck may be bilingual, reveal an alphabet and a language, and when deciphered and translated may yield undreamt-of information about the events of the past, to commemorate which these monuments were built. *Saxa loquuntur!*

If one tries in something the same way to let the symptoms of a case of hysteria tell the tale of the development of the disease, we must start from the momentous discovery of J. Breuer: that the symptoms of hysteria (apart from stigmata) are determined by certain experiences of the patient's which operate traumatically and are reproduced in his psychic life as memory-symbols of these experiences. We must adopt Breuer's method – or one of a similar kind – in order to lead the patient's attention from the symptom back to the scene in and through which it originated; and having thus discovered it, we proceed when the traumatic scene is reproduced to correct the original psychical reaction to it and thus remove the symptom.

It is no part of my intention today to treat of the difficult technique of this therapeutic method or the psychological revelations it has achieved. I had to start from this point, simply because analyses conducted on Breuer's method seem at the same time to open up the way to the causes of hysteria. If we subject a large number of symptoms in many people to this analysis, we shall come to know of a correspondingly large number of traumatically operative scenes. We have learnt to recognize in these experiences the efficient causes of hysteria; hence we may hope to discover from the study of these traumatic scenes by what influences and in what ways hysterical symptoms are produced.

That this expectation is justified follows from the fact that Breuer's theses, when put to the test in more numerous cases, prove to be actually correct. But the way from the symptoms of hysteria to its aetiology is longer and introduces us to all sorts of unexpected connections.

For let us be quite clear that tracing an hysterical symptom back to a traumatic scene assists our understanding only if the scene in question fulfils two conditions – if it possesses the

6

required *determining quality* and if we can credit it with the necessary *traumatic power*. Let me give an illustration instead of a mere explanation of terms. Suppose that the symptom in question is that of hysterical vomiting, we think we can apprehend its cause (or at any rate leave only a certain part unexplained) if analysis traces the symptom to an experience which justifiably gave rise to a high degree of disgust, for instance the sight of a decomposing corpse. Supposing, instead of this, analysis traces back the vomiting to some great shock, e.g. a railway accident, this explanation will be unsatisfactory and we shall have to ask ourselves how it is that the shock led to the particular symptom of vomiting. This derivation of the symptom lacks determining quality. We have another instance of an unsatisfactory explanation when the vomiting is said to have originated in eating a fruit which had a rotten spot in it. Then the vomiting is indeed determined by disgust, but we cannot understand how the disgust in this case could be so powerful as to perpetuate itself in an hysterical symptom; the experience lacks traumatic power.

Now let us consider to what extent the traumatic scenes of hysteria which are revealed in analysis fulfil the two above requirements in a large number of symptoms and cases. Here we encounter our first great disappointment. It does sometimes happen that the traumatic scene in which the symptom originated really possesses both properties which we require in order to understand the symptom: determining quality and traumatic force. But far oftener – incomparably so – we find realized one of three other possibilities which are very difficult to understand: either the scene indicated by analysis in which the symptom first made its appearance seems to us not qualified to determine the symptom, for its content bears no relation to the form of that symptom; or the ostensibly traumatic experience whose content is so related proves to be a normally harmless impression, one which ordinarily would have no effect; or finally the 'traumatic scene' disconcerts us in both directions, appearing both harmless and altogether unrelated to the peculiar form of the hysterical symptom.

(Here I may remark in passing that Breuer's conception of the origin of hysterical symptoms is not affected by the discovery of traumatic scenes which represent experiences in themselves insignificant. For Breuer assumed – in agreement with Charcot – that even a harmless experience may acquire the significance of a trauma and may develop determining power when the subject is in a particular psychic condition, the so-called *hypnoid state*. I find, however, that often there are no grounds for presupposing such hypnoid states. What is definite is that the theory of hypnoid states contributes nothing to the solution of the other difficulties, namely, that so often the traumatic scenes are lacking in determining quality.)

Moreover, this first disappointment in the practice of Breuer's method is followed immediately by another which must be specially grievous to a physician. Such derivations as these which do not contribute to our understanding of the case in respect of determining quality and traumatic force are also of no therapeutic advantage; the patient keeps his symptoms unaltered, in spite of the first result yielded by analysis. You will understand how great the temptation then is to go no further with work which, apart from this, is laborious.

But perhaps we only need a fresh inspiration to help us out of our dilemma and lead to valuable results. Here it is: we know indeed through Breuer that hysterical symptoms may be resolved if, starting from them, we can find our way back to the memory of a traumatic experience. If the memory so revealed does not answer our expectations, possibly we must pursue the same path a little further; perhaps there is hidden behind the first traumatic scene the recollection of a second, which satisfies our requirements better and the reproduction of which has a better therapeutic result, so that the scene first discovered has only the significance of a link in the chain of association. And perhaps this situation repeats itself, inoperative scenes being in several places interpolated as necessary transitions in the reproduction, till finally, starting from the hysterical symptom, we arrive at the scene which really operates traumatically and is in every respect, from both the therapeutic and the analytic point of view, satisfactory. Well, this supposition is correct. When the scene first revealed does not satisfy our requirements, we say to the patient that this experience does not explain anything, but that there must be hidden behind it an earlier and more significant experience, and, following the same technique, we direct his attention to that strand in the associations which unites both memories – that which we have found and that which we have still to find.[2] Continuation of the analysis then leads in every instance to the reproduction of new scenes of the kind we should expect; for example, to instance again the case of hysterical vomiting which I selected before and which was first referred by analysis to the shock of a railway accident. Now although this experience lacks the determining quality, I find on further analysis that this accident woke the memory of another which had happened previously, in which the patient had not, it is true, been himself involved, but which was the occasion of his seeing a corpse, a sight which aroused in him horror and disgust. It is as though the combined influence of these two scenes led to the fulfilment of our two postulates, the one experience supplying, in the shock, the traumatic force and the other, in its content, the determining influence. The other instance, where the vomiting was traced to eating an apple in which there was a rotten spot, is amplified through analysis somewhat as follows: the rotting apple roused the memory of a former experience of picking up fallen apples in a garden when the patient happened to come on the loathsome carcase of an animal.

I will not again return to these examples, for I must admit that they are not taken from any case in my experience, but that I invented them, and most probably they are bad inventions; I myself regard such explanations of hysterical symptoms as impossible. But there were several reasons why I had to make up examples, and one reason I can state at once. The real examples are all of them far and away more complicated; to relate a single one of them in detail would occupy the whole of this lecture hour. The chain of associations has always more than two links; the traumatic scenes do not form simple rows like a pearl necklace, but they branch out and are interconnected like genealogical trees, a new experience being influenced by two or more earlier ones in the form of memories; in short, to give an account of the resolution of a single symptom is practically synonymous with the task of giving a complete history of a case.

But now I must not neglect to lay special emphasisis on the one conclusion derived, quite unexpectedly, from analytic work by means of these chains of recollections. We have found out that no hysterical symptom can originate in one real experience alone, but that in every instance the memory roused by association co-operates with earlier experiences in causing the symptom. If this conclusion is (as I believe) *without exception* correct, it indicates the foundation upon which a psychological theory of hysteria is to be built.

You might think that those rare instances in which analysis can trace the symptom immediately to a traumatic scene of satisfactory determining quality and traumatic force and, by so tracing it, at the same time remove it (as described in Breuer's history of the case of Anna O.) would surely constitute powerful objections to the general validity of the conclusion just propounded. Certainly it looks as if that were so; but I can assure you I have the best of reasons for assuming that even in these cases there exists a chain of operative memories which stretches far back behind the traumatic scene, even though the reproduction of the latter alone may result in the removal of the symptom.

In my opinion it is really astonishing that hysterical symptoms should arise only where memories are at work, especially when we reflect that these memories, according to all the statements of the patients themselves, did not come into consciousness at the moment when the symptom first made its appearance. Here is food for much reflection, but for the present we must not let these problems deflect the course of our discussion of the aetiology of hysteria. Rather we must ask ourselves: where shall we get to if we follow the chain of associated memories revealed to us by analysis? How far do they go? Is there any point at which they come naturally to an end? Do they perhaps lead to experiences which are in any way similar, whether by relation of time or of content, so that in these universally similar factors we may discern that aetiology of hysteria for which we are seeking?

My experience up till now enables me already to answer these questions. Taking a case which presents several symptoms, from whatever symptom we start we arrive by means of analysis at a series of experiences the memories of which are linked together by association. At first the memory-chains are distinct from one another as they lead backwards, but, as we said before, they branch out; from a single scene two or more memories may be reached at the same time, and from these again there issue side-chains the single links of which may in their turn be joined by association to links of the main chain. The metaphor of a family tree of which the members have also intermarried is really not a bad one. Other complications in the linking up of the chains arise from the circumstance that a single scene in the same chain may be several times recalled to memory, so that it is related in more than one way to a later scene, and may prove both to be directly connected with it and also to be joined by means of intermediate links. In short, the connection is by no means a simple one, and the fact that the scenes are discovered in reverse chronological order (the very feature which justifies our comparison with the excavation of ruins) certainly does not contribute to a more rapid understanding of the process.

New complications are met if the analysis is pursued further. The chains of associations for the separate symptoms then begin to enter into relation with one another; the family trees intertwine. When we come to a certain experience in the memory-chain which has reference, for instance, to the symptom of vomiting, besides the backward-leading links in this chain, there is revived a memory which belongs to another chain and which is the basis of another symptom, perhaps that of headaches. So that experience belongs to both series and thus constitutes a *nodal point*, several of which are to be found in every analysis. Its clinical correlation may perhaps be that from a certain time on the two symptoms occur together, symbiotically, really without any inner mutual dependence. Still further back we find nodal points of another sort. There the chains of associations converge; we find experiences in which two or more symptoms have originated. One chain has attached itself to one detail of the scene and a second chain to another detail.

But the most important result arrived at by such a consistent pursuit of analysis is this: whatever case and whatever symptom we take as our starting-point, *in the end we infallibly come to the realm of sexual experience.* So here for the first time we would seem to have discovered an aetiological condition of hysterical symptoms.

From previous experience I can foresee that it is just against this conclusion or against its universal validity that your opposition will be directed. Perhaps it would be more correct to say: your inclination to opposition, for probably none of you can refer to investigations which, if the same method had been employed, would have yielded a different result. On the actual matter in dispute I will only remark that in my case at least there was no preconceived opinion which led me to single out the sexual factor in the aetiology of hysteria. The two investigators as whose pupil I began my work on the subject, Charcot and Breuer, emphatically had no such presupposition, in fact they had a personal disinclination to it which I originally shared. Only the most laborious and detailed investigations have converted me, and that slowly enough, to the opinion which I defend today. If you subject to the closest scrutiny my assertion that the aetiology of hysteria is to be sought in the sexual life, it amounts to the statement that I can assure you that, in some eighteen cases of hysteria, I was able to recognize this connection to hold for every single symptom and, when circumstances permitted, to confirm the fact by therapeutic success. You may of course object that the nineteenth and twentieth analyses would perhaps show that hysterical symptoms can be derived from other sources also, and that thus the validity of the sexual aetiology would not be universal but would be reduced to 80 per cent. By all means let us wait and see, but since those eighteen cases are at the same time *all* those which I was able to analyse, and since nobody picked them out to please me, you will understand that I do not share any such expectation, but am prepared to let my belief outrun the evidential force of my discoveries up to the present time. Besides, I am influenced by yet another motive, which for the moment is of merely subjective value. In the single attempt to explain the physiological and psychical mechanism of hysteria that I have made for the purpose of embracing the results of my observations, I have found the participation of sexual impulses an indispensable hypothesis.

So, the memory-chains having converged, we come at last to sexual things and to some few experiences which for the most part occur at the same period of life, namely, the age of puberty. In these experiences we are to find the aetiology of hysteria and through them learn to understand how hysterical symptoms originate. But here we meet with a fresh disappointment and a grave one. It is true that these experiences which have been discovered and extracted from the whole mass of memories with such difficulty and seemed to be the ultimate traumata, have two characteristics in common: they are sexual and they occur at the time of puberty, but otherwise they are very different in kind and unequal in importance. In some cases it was a matter of experiences which must be recognized as serious traumata – an attempt at rape, revealing at one blow to the immature girl the whole brutality of sexual desire; or the involuntary witnessing of sexual acts on the part of the parents, which at one and the same time reveals unsuspected ugliness and wounds both the childish and the moral sensibility; and so forth. In other cases these experiences are astonishingly trivial. The experience on which the neurosis of one of my patients was shown to be based was that a boy friend had stroked her hand caressingly and on another occasion had pressed his leg against her dress as they sat side by side at table, his expression at the same time leading her to guess that this was something forbidden. With another young lady, hearing a riddle which suggested an obscene answer actually sufficed to call forth the first anxiety-attack with which the illness began. Clearly, discoveries such as these are not favourable to an understanding of the cause of hysterical symptoms. If both serious and trifling occurrences, experiences undergone by the patient in person as well as visual impressions and verbal communications may be recognized as the ultimate traumata of hysteria, we may perhaps put forward the explanation that hysterics are peculiarly constituted human beings – probably on account of some hereditary disposition or process of degeneration – in whom the shrinking from sexuality which normally plays a certain part at the age of puberty is developed to a pathological extent and is permanently retained; so to speak, persons who are not adequate mentally to the demands of sexuality. It is true that in this statement we pass over hysteria in men; but, even without such an obvious objection, it would scarcely be a very great temptation to halt at this solution. We are only too conscious intellectually that we have here something only half understood, something obscure and unsatisfactory.

Luckily for our explanation, certain of these sexual experiences at puberty display a further inadequacy likely to stimulate us to continue our analytic work. For we find that these experiences may also too lack the determining quality, though this is much rarer than in the traumatic scenes of later life. So, for example, the two patients whom I spoke of above as cases in which the experiences of puberty were actually harmless began, in consequence of those experiences, to suffer from peculiar painful sensations in the genital organs. These sensations had persisted as main symptoms of the neurosis, but it could not be shown that they were determined either by the scenes at puberty or by later ones; certainly they were neither normal organic sensations nor manifestations of sexual excitation. Does it not then seem obvious to say that we must look for the determining quality of these symptoms in yet other experiences, dating from an even earlier period; that here, for the second time, we must follow that saving inspiration which led us before from the first traumatic scenes to the memory-chains? To be sure, by so doing, we get back to the time of earliest childhood, the time before the sexual life developed, and this would seem to involve abandoning our sexual aetiology. But have we no right to assume that even the age of childhood is not without delicate sexual excitations, more, that perhaps the later sexual development is decisively influenced by childish experiences? Injuries sustained by an organ as yet immature, or a function in process of development, do indeed so often cause graver and more lasting effects than can ensue in riper years. Perhaps the abnormal reaction to sexual impressions which surprises us in hysterics at puberty is always due to such sexual experiences in childhood, experiences which might then prove to be significant and similar in kind? We should then come to the view that certain things must be regarded as having been acquired in early life which hitherto have been laid to the charge of some by no means clearly understood hereditary predisposition. And, since infantile experiences of a sexual nature can surely manifest a psychic influence only through their memory-traces, would not this view bear out in a gratifying manner the result reached in analysis – namely, that the influence of memories is essential for the production of hysterical symptoms?

II

You will doubtless have suspected that I should not have developed this last train of thought at such length, if I had not wished to prepare you for the idea that this path alone, after our many delays, can lead us to the goal. For now we really stand at the end of our lengthy and laborious analytic work and find fulfilled here all that we have so far maintained and expected. When we are persevering enough to carry our analysis back into early childhood, to the very furthest point which human memory can reach, we thereby in every instance cause the patient to reproduce the experiences which, on account both of their special features and of their relation to subsequent morbid symptoms, must be regarded as the aetiology for which we are looking. These *infantile* experiences are once more *sexual* in content, but are far more uniform in kind than was the case in the scenes of puberty which we had lately discovered; it is now no longer a question of sexual thoughts being awakened by any chance sensory impression, but of sexual experiences undergone by the patient personally, of sexual intercourse (in a wide sense). You will admit that the importance of such scenes needs no further argument; to this you may now add that in the details of this scene you can invariably discover the determining factors which were perhaps still lacking in those other scenes that had taken place later and were reproduced earlier.

I put forward the proposition, therefore, that at the bottom of every case of hysteria will be found one or more experiences of premature sexual experience, belonging to the first years of childhood, experiences which may be reproduced by analytic work though whole decades have intervened. I believe this to be a momentous revelation, the discovery of a *caput Nili* of neuropathology, but I hardly know from what point to continue the discussion of the situation. Shall I set out before you the actual material I have obtained from the analyses I have conducted, or ought I not rather first of all to try to meet the mass of objections and doubts which I am probably right in supposing to be at this moment absorbing your attention? I choose the latter course; perhaps we shall then be able to dwell on the facts with a more objective mind.

(*a*) Anyone who is altogether opposed to the psychological conception of hysteria, who is unwilling to give up the hope of one day tracing its symptoms to 'finer anatomical changes' and has rejected the view that the material foundations of hysterical changes must necessarily be similar in kind to those of our normal mental processes – anyone who adopts this attitude will naturally put no faith in the results of our analyses; but the difference in principle between his premises and ours absolves us from any obligation to convince him on single points.

But someone else, less determined to reject psychological theories of hysteria, will when considering our analytical results be tempted to ask what degree of certainty the application of psycho-analysis involves; whether it is not very possible either that the physician forces such scenes upon the docile patient, alleging them to be recollections, or that the patient tells him things which he has purposely invented or spontaneous phantasies which the physician accepts as genuine facts. Well, my answer is that the general misgiving about the reliability of the psycho-analytic method can be appraised and removed only when a complete presentation of its technique and results is available; doubts about the genuine nature of the infantile sexual scenes, however, can be deprived of their force here and now by more than one argument. In the first place, the behaviour of the patients who reproduce these infantile experiences is in every respect incompatible with the assumption that the scenes are anything but a most distressing reality which is recalled with the utmost reluctance. Before they are analysed, the patients know nothing of these scenes; they are generally indignant if we tell them that something of the sort is now coming to light; they can be induced only under the very strongest compulsion of the treatment to engage in reproducing the scenes; whilst calling these infantile experiences into consciousness they experience the most violent sensations, of which they are ashamed and which they endeavour to hide, and they still try, even after going through them again in so convincing a fashion, to withhold belief by emphasizing the fact that they have no feeling of recollecting these scenes as they had in the case of other forgotten material.

Now this last attitude on their part seems absolutely decisive.

Why should patients assure me so emphatically of their unbelief, if from any motive they had invented the very things that they wish to discredit?

It is less easy to refute the charge that the physician forces reminiscences of this sort upon the patient and influences him by suggestion to imagine and recount them; nevertheless I think this position is just as untenable. I have never yet succeeded in forcing on a patient a scene that I expected to find in such a way that he appeared to live through it again with all the appropriate emotions; perhaps others are more successful.

There is however a whole series of further evidence which vouches for the reality of the infantile sexual scenes. First, they display just the uniformity in certain details that would necessarily follow from the identically recurring conditions of the existence of these experiences; otherwise we should have to believe in a secret conspiracy between the individual patients. And again, patients often describe them as if they were harmless events, the significance of which they obviously do not perceive, for if they did they would be shocked; or they mention details to which they attach no importance but which only someone with experience of life knows of and can appreciate as subtle indications of reality.

Such occurrences strengthen the impression that patients must actually have experienced what they reproduce under the compulsion of analysis as scenes from childhood, and we have yet another and even more convincing proof when we examine the relation of the infantile scenes to the content of the whole subsequent history of the illness. Just as when putting together children's picture-puzzles, we finally after many attempts become absolutely certain which piece belongs to the gap not yet filled – because only that particular piece at the same time completes the picture and can be fitted in with its irregular edges to the edges of the other pieces in such a way as neither to leave a space nor to overlap – so the content of the infantile scenes proves to be an inevitable completion of the associative and logical structure of the neurosis; and only after they have been inserted does its origin become evident – one might often say, self-evident.

Without wishing to lay special stress on the fact, I will add that in a number of cases the therapeutic test also speaks for the genuine nature of the infantile scenes. There are cases in which a complete or partial cure can be achieved without going down as far as the infantile experiences; others in which there is no success at all until the analysis comes to its natural end with the discovery of the earliest traumata. I think that in the former cases we are not secure against relapses; my belief is that a complete psycho-analysis implies the radical cure of a case of hysteria. However, do not let us here anticipate what experience will show.

There would be yet one more proof, one which is really unassailable, of the genuineness of the childish sexual experiences – namely, the confirmation of the statements of the person analysed by the account of someone else who is, or is not, under treatment. These two persons must have taken part in the same experience in their childhood, perhaps had stood in a sexual relation to one another. Such relations between children are, as you will hear in a moment, by no means rare; moreover, it quite often happens that both persons concerned suffer subsequently from neuroses; and yet I regard it as a fortunate accident that I have had objective confirmation of this kind in two out of my eighteen cases. In one instance, the brother, who had not fallen ill, of his own accord confirmed for me not, it is true, the earliest sexual experiences with his sister, the patient, but at least scenes of this kind from their later childhood and the fact of sexual relations dating further back. Another time it happened that two women whom I was treating had as children had sexual intercourse with the same man, when certain scenes had occurred in which all three took part. A particular symptom which could be traced to these childish experiences had been developed in both cases and bore witness to this common experience.

(*b*) Sexual experiences in childhood consisting of stimulation of the genitals, coitus-like activities, etc. are therefore in the final analysis to be recognized as the traumata from which proceed hysterical reactions against experiences at puberty and hysterical symptoms themselves. Two objections which contradict each other are sure to be raised from different quarters against this statement. Some will say that such sexual abuses, practised on children or by children on one another, happen too seldom to be regarded as conditioning so common a neurosis as hysteria; others will perhaps maintain that such experiences are, on the contrary, very frequent, far too frequent for us to ascribe aetio-logical significance to them where their existence is proved. Further, it will be urged that it is easy enough on inquiry to find people who remember scenes of sexual seduction and abuse in their childhood, but yet have never suffered from hysteria; finally, as a weighty argument, that in the lower strata of the population hysteria certainly does not appear more frequently than in the highest, while surely everything goes to show that the rule of keeping a child from everything sexual is transgressed far more commonly among the proletariat.

Let us begin our defence with the easier part of our task. It seems to me certain that our children are far oftener exposed to sexual aggressions than we should suppose, judging by the scanty precautions taken by parents in this matter. When I first made inquiries about what was known on the subject, I learnt from colleagues that there are several publications by children's phys-icians in which the frequency of sexual practices by nurses and attendants with their charges, even with infants, is complained of and in the last few weeks I have come across a study by Dr Stekel of Vienna on 'Coitus in Childhood'.[3] I have not had time to collect other published evidence, but even if only isolated testimony were forthcoming, we might expect that increased attention to this subject would confirm the great frequency of sexual experiences and sexual activity in childhood.

Lastly, the results of my analysis may speak for themselves. In all the eighteen cases (of pure hysteria and hysteria combined with obsessions: six men and twelve women) I have, as I said, discovered such sexual experiences in childhood. I may divide my cases into three groups, according to the source of the sexual excitation. In the first group it was a question of assaults – single or at any rate isolated instances of abuse by grown-up strangers (who took care to avoid gross mechanical injury) where consent by the children did not enter into the matter and the first and preponderating result of the experience was terror. A second group consists of those far more numerous cases in which some adult attendant of the child – a maid, nurse, governess, teacher, unhappily only too often a near relation – initiated the child into sexual intercourse and maintained a regular love-relation with him, often for years, which had its mental counterpart. To the third group belong finally the real child-relations, sexual relations between two children of different sex, mostly between brother and sister, which are often continued past the age of puberty and have far-reaching consequences for the two concerned. In most of my cases I could trace the combined influences of two or more such aetiologies; in certain instances the accumulation of sexual experiences from different quarters was really amazing. You will understand this peculiarity in my observations more easily when you consider that the cases were all of severe forms of neurosis involving almost complete incapacity for life.

Where there had been a relation between two children I was sometimes able to prove that the boy – who played the aggressive part – had previously been seduced by a woman, and that then, urged on by his prematurely aroused libido and in consequence of the obsessive memory, he tried to repeat with the little girl exactly the same practices as he had learnt from the adult, without attempting any independent modification in the form of the sexual activity.

So I am inclined to assume that without previous seduction children cannot find the way to acts of sexual aggression. The foundation of the neurosis would accordingly have been laid in childhood by adults, and the children themselves have transmitted to one another the disposition to suffer later from hysteria. I ask you to pause for a moment upon the special frequency of sexual relations in childhood between brothers and sisters, or cousins, due to the opportunity afforded by their being constantly together; now suppose that ten or fifteen years later several of the younger generation of the same family are found to be ill, and then ask yourselves whether this familial type of neurotic manifestation would not naturally lead us to assume an hereditary disposition, where there is actually only *pseudo-heredity*, a transmission or infection having taken place in childhood.

Now let us turn to the other objection which is based upon the very frequency – freely admitted – of infantile sexual experiences and the fact that many people who have not developed hysteria remember such scenes.

We shall reply in the first place that excessive frequency in an aetiological factor cannot possibly be used as an objection to its aetiological significance. Is not the tubercle bacillus ubiquitous, inhaled by many more human beings than suffer from tuberculosis? And is its aetiological significance impaired by the fact that it clearly needs the concurrence of other factors to produce the disease that is its specific effect? It is enough to establish it as the specific cause that tuberculosis is never found where the bacillus is not active. The same is probably true of our problem also. It makes no difference that many people go through infantile sexual experiences without developing hysteria, so long as all those who do become hysterics have had such experiences. The radius of an aetiological factor may be wider, but not less wide than its effect. Not everyone who touches or comes near a smallpox patient develops smallpox, and yet infection from an actual case of it is almost the only known aetiology of the disease.

Of course if infantile sexual activity were an almost universal occurrence, it would prove nothing to find it in every case. But first, such a statement would be a grave exaggeration, and secondly, the aetiological pretensions of infantile scenes rest not only on their constant appearance in the anamnesis of hysterics, but above all on the evidence of the associative and logical connections between these scenes and the hysterical symptoms, connections which would be as clear as daylight to you if you had the complete history of the illness.

What are the other factors that are necessary to the 'specific aetiology' of hysteria in order actually to produce the neurosis? Now this is really a theme in itself, one which I do not propose to discuss; today I need only indicate the point of contact at which the sides of the question – the specific and the subsidiary aetiology – fit into one another. Probably a considerable number of factors will have to be considered: inherited and personal constitution; the importance of the infantile sexual experiences in themselves and particularly their number – a short relation with a boy outside the patient's family to whom she later becomes indifferent will not have so powerful an effect as intimate sexual relations with a brother lasting for several years. In the aetiology of the neurosis quantitative conditions are just as important as qualitative; there are thresholds which have to be crossed if the illness is to manifest itself. Moreover, I myself do not regard the aetiological series mentioned above as complete, nor do I think it solves the problem why hysteria is not more common in the lower classes. (You will remember, by the way, how surprisingly frequent Charcot declared it to be in the *men* of the working classes.) But I may also remind you that I myself a few years ago indicated a factor hitherto but little remarked, to which I ascribe the leading part in the production of hysteria *after* puberty. At that time I put forward the view that the outbreak of hysteria may almost invariably be traced to a *psychic conflict*, arising through an unbearable idea having called up the *defences* of the ego and demanding repression. In what circumstances this attempt at defence has the pathological effect of actually thrusting into the unconscious a memory painful to the ego and creating an hysterical symptom in its place I could not at that time say. I can complete my statement today: The defence achieves its purpose of thrusting the unbearable idea out of consciousness, if in the (hitherto normal) person concerned infantile sexual scenes exist in the form of unconscious memories and if the idea to be repressed can be brought into logical or associative connection with any such infantile experience.

Since the ego's attempt at defence depends on the whole moral and intellectual development of the person concerned, the fact that hysteria is so much rarer in the lower classes than would follow from its specific aetiology is no longer entirely incomprehensible.

Let us go back once more to the last group of objections, the answer to which has led us so far afield. We have heard and acknowledged that there are many people who have a very clear recollection of infantile sexual experiences and yet do not suffer from hysteria. This objection has really no weight at all, but it provides an occasion for a valuable comment. People of this type *should* not (according to our understanding of neurosis) be hysterical at all, at least not in consequence of scenes which they consciously remember. In our patients these memories are never conscious; we cure their hysteria, however, by converting their unconscious memories of infantile scenes into conscious recollection. We could not in any way alter the fact that they had such memories nor need we. From this you perceive that it is not merely a question of the existence of the infantile sexual experiences, but that a certain psychological condition enters into the case. These scenes must exist as *unconscious memories*; only so long and in so far as they are unconscious can they produce and maintain hysterical symptoms. But upon what the consciousness or unconsciousness of these memories depends, whether it be conditioned by their content, or by the time at which they occur, or by some later influences, is a fresh problem which we will take care to avoid. Let me just remind you that the first result of analysis is embodied in the conclusion: hysterical symptoms are derivatives of memories operating unconsciously.

(c) If we hold fast to the assumption that infantile sexual experiences are the fundamental condition of hysteria – constitute, if I may say so, the *disposition* to that disease – they yet do not produce hysterical symptoms directly, for in the first instance they have no effect and exercise a pathogenic influence only later when they are roused after puberty in the form of unconscious memories – then we have to deal with the numerous observations which prove that hysterical illness may already make its appearance in childhood and before puberty. But this difficulty is solved when we examine more closely the particulars gathered in analysis about the period when these infantile sexual experiences took place. We then find that in our severe cases the formation of hysterical symptoms begins, not exceptionally but regularly, with the eighth year, and that those sexual experiences which show no direct result invariably date further back, to the third and fourth or even the second year. Since in no single instance does the chain of effective experiences break off with the eighth year, I must assume that this time of life, the period of growth in which the second dentition occurs, forms a boundary line for hysteria, which cannot be caused when once this line is passed. Anyone who has not had sexual experiences before this cannot be disposed to hysteria after this; anyone who has had them is ready to develop hysterical symptoms. The isolated instances of the occurrence of hysteria on the other side of the dividing line of age (before eight years) may be interpreted as evidence of premature development. The existence of this dividing line has probably some connection with processes of development in the sexual system. Premature sexual development on the physical side may often be observed and we may even suppose that it may in general be promoted by premature sexual excitation.

So we have an indication that a certain infantile condition of the psychic functions, as of the sexual system, is necessary in order that a sexual experience occurring within this period should subsequently, in the form of a memory, exercise a pathogenic influence. Still I do not as yet venture to make any more precise statement about the nature of this psychic infantilism and its temporal limits.

(d) Another of our critics might possibly take exception to the idea that the memory of infantile sexual experiences should have so tremendous a pathogenic effect, while the experience itself had none. True, we are not accustomed to find that a memory-picture has a power that the real impression lacked. Here, however, we note, by the way, with what consistency the proposition that symptoms can only proceed from memories is borne out in hysteria. All the later scenes at which the symptoms begin are not the causative ones: those which really are causative do not at first have any effect. But here we are confronted by a problem which we may justifiably keep separate from our main theme. We feel indeed that synthesis is required of us when we reflect upon the number of remarkable conditions we have come to recognize: that in order to form an hysterical symptom there must be an effort of defence against a painful idea; that this idea must be shown to have an associative and logical connection with an unconscious memory, many or few links being present, all of which remain unconscious too for the time being; that the content of the unconscious memory must be sexual; that that content is an experience which occurred at a certain infantile period of life; and we cannot help asking how it comes about that this memory of an experience which was harmless at the time can subsequently have the abnormal effect of conducting to a pathological issue a psychic process like that of defence, while itself remaining all the time unconscious.

But one must say to oneself that this is a purely psychological problem, the solution of which may perhaps require certain assumptions about normal psychic processes and the part played in them by consciousness; for the time, however, it may remain unsolved without robbing of its value the insight so far acquired into the aetiology of hysterical phenomena.

III

The problem I have just formulated concerns the *mechanism* of hysterical symptom-formation. But I have to present the causation of these symptoms without taking this mechanism into consideration, and the conclusions are consequently bound to forfeit something in clearness and completeness. Let us go back to the part played by the infantile sexual scenes. I am afraid that I may have misled you in the direction of over-estimating their power to form symptoms. So I will again emphasize the fact that every case of hysteria displays symptoms which are determined not by infantile, but by later, often by recent experiences. Other symptoms, of course, date from the very earliest experiences, have, so to speak, the longest pedigree. Such are especially the numerous and manifold sensations and paraesthesias of the genital organs and other parts of the body, sensations which simply correspond to those belonging to the infantile scenes, reproduced in hallucinatory fashion and often intensified to a painful degree.

Another series of exceedingly common hysterical phenomena – painful bladder pressure, painful sensations in defecation, intestinal disturbances, choking and vomiting, indigestion and nausea – could similarly be recognized in my analyses (and that with surprising regularity) as derivatives of the same childhood-experiences and were explained without difficulty by certain invariable features of these episodes. Now the feeling of a sexually normal human being recoils from the idea of these infantile sexual scenes, containing, as they do, all the abuses known to libertines and impotent persons, whose sexual practices include the improper use of the mouth and the rectum. The physician's astonishment at this soon gives place to complete understanding. We cannot expect that people who do not scruple to gratify their sexual desires upon children will be repelled by any lack of refinement, in the manner of that gratification, and the natural sexual impotence of childhood inevitably impels towards those surrogate activities to which the adult degrades himself in the case of acquired sexual impotence. All the peculiar circumstances in which the ill-matched pair carry on their love-relation: the adult – who cannot escape his share in the mutual dependence inherent in a sexual relation and yet is endued with complete authority and the right of punishment, and can exchange the one role for the other in unbridled gratification of his moods; the child – helpless victim of this capriciousness, prematurely awakened to every kind of sensation and exposed to every kind of disappointment, often interrupted in the practice of the sexual activities assigned to him by his imperfect control of his natural needs – all these grotesque, yet tragic, incongruities become stamped upon the further development of the person concerned and his neurosis, manifesting themselves in innumerable lasting consequences which deserve to be carefully traced out. Where the relation is one between two children, the character of the sexual scenes is still repulsive, since every relation of the sort between children postulates a previous seduction of one of them by an adult. The psychic consequences of such a childhood-relation are quite extraordinarily far-reaching; the two persons remain all their lives united by an invisible bond.

Sometimes it is the accidental circumstances of these infant-ile sexual scenes which in later years exercise a determining influence upon the symptoms of the neurosis. Thus in one of my cases the circumstance that the child was required to stimu-late the genitals of an adult woman with his foot sufficed for years to fix neurotic attention on the legs and their functions and finally to produce an hysterical paraplegia. In another case a patient suffering from anxiety-attacks which tended to come on at certain hours of the day could not be calmed unless one particular sister remained at her side. It would have remained a problem why she would not allow this one of her many sisters to leave her, had not analysis revealed that formerly the man who seduced the patient used to ask every time he came whether this sister, from whom he anticipated an interruption, was at home.

It may happen that the determining power of the infantile scenes disguises itself so effectually that it would certainly be overlooked in a superficial analysis. We imagine that we have found the explanation of a certain symptom in the content of one of the later scenes, but in the course of the analysis we come upon the same content in one of the infantile scenes, so that finally we have to admit that after all the later scene owes its power of determining the symptoms only to its agreement with the earlier one. I do not wish for this reason to represent the later scene as of no importance; if my task were to discuss the laws of hysterical symptom-formation, I should have to recognize as one of these laws that the idea chosen as the basis of a symptom will be one which various factors combine to arouse and which is stirred up from several directions simultaneously – a state of affairs I have elsewhere tried to formulate by saying that *hysterical symptoms are over-determined*.

One thing more. It is true that so far I have set aside the relation between recent and infantile aetiology as a theme apart; nevertheless I cannot leave the subject without making at least one remark on this point. You will admit that there is one fact in particular which is apt to mislead us in the understanding of the psychology of hysterical phenomena, which so often seem to warn us not to judge by the same standard psychic acts in hysterics and in normal people. I refer to the discrepancy between psychic excitation and psychic reaction which we observe in hysterics and for which we try to account by assuming in them a general abnormal sensibility to stimulation; we often attempt to explain it in terms of physiology, as though in such patients certain organs of the brain which serve to transmit stimuli were in a peculiar morbid state (something like the spinal centres of a frog which has been injected with strychnine) or else had withdrawn from the influence of the higher, inhibiting centres, as in animals experimented upon in vivisection. Here and there either of these conceptions may be a perfectly valid explanation of hysterical phenomena: I do not deny it. But the most important part of the phenomenon, that is, of the abnormal, exaggerated, hysterical reaction to psychic stimuli admits of another explanation, supported by countless instances taken from the analyses of patients. This explanation is as follows: the reaction of hysterics only appears exaggerated; it is bound to appear so to us, because we know only a small part of the motive forces behind it.

In reality, this reaction is proportionate to the exciting stimulus, and therefore normal and psychologically intelligible. We immediately perceive this when analysis has added to the manifest causes of which the patient is conscious those other causes which have contributed to the result, though the patient knows nothing about them and is therefore unable to tell us anything.

I could spend hours demonstrating the validity of this important assertion for the whole range of psychic activity in hysterics, but here I must confine myself to a few examples. You will remember the mental 'hypersensitiveness' so common in hysterics, which leads them to react to the least suggestion of depreciation as to a deadly insult. Now what would you think if you observed such a readiness to take offence in two normal people, for instance husband and wife? You would certainly infer that the conjugal scene you witnessed was not simply the result of the present trifling occasion, but that, for a long time, inflammable material had been accumulating and that the whole mass had now been brought to an explosion by this last shock.

Now apply this train of thought to hysterics. It is not the

last, in itself infinitesimal, mortification which produces the fit of crying, the outbreak of despair, the attempted suicide – regardless of the axiom that effect must be proportioned to cause, but this trivial actual mortification has roused and set working the memories of so many, far more intense, previous mortifications, behind all of which lies the memory of a serious one in childhood, one which the patient never got over. Or, when a young girl reproaches herself most bitterly for allowing a boy secretly to caress her hand, and from that moment is the victim of neurosis, you can of course explain it by pronouncing her to be an abnormal, eccentric, hypersensitive person; but you will take a different view when analysis shows that the touch reminded her of a similar one felt in very early youth, which was part of a less harmless story, so that really the reproaches belong to that former occasion. Finally, the problem of hysterogenic areas is another of the same kind; if you touch one particular spot, you do something you did not intend: i.e. you wake a memory which may bring on an hysterical attack, and since you know nothing of the psychic connecting link you refer the attack directly to your touch. The patients are equally ignorant and therefore fall into similar errors; they constantly establish 'false connections' between the last recent cause of which they are conscious and the effect which depends on so many intermediate links. But if the physician succeeds in linking up the unconscious and the conscious determinants of an hysterical reaction, he nearly always has to recognize that this seemingly exaggerated reaction is appropriate and is abnormal only in form.

You may now rightly object to this justification of the hysterical reaction to psychic stimuli that it is none the less abnormal, for why do healthy people behave differently? Why do not all the long-past excitations in them also combine afresh to operate when there is a real new excitation? We do indeed get the impression that in hysterics all the former experiences, to which there has so often already been such a violent reaction, retain their power of producing an effect, as though these people were incapable of discharging psychic stimuli. That is so; we must indeed assume something of the sort. Do not, however, forget that the former experiences of hysterics become operative on some actual occasion, in the form of *unconscious memories*. It seems as though the difficulty of discharge, the impossibility of transforming an actual impression into a powerless memory, was related to the nature of the unconscious part of the mind. You see that the rest of the problem is again psychology, a psychology too for which philosophers have done little to prepare the way.

To this psychology, which has yet to be constructed to meet our requirements – the future *pathopsychology* – I must also refer you when in conclusion I tell you something which at first will make you apprehensive lest it should confuse our dawning understanding of the aetiology of hysteria. For I must state that the aetiological role of infantile sexual experiences is not confined to hysteria, but holds good equally for the remarkable obsessional neurosis and perhaps even for the different forms of chronic paranoia and other functional psychoses. I express myself on this point less definitely, because I have analysed far fewer cases of obsessional neurosis than of hysteria; I have actually only a single full analysis and several fragmentary ones of cases of paranoia to which to refer. But what I discovered in these cases seemed to me reliable evidence and gave me confident expectations for future cases. You will perhaps remember that I had already placed both hysteria and obsessions under the single heading of 'defence neuroses', even before I knew of common features in the infantile aetiology of both. Now I must add – though this is a thing which of course need not be of general occurrence – that every one of my cases of obsessional neurosis revealed a substratum of hysterical symptoms, mainly sensations and pains, which were traced to those earliest experiences of childhood. What then determines whether the subsequent developments of the infantile sexual scenes shall take the form of hysteria or obsessional neurosis, or even paranoia, when the other pathogenic factors supervene? These additions to our knowledge would seem to diminish the aetiological significance of these scenes, for the aetiological relation would lose its specific character.

I am not yet able to give a positive answer to this question. The number of cases I have analysed is not large enough, nor have the conditioning factors been sufficiently various. So far I have noted that obsessional ideas can regularly be shown by analysis to be disguised and transformed self-reproaches for sexual aggressions in childhood, that they are therefore more frequently met with in men than in women, and that men develop them more often. From this I might conclude that the character of the infantile scenes – whether the experience was pleasurable or was merely passively submitted to – has a determining influence upon the choice of the subsequent neurosis, but again I do not wish to under-estimate the significance of the age at which these childish activities take place, and of certain other factors. On these points we need discussion of further analyses to guide us to a conclusion; but when it becomes clear which are the decisive factors in the choice between the possible forms of defence neurosis, the mechanism by which that particular form develops will once more be a purely psychological problem.

I have now come to the end of my subject for today's discussion. I am prepared for contradiction and unbelief, and will therefore say one thing more in support of my position. Whatever you may think of my conclusions, I have the right to ask you not to look upon them as the fruit of idle speculation. They are based on laborious individual examination of patients, which in most cases has taken a hundred hours and more of work. Even more important to me than your estimation of my results is the direction of your attention to the method I have used, which is novel, difficult to handle and yet irreplaceable for scientific and therapeutic purposes. I am sure you will realize that one cannot gainsay the conclusions reached by the use of this modification of Breuer's original method if one neglects that method and uses only the ordinary one of questioning the patient. To do so would be like trying to refute the discoveries of histological technique by the aid of macroscopic investigations. Since the new method of research gives access to a new element in psychic processes, namely, to that which remains unconscious or, to use Breuer's expression, is *incapable of entering consciousness*, it beckons to us with the hope of a new and better understanding of all functional mental disturbances. I cannot believe that psychiatry will long hold back from this new path to knowledge.

Clinical Papers

The Sexual Enlightenment of Children[1]

(1907)

An Open Letter to Dr M. Fürst, Editor of
Soziale Medizin und Hygiene

DEAR SIR – When you ask me for an expression of opinion
on the matter of sexual enlightenment for children, I assume
that what you want is the independent opinion of an individual
physician whose professional work offers him special opportunities for studying the subject, and not a regular conventional
treatise dealing with all the mass of literature that has grown
up around it. I am aware that you have followed my scientific
efforts with interest, and that, unlike many other colleagues, you
do not dismiss my ideas without a hearing because I regard the
psycho-sexual constitution and certain noxiae in the sexual life
as the most important causes of the neurotic disorders that are
so common. My *Drei Abhandlungen zur Sexualtheorie*, in which
I describe the components of which the sexual instinct is made

47

up, and the disturbances which may occur in its development into the function of sexuality, has recently received favourable mention in your Journal.

I am therefore to answer the questions whether children may be given any information at all in regard to the facts of sexual life, and at what age and in what way this should be done. Now let me confess at the outset that discussion with regard to the second and third points seems to me perfectly reasonable, but that to my mind it is quite inconceivable how the first of these questions could ever be the subject of debate. What can be the aim of withholding from children, or let us say from young people, this information about the sexual life of human beings? Is it a fear of arousing interest in such matters prematurely, before it spontaneously stirs in them? Is it a hope of retarding by concealment of this kind the development of the sexual instinct in general, until such time as it can find its way into the only channels open to it in the civilized social order? Is it supposed that children would show no interest or understanding for the facts and riddles of sexual life if they were not prompted to do so by outside influence? Is it regarded as possible that the knowledge withheld from them will not reach them in other ways? Or is it genuinely and seriously intended that later on they should consider everything connected with sex as something despicable and abhorrent, from which their parents and teachers wish to keep them apart as long as possible?

I am really at a loss to say which of these can be the motive for the customary concealment from children of everything connected with sex. I only know that these arguments are one and all equally foolish, and that I find it difficult to pay them the compliment of serious refutation. I remember, however, that in the letters of that great thinker and friend of humanity, Multatuli, I once found a few lines which are more than adequate as an answer:

To my mind it seems that certain things are altogether too much wrapped in mystery. It is well to keep the fantasies of children pure, but their purity will not be preserved by ignorance. On the contrary, I believe that concealment leads a girl or boy to suspect the truth more than ever. Curiosity leads to prying into things which would have roused little or no interest if they were talked of openly without any fuss. If this ignorance could be maintained I might be more reconciled to it, but that is impossible; the child comes into contact with other children, books fall into his hands which lead him to reflect, and the mystery with which things he has already surmised are treated by his parents actually increases his desire to know more. Then this desire that is only incompletely and secretly satisfied gives rise to excitement and corrupts his imagination, so that the child is already a sinner while his parents still believe he does not know what sin is.[2]

I do not know how the case could be better stated, though perhaps one might amplify it. It is surely nothing else but habitual prudery and a guilty conscience in themselves about sexual matters which causes adults to adopt this attitude of mystery towards children; possibly, however, a piece of theoretical ignorance on their part, to be counteracted only by fresh information, is also responsible. It is commonly believed that the sexual instinct is lacking in children, and only begins to arise in them when the sexual organs mature. This is a grave error, equally serious from the point of view both of theory and of actual practice. It is so easy to correct it by observation that one can only wonder how it can ever have arisen. As a matter of fact, the new-born infant brings sexuality with it into the world; certain sexual sensations attend its development while at the breast and during early childhood, and only very few children would seem to escape some kind of sexual activity and sexual experiences before puberty. A more complete exposition of this statement can be found in my *Drei Abhandlungen zur Sexualtheorie*, to which reference has been made above. The reader will learn that the specific organs of reproduction are not the only portions of the body which are a source of pleasurable sensation, and that Nature has stringently ordained that even stimulation of the genitals cannot be avoided during infancy. This period of life, during which a certain degree of directly sexual pleasure is produced by the stimulation of various cutaneous areas (erotogenic zones), by the activity of certain biological impulses and as an accompanying excitation during many affective states, is designated by an expression introduced by Havelock Ellis as the period of auto-erotism. Puberty merely brings about attainment of the stage at which the genitals acquire supremacy among all the zones and sources of pleasure, and in this way presses erotism into the service of reproduction, a process which naturally can undergo certain inhibitions; in the case of those persons who later on become perverts and neurotics this process is only incompletely accomplished. On the other hand, the child is capable long before puberty of most of the mental manifestations of love, for example, tenderness, devotion, and jealousy. Often enough the connection between these mental manifestations and the physical sensation of sexual excitation is so close that the child cannot be in doubt about the relation between the two. To put it briefly, the child is long before puberty a being capable of mature love, lacking only the ability for reproduction; and it may be definitely asserted that the mystery which is set up withholds him only from intellectual comprehension of achievements for which he is psychically and physically prepared.

The intellectual interest of a child in the riddle of sexual life, his desire for knowledge, finds expression at an earlier period of life than is usually suspected. If they have not often come across such cases as I am about to mention, parents must either be afflicted with blindness in regard to this interest in their children, or, when they cannot overlook it, must make every effort to stifle it. I know a splendid boy, now four years old, whose intelligent parents abstain from forcibly suppressing one side of the child's development. Little Herbert, who has certainly not been exposed to any seducing influence from servants, has for some time shown the liveliest interest in that part of his body which he calls his wee-wee-maker. When only three years old he asked his mother, 'Mamma, have you got a wee-wee-maker, too?' His mother answered, 'Of course, what did you think?' He also asked his father the same question repeatedly. At about the same age he was taken to a barn and saw a cow milked for the first time. 'Look, milk is coming out of the wee-wee-maker!' he called in surprise. At the age of three and three-quarters he was well on the way to establish correct categories by means of his own independent observation. He saw how water is run off from a locomotive and said, 'See, the engine is making wee-wee, but where is its wee-wee-maker?' Later on he added thoughtfully, 'Dogs and horses have wee-wee-makers, but tables and chairs don't have them.' Recently he was watching his little sister of one week old being bathed, and remarked, 'Her wee-wee-maker is still tiny; it will get bigger when she grows.' (I have heard of this attitude towards the problem of sex difference in other boys of the same age.) I must expressly assert that Herbert is not a sensual child nor even morbidly disposed; in my opinion, since he has never been frightened or oppressed with a sense of guilt, he gives expression quite ingenuously to what he thinks.

The second great problem which exercises a child's mind

– probably at a rather later date – is that of the origin of children, and is usually aroused by the unwelcome arrival of a baby brother or sister. This is the oldest and most burning question that assails immature humanity; those who understand how to interpret myths and legends can detect it in the riddle which the Theban Sphinx set to Oedipus. The answers usually given to children in the nursery wound the child's frank and genuine spirit of investigation, and generally deal the first blow at his confidence in his parents; from this time onwards he commonly begins to mistrust grown-up people and keeps to himself what interests him most. The following letter may show how torturing this very curiosity may become in older children; it was written by a motherless girl of eleven and a half who had been puzzling over the problem with her younger sister.

DEAR AUNT MALI – Please will you be so kind as to write and tell me how you got Chris or Paul. You must know because you are married. We were arguing about it yesterday, and we want to know the truth. We have nobody else to ask. When are you coming to Salzburg? You know, Aunt Mali, we simply can't imagine how the stork brings babies. Trudel thought the stork brings them in a shirt. Then we want to know, too, how the stork gets them out of the pond, and why one never sees babies in ponds. And please will you tell me, too, how you know beforehand when you are going to have one. Please write

and tell me *all* about it. Thousands of kisses from all of
us. – Your inquiring niece,

LILY.

I do not think that this touching request brought the two sisters
the information they wanted. Later on the writer developed
the neurosis that arises in unanswered unconscious questions –
obsessive speculating.

I do not think that there is even one good reason for denying
children the information which their thirst for knowledge
demands. To be sure, if it is the purpose of educators to stifle
the child's power of independent thought as early as possible, in
order to produce that 'good behaviour' which is so highly prized,
they cannot do better than deceive children in sexual matters
and intimidate them by religious means. The stronger characters will, it is true, withstand these influences; they will become
rebels against the authority of their parents and later against
every other form of authority. When children do not receive
the explanations for which they turn to their elders, they go on
tormenting themselves in secret with the problem, and produce
attempts at solution in which the truth they have guessed is mixed
up in the most extraordinary way with grotesque inventions; or
else they whisper confidences to each other which, because of
the sense of guilt in the youthful inquirers, stamp everything
sexual as horrible and disgusting. These infantile sexual theories
are well worth collecting and examining. After these experiences

children usually lose the only proper attitude to sexual questions, many of them never to find it again.

It would seem that the overwhelming majority of writers, both men and women, who have dealt with the question of explaining sexual matters to children have expressed themselves in favour of enlightenment. The clumsiness, however, of most of their proposals how and when this enlightenment should be carried out leads one to conclude that they have not found it very easy to venture this admission. As far as my knowledge of the literature goes, the charming letter of explanation which a certain Frau Emma Eckstein gives as written to her ten-year-old boy stands out conspicuously.[3] The customary method is obviously not the right one. All sexual knowledge is kept from children as long as possible, and then on one single occasion an explanation, which is even then only half the truth and generally comes too late, is proffered them in mysterious and solemn language. Most of the answers to the question 'How can I tell my children?' make such a pitiful impression, at least upon me, that I should prefer parents not to concern themselves with the explanation at all. It is much more important that children should never get the idea that one wants to make more of a secret of the facts of sexual life than of any other matter not suited to their understanding. To ensure this it is necessary that from the very beginning everything sexual should be treated like everything else that is worth knowing about. Above all, schools should not evade the task of mentioning sexual matters; lessons about the animal kingdom should include the great facts of reproduction, which should be given their due significance, and emphasis should be laid at the same time on the fact that man shares with the higher animals everything essential to his organization. Then, if the atmosphere of the home does not make for suppression of all reasoning, something similar to what I once overheard in a nursery would probably occur oftener. A small boy said to his little sister, 'How can you think the stork brings babies! You know that man is a mammal, do you suppose that storks bring other mammals their young too?' In this way the curiosity of children will never become very intense, for at each stage in its inquiries it will find the satisfaction it needs. Explanations about the specific circumstances of human sexuality and some indication of its social significance should be provided before the child is eleven years old.[4] The age of confirmation would be a more suitable time than any other at which to instruct the child, who already has full knowledge of the physical facts involved, in those social obligations which are bound up with the actual gratification of this instinct. A gradual and progressive course of instruction in sexual matters such as this, at no period inter-rupted, in which the school takes the initiative, seems to me to be the only method of giving the necessary information that takes into consideration the development of the child and thus successfully avoids ever-present dangers.

I consider it a most significant advance in the science of education that in France, in place of the catechism, the State should have introduced a primer which gives the child his first instruction in his position as a citizen and in the ethical obligations which will be his in time to come. The elementary instruction provided there, however, is seriously deficient in that it includes no reference to sexual matters. Here is the omission which stands in such need of attention on the part of educators and reformers. In those countries which leave the education of children either wholly or in part in the hands of the priesthood, the method urged would of course not be practicable. No priest will ever admit the identity in nature of man and beast, since to him the immortality of the soul is a foundation for moral training which he cannot forgo. Here again we clearly see the unwisdom of putting new wine into old bottles, and perceive the impossibility of carrying through a reform in one particular without altering the foundations of the whole system.

A Case of Paranoia Running Counter to the Psycho-Analytical Theory of Disease[1]

(1915)

SOME YEARS AGO a well-known lawyer consulted me about a case which had raised some doubts in his mind. A young woman had asked him to protect her from the molestations of a man who had drawn her into a love-affair. She declared that this man had abused her confidence by getting invisible witnesses to photograph them in the act of love-making, and that by exhibiting these pictures he could bring shame upon her and force her to resign her position. Her legal adviser was experienced enough to recognize the pathological stamp of this accusation; he remarked, however, that, as what appears to be incredible often actually happens, he would appreciate the opinion of a psychiatrist in this matter. He promised to call on me again, accompanied by the plaintiff.

Before I continue the account, I will say that I have altered the *milieu* of this case in order to preserve the incognito of those concerned, but that I have altered nothing else. I consider it an undesirable practice, however excellent the motive may be, to alter any detail in the presentation of a case. One can never tell which aspect of a case may be picked out by a reader of independent judgement, and one runs the risk of giving the latter a false impression.

Shortly afterwards I met the patient in person. She was thirty years old, a singularly attractive and handsome girl, who looked much younger than her age and was of a distinctly feminine type. She obviously resented the interference of a doctor and took no trouble to hide her distrust. It was clear that only the influence of her legal adviser, who was present, induced her to tell the following story, one which set me a problem to be referred to later. Neither in her manner nor by any kind of expression of emotion did she betray the slightest shame or shyness, although some such state of mind would naturally arise on such an occasion in the presence of a stranger. She was completely under the spell of the apprehension that her experience had induced in her.

For many years she had been on the staff of a big institution, where she held a responsible post. Her work had given her satisfaction and had been appreciated by her employers. She had never sought any love-affairs with men, but had lived quietly with her old mother whose only support she was. She had no brothers or sisters; her father had died many years before. Recently an official in the same institution, a cultured and attractive man, had paid her attentions and she had inevitably been drawn towards him. For external reasons, marriage was out of the question, but the man would not hear of giving up their relationship on that account. He had pleaded that it was senseless to sacrifice to social convention all that they longed for, that they had an indisputable right to enjoy and that could enrich their life as nothing else could. As he had promised not to expose her to any risk, she had at last consented to go to his bachelor rooms in the daytime. There they kissed and embraced as they lay side by side, and he began to admire the charms which were now partly revealed. In the midst of their love-making she was suddenly frightened by a noise, a kind of knock or tick. It came from the direction of the writing-desk, which was standing sideways in front of the window; the space between desk and window was partly filled up by a heavy curtain. She had at once asked her friend what this noise meant, and was told, so she said, that it probably came from the small clock on the writing-desk. I shall take the liberty, however, of commenting below on this part of her narrative.

As she left the house she had met two men on the staircase who whispered to each other as she passed. One of the strangers was carrying something which was wrapped up and looked rather like a box. She was much exercised over this meeting, and even on the way home her thoughts had already taken the following shape: the box could easily have been a camera, and the man a photographer who had been hidden behind the curtain while she was in the room; the tick had been the noise of the shutter; the photograph had been taken as soon as he saw her in a particularly compromising position of which he had wished to obtain pictorial evidence. From that moment nothing could abate her suspicion. She pursued her lover with reproaches and pestered him for explanations and reassurances, not only when they met but also by letter. In vain did he try to convince her that his feelings were sincere and that her suspicions were entirely without foundation. At last she called on the lawyer, told him of her experience and handed over the letters which the accused had written to her about the incident. Later I had an opportunity of seeing some of these letters. They made a very favourable impression on me, and contained mainly expressions of regret that such an unspoilt and tender understanding should have been destroyed by this 'unfortunate morbid idea'.

I need hardly justify my agreement with this view. But the case had a special interest for me other than a merely diagnostic one. The view had already been put forward in psycho-analytical literature that patients suffering from paranoia are struggling against an intensification of their homosexual trends, this pointing back to a narcissistic object-choice. And a further interpretation had been made: that the persecutor is in reality the loved person, past or present. A synthesis of the two propositions would lead us to expect that the persecutor must be of the same sex as the persecuted. We had not, it is true, asserted that paranoia is always without exception conditioned by homosexuality; but only because our observations were not sufficiently numerous. It was one of those conceptions which in view of certain connections become important only when universal application can be claimed for them. In psychiatric literature there is certainly no lack of cases in which the patient imagines himself persecuted by a person of the opposite sex. It is one thing, however, to read of such cases, and quite a different thing to come into personal contact with one. The relation between paranoia and homosexuality had so far been easily confirmed by my own observations and analyses and by those of my friends. But the present case emphatically contradicted it. The girl seemed to defend herself against love for a man by transforming the lover straight away into a persecutor: there was no sign of the influence of a woman, no trace of a struggle against a homosexual attachment.

In these circumstances the simplest thing to do would have been to abandon the theory that the delusion of persecution invariably depends on homosexuality, and with it everything based on this view. Either that theory must be given up or else, in view of this lack of conformation to rule, one must side with the lawyer and assume that this was no paranoiac combination but an actual experience which had been accurately interpreted. But I saw another way out, by which a final verdict could for the moment be postponed. I recollected how often wrong views were taken about psychotic patients simply because they had not been studied carefully enough and had not told enough about themselves. I therefore said that I could not form an immediate opinion, and asked the lady to call on me a second time, when she could relate her story again and add any details that had perhaps been omitted. Thanks to the lawyer's influence I secured this promise from the reluctant patient; while the former aided me in another way by saying that at our second meeting his presence would be superfluous.

The story told on this second occasion did not conflict with the previous narrative, but the additional details supplied resolved all doubts and difficulties. To begin with, she had visited the young man not once but twice. It was on the second occasion that she had been disturbed by the suspicious noise: she had suppressed, or omitted to mention, the first visit because it had no longer seemed of importance to her. On the first day nothing had happened, but something did happen on the day following. Her department in the business concern was under the direction of an elderly lady whom she described as follows: 'She has white hair like my mother.' This elderly superintendent had a great liking for her and treated her with affection, though sometimes she teased her; the girl regarded herself as her particular favourite. On the day after her first visit to the young man's rooms he appeared in the office to discuss some business matter with this elderly woman. During their whispered conversation the patient suddenly felt convinced that he was telling her about their adventure of the previous day, and even concluded that there had been for some time a love-relationship between the two which she had overlooked. The white-haired motherly old lady now knew everything, and her speech and conduct throughout the rest of the day seemed to confirm the patient's suspicion. At the first opportunity she took her lover to task about his treachery. He naturally raised a vigorous protest against what he called a senseless accusation. This time he succeeded in freeing her from her delusion and she regained enough confidence to repeat her visit to his room a short time, I believe a few weeks, afterwards. The rest we know from her first narrative.

These new details remove first of all any doubts as to the pathological nature of her suspicion. It is easy to see that the white-haired elderly manageress is a mother-substitute, that in spite of his youth the lover has been put in the place of the father, and that the strength of the mother-complex has driven the patient to suspect a love-relationship between these ill-matched partners, however unlikely such a relation might be. Moreover, this fresh information resolves the apparent contradiction with the view maintained by psycho-analysis, that the development of a delusion of persecution is conditioned by an over-powerful homosexual bond. The *original* persecutor – the agency whose influence the patient wishes to escape – is here again not a man but a woman. The manageress knows about the girl's love-affairs, disapproves of them, and shows her disapproval by mysterious allusions. The woman's attachment to her own sex hinders her attempts to adopt a person of the other sex as a love-object. Love for the mother becomes the protagonist of all those tendencies which, acting as her 'conscience', would arrest the girl's first step along the new road to normal sexual satisfaction, in many respects a dangerous one; and indeed it succeeds in destroying her relation with the man.

When the mother hinders or arrests a daughter's sexual activity she fulfils a normal function. This function is outlined in the early relationship between mother and infant; it is based on powerful, unconscious motivations, and has the sanction of society. It is the daughter's business to emancipate herself from this influence and to decide for herself on broad and rational grounds what her share of enjoyment or denial of sexual pleasure shall be. If in the attempt to emancipate herself she falls a victim to a neurosis there is present a mother-complex, which is as a rule over-powerful, and is certainly unmastered. This conflicts with the new direction taken by the libido, and the conflict is disposed of in the form of this or that neurosis, according to the disposition present. The manifestations of the neurotic reaction will always be determined, however, not by the actual relation to the actual mother, but by the infantile relation to the original mother-imago.

We know that our patient had been fatherless for many years: we may also assume that she would not have kept away from men up to the age of thirty if she had not been sustained by a powerful emotional attachment to her mother. This supporting tie becomes a burdensome obstacle when her libido begins to respond to the call of a man's insistent wooing. She tries to free herself, to throw off her homosexual bond; and her disposition, which need not be discussed here, enables her to achieve this by the formation of a paranoiac delusion. The mother thus becomes the hostile and jealous watcher and persecutor. As such she could be overcome, were it not that the mother-complex retained power enough to carry out its purpose of keeping her at a distance from men. At the end of the first phase of the conflict the patient has thus become estranged from the mother without having definitely gone over to the man. Indeed, both of them are plotting against her. Then with a vigorous effort the man draws her to himself. She conquers the mother's opposition in her mind and is willing to grant her lover a second meeting. In the later developments the mother does not reappear, but we may rightly assume that in this earlier phase the lover was not a persecutor directly; his character as such was acquired, as it were, through the mother and in virtue of his relationship to the mother, a factor which played the chief part in the formation of the first delusion.

One would think that the resistance was now definitely overcome, that the girl who had until now been bound to her mother had succeeded in coming to love a man. But after the second visit a new delusion appears, which by making ingenious use of accidental circumstances, destroys this love and thus successfully carries through the purpose of the mother-complex. It still seems strange that a woman should protect herself against the love of a man by means of a paranoiac delusion; but before examining this state of things more closely, let us glance at the accidental circumstances that form the basis of this second delusion, the one aimed exclusively against the man.

Lying partly undressed on the sofa alongside her lover, she hears some noise, a tick, knock, or tap. She does not know its cause but she arrives at an interpretation of it after meeting on the staircase two men, one of whom carries something that looks like a covered box. She is convinced that someone acting on instructions from her lover has watched and photographed her during their intimate tête-à-tête. We, of course, are far from thinking that had the fatal noise not occurred the delusion would not have been formed; on the contrary, we see behind this accidental circumstance something compulsive, asserting itself again as inevitably as when the patient divined a love-relationship between her lover and the elderly manageress, her mother-substitute. Among the wealth of unconscious phantasies of neurotics, and probably of all human beings, there is one which is seldom absent and can be disclosed by analysis, concerning the watching of sexual intercourse between the parents. I call these phantasies, together with those of seduction, castration, and others, *primal phantasies*; and I shall discuss more fully elsewhere their origin and the relation of them to individual experience. The accidental noise is merely a stimulus which activates the typical phantasy of eavesdropping, itself a component of the parental complex. Indeed, it is doubtful whether we can rightly call it 'accidental'. As O. Rank has remarked to me, it is an essential part of the phantasy of listening, and it reproduces either the sounds which betray parental intercourse or those by which the listening child fears to betray itself. But now we know at once where we stand. The lover is still the father, but the patient herself has taken the mother's place. The part of the listener must then be allotted to a third person. We can see by what means the girl has freed herself from her homosexual dependence on the mother. A partial regression has taken place; instead of choosing her mother as a love-object, she has identified herself with her, she herself has become the mother. The possibility of this regression points to the narcissistic origin of her homosexual object-choice and with that to the paranoiac disposition in her. One might sketch a train of thought which would bring about a similar result: 'If mother does it, I can do it too; I've just as good a right as she.'

One can go a step further in disproving the accidental nature of the noise. We do not, however, ask our readers to follow us, since the absence of thorough analytic investigation makes it impossible in this case to go beyond a certain probability. The patient mentioned in her first interview with me that she had immediately demanded an explanation of the noise, and had been told that it was probably the ticking of the little clock on the table. I take the liberty of assuming that this piece of information was a mistaken memory. It seems to me much more likely that at first she did not react to the noise at all, and that it became significant only after she met the two men on the staircase. Her friend, who had probably not even heard the noise, ventured the explanation, perhaps on some later occasion when she assailed him with her suspicions, 'I don't know what noise you can have heard. Perhaps it was the little clock; it sometimes ticks like that.' A subsequent use of impressions and displacement of recollections such as this occurs frequently in paranoia and is characteristic of it. But as I never met the man and did not continue the analysis of the woman, my hypothesis cannot be proved.

I might go still further in the analysis of this apparently real 'accident'. I do not believe that the clock ever ticked or that any noise was to be heard at all. The woman's situation justified a sensation of throbbing in the clitoris. This was what she subsequently projected as a perception of an external object. Similar things occur in dreams. An hysterical patient of mine once related to me a short 'awakening' dream to which she could bring no spontaneous associations. She dreamt simply that someone knocked and then she awoke. Nobody had knocked, but during the previous nights she had been awakened by unpleasant sensations of pollutions: she had thus a motive for awakening as soon as she felt the first sign of genital excitation. There had been a 'knocking' of the clitoris. In the case of our paranoiac patient, I should substitute for the accidental noise a similar process of projection. I certainly cannot guarantee that during our short acquaintance the patient, who was reluctantly yielding to necessity, gave me a truthful account of all that had taken place during the two meetings. But an isolated clitoris-contraction would be in keeping with her statement that no contact of the genitals had taken place. In her subsequent rejection of the man, lack of satisfaction undoubtedly played a part as well as 'conscience'.

Let us consider again the outstanding fact that the patient protects herself against her love for a man by means of a paranoiac delusion. The key to the understanding of this is to be found in the evolution of the delusion. As we might have expected, the latter was at first aimed against the woman; *the subsequent progression from a female to a male object* was, however, made on a *paranoiac basis*. Such a progression is unusual in paranoia; as a rule we find that the victim of persecution remains fixated to the same persons and therefore to the same sex as before the paranoiac transformation set in. But neurotic disorder does not preclude a progression of this kind, and our observation may be the prototype of many others. There are many similar processes beside that in paranoia which have never yet been classified under this heading, amongst them some which are very familiar. The so-called neurasthenic, for example, is prevented by his unconscious incestuous fixation from choosing a strange woman as a love-object; his sexual activity must remain within the limits of phantasy. But within the limits of this phantasy he achieves the progress denied him in reality and he succeeds in replacing mother and sister by new objects. Since the veto of the censorship does not then come into action, he can become conscious of his choice of these substitute-figures.

Alongside the phenomena of attempted progression from a position recently achieved, as a rule by regression, we may group the efforts made in some neuroses to regain a libido-position once held and subsequently lost. Indeed we can hardly draw any abstract distinction between these two categories. We are too apt to think that the conflict underlying a neurosis is removed when the symptom has been formed. In reality the struggle often goes on after this. Fresh instinctual components arise on both sides, and these continue it. The symptom itself becomes an object of this struggle; certain trends anxious to preserve it conflict with others which strive to remove it and to re-establish the *status quo*. In the attempt to render the symptom nugatory the expedient is often adopted of trying to regain through new channels what has been lost and is now frustrated by the symptom. These facts throw much light on a statement made by C. G. Jung to the effect that a peculiar psychic inertia, hostile to change and progress, is the fundamental condition of neurosis. This inertia is in fact most peculiar; it is not a general one, but is highly specialized; it is not even all-powerful within its own scope, but fights against tendencies towards progress and reconstruction which remain active even after the formation of neurotic symptoms. If we search for the starting-point of this specialized inertia, we discover that it is the expression of a conjunction of instincts with impressions and with the objects connected with these impressions. This conjunction has been effected very early, is very hard to resolve, and has the effect of bringing the development of the instincts concerned to a standstill. Or in other words, this specialized 'psychic inertia' is only a different term, though hardly a better one, for what in psycho-analysis we are accustomed to call a *fixation*.

The Psychogenesis of a Case
of Homosexuality in a Woman[1]

(1920)

I

HOMOSEXUALITY in women, which is certainly not less common than in men, although much less glaring, has not only been ignored by the law, but has also been neglected by psycho-analytic research. The narration of a single case, not too pronounced in type, in which it was possible to trace its origin and development in the mind with complete certainty and almost without a gap may, therefore, have a certain claim to attention. If this presentation of it furnishes only the most general outlines of the various events concerned and of the conclusions reached from a study of the case, while suppressing all the characteristic details on which the interpretation is founded, this limitation is easily to be explained by the medical discretion necessary in discussing a recent case.

A beautiful and clever girl of eighteen, belonging to a family of good standing, had aroused displeasure and concern in her parents by the devoted adoration with which she pursued a certain lady 'in society' who was about ten years older than herself. The parents asserted that, in spite of her distinguished name, this lady was nothing but a *cocotte*. It was said to be well known that she lived with a married woman as her friend, having intimate relations with her, while at the same time she carried on promiscuous affairs with a number of men. The girl did not contradict these evil reports, but neither did she allow them to interfere with her worship of the lady, although she herself was by no means lacking in a sense of decency and propriety. No prohibitions and no supervision hindered the girl from seizing every one of her rare opportunities of being together with her beloved, of ascertaining all her habits, of waiting for her for hours outside her door or at a tram-halt, of sending her gifts of flowers, and so on. It was evident that this one interest had swallowed up all others in the girl's mind. She did not trouble herself any further with educational studies, thought nothing of social functions or girlish pleasures, and kept up relations only with a few girl friends who could help her in the matter or serve as confidantes. The parents could not say to what lengths their daughter had gone in her relations with the questionable lady, whether the limits of devoted admiration had already been exceeded or not. They had never remarked in their daughter any interest in young men, nor pleasure in their attentions, while, on the other hand, they were sure that her present attachment to a woman was only a continuation, in a more marked degree, of a feeling she had displayed of recent years for other members of her own sex which had already aroused her father's suspicion and anger.

There were two details of her behaviour, in apparent contrast with each other, that most especially vexed her parents. On the one hand, she did not scruple to appear in the most frequented streets in the company of her questionable friend, being thus quite neglectful of her own reputation; while, on the other hand, she disdained no means of deception, no excuses and no lies that would make meetings with her possible and cover them. She thus showed herself too brazen in one respect and full of deceitfulness in the other. One day it happened, indeed, as was sooner or later inevitable in the circumstances, that the father met his daughter in the company of the lady. He passed them by with an angry glance which boded no good. Immediately after, the girl rushed off and flung herself over a wall down the side of a cutting on to a railway line. She paid for this undoubtedly serious attempt at suicide with a considerable time on her back in bed, though fortunately little permanent damage was done. After her recovery she found it easier to get her own way than before. The parents did not dare to oppose her with so much determination, and the lady, who up till then had received her advances coldly, was moved by such an unmistakable proof of serious passion and began to treat her in a more friendly manner.

About six months after this episode the parents sought

medical advice and entrusted the physician with the task of bringing their daughter back to a normal state of mind. The girl's attempted suicide had evidently shown them that the instruments of domestic discipline were powerless to overcome the existing disorder. Before going further it will be desirable, however, to deal separately with the attitude of her father and of her mother to the matter. The father was an earnest, worthy man, at bottom very tender-hearted, but he had to some extent estranged his children by the sternness he had adopted towards them. His treatment of his only daughter was too much influenced by consideration for his wife. When he first came to know of his daughter's homosexual tendencies he flared up in rage and tried to suppress them by threatening her; at that time perhaps he hesitated between different, though equally painful, views – regarding her either as vicious, as degenerate, or as mentally afflicted. Even after the attempted suicide he did not achieve the lofty resignation shown by one of our medical colleagues who remarked of a similar irregularity in his own family, 'It is just a misfortune like any other.' There was something about his daughter's homosexuality that aroused the deepest bitterness in him, and he was determined to combat it with all the means in his power; the low estimation in which psycho-analysis is so generally held in Vienna did not prevent him from turning to it for help. If this way failed he still had in reserve his strongest countermeasure; a speedy marriage was to awaken the natural instincts of the girl and stifle her unnatural tendencies.

The mother's attitude towards the girl was not so easy to grasp. She was still a youngish woman, who was evidently unwilling to relinquish her own claim to find favour by means of her beauty. All that was clear was that she did not take her daughter's passion so tragically as did the father, nor was she so incensed at it. She had even for a long time enjoyed her daughter's confidence concerning the love-affair, and her opposition to it seemed to have been aroused mainly by the harmful publicity with which the girl displayed her feelings. She had herself suffered for some years from neurotic troubles and enjoyed a great deal of consideration from her husband; she was quite unfair in her treatment of her children, decidedly harsh towards her daughter and over-indulgent to her three sons, the youngest of whom had been born after a long interval and was then not yet three years old. It was not easy to ascertain anything more definite about her character, for, owing to motives that will only later become intelligible, the patient was always reserved in what she said about her mother, whereas in regard to her father she showed no feeling of the kind.

To a physician who was to undertake psycho-analytic treatment of the girl there were many grounds for a feeling of discomfort. The situation he had to deal with was not the one that analysis demands, in which alone it can demonstrate its effectiveness. As is well known, the ideal situation for analysis is when someone who is otherwise master of himself is suffering from an inner conflict which he is unable to resolve alone, so that he brings his trouble to the analyst and begs for his help. The physician then works hand in hand with one part of the personality which is divided against itself, against the other partner in the conflict. Any situation but this is more or less unfavourable for psycho-analysis and adds fresh difficulties to those already present. Situations like that of a proprietor who orders an architect to build him a villa according to his own tastes and desires, or of a pious donor who commissions an artist to paint a picture of saints, in the corner of which is to be a portrait of himself worshipping, are fundamentally incompatible with the conditions of psycho-analysis. It constantly happens, to be sure, that a husband informs the physician as follows: 'My wife suffers from nerves, so that she gets on badly with me; please cure her, so that we may lead a happy married life again.' But often enough it turns out that such a request is impossible to fulfil, i.e. that the physician cannot bring about the result for which the husband sought the treatment. As soon as the wife is freed from her neurotic inhibitions she sets about dissolving the marriage, for her neurosis was the sole condition under which maintenance of the marriage was possible. Or else parents expect one to cure their nervous and unruly child. By a healthy child they mean one who never places his parents in difficulties, but only gives them pleasure. The physician may succeed in curing the child, but after that it goes its own way all the more decidedly, and the parents are now far more dissatisfied than before. In short, it is not a matter of indifference whether someone comes to analysis of his own accord or because he is brought to it, whether he himself desires to be changed, or only his relatives, who love him (or who might be expected to love him), desire this for him.

Further unfavourable features in the present case were the facts that the girl was not in any way ill – she did not suffer from anything in herself, nor did she complain of her condition – and that the task to be carried out did not consist in resolving a neurotic conflict but in converting one variety of the genital organization of sexuality into the other. The removal of genital inversion or homosexuality is in my experience never an easy matter. On the contrary, I have found success possible only under specially favourable circumstances, and even then the success essentially consisted in being able to open to those who are restricted homosexually the way to the opposite sex, which had been till then barred, thus restoring to them full bisexual functions. After that it lay with themselves to choose whether they wished to abandon the other way that is banned by society, and in individual cases they have done so. One must remember that normal sexuality also depends upon a restriction in the choice of object; in general, to undertake to convert a fully developed homosexual into a heterosexual is not much more promising than to do the reverse, only that for good practical reasons the latter is never attempted.

In actual numbers the successes achieved by psycho-analytic treatment of the various forms of homosexuality, which, to be sure, are manifold, are not very striking. As a rule the homosexual is not able to give up the object of his pleasure, and one cannot convince him that if he changed to the other object he would find again the pleasure that he has renounced. If he comes to be treated at all, it is mostly through the pressure of external motives, such as the social disadvantages and dangers attaching to his choice of object, and such components of the instinct of self-preservation prove themselves too weak in the struggle against the sexual impulses. One then soon discovers his secret plan, namely, to obtain from the striking failure of his attempt the feeling of satisfaction that he has done everything possible against his abnormality, to which he can now resign himself with an easy conscience. The case is somewhat different when consideration for beloved parents and relatives has been the motive for his attempt to be cured. Then there really are libidinal tendencies present which may put forth energies opposed to the homosexual choice of object, though their strength is rarely sufficient. It is only where the homosexual fixation has not yet become strong enough, or where there are considerable rudiments and vestiges of a heterosexual choice of object, i.e. in a still oscillating or in a definitely bisexual organization, that one may make a more favourable prognosis for psycho-analytic therapy.

For these reasons I declined altogether holding out to the parents any prospect of their wish being fulfilled. I merely said I was prepared to study the girl carefully for a few weeks or months, so as then to be able to pronounce how far a continuation of the analysis might influence her. In quite a number of cases, indeed, the analysis divides itself into two clearly distinguishable stages: in the first, the physician procures from the patient the necessary information, makes him familiar with the premises and postulates of psycho-analysis, and unfolds to him the reconstruction of the genesis of his disorder as deduced from the material brought up in the analysis. In the second stage the patient himself lays hold of the material put before him, works on it, recollects what he can of the apparently repressed memories, and behaves as if he were living the rest over again. In this way he can confirm, supplement, and correct the inferences made by the physician. It is only during this work that he experiences, through overcoming resistances, the inner change aimed at, and acquires for himself the convictions that make him independent of the physician's authority. These two stages in the course of the analytic treatment are not always sharply divided from each other; this can only happen when the resistance maintains certain conditions. But when this is so, one may institute a comparison with two stages of a journey. The first comprises all the necessary preparations, today so complicated and hard to effect, before, ticket in hand, one can at last go on to the platform and secure a seat in the train. One then has the right, and the possibility, of travelling into a distant country, but after all these preliminary exertions one is not yet there – indeed, one is not a single mile nearer to one's goal. For this to happen one has to make the journey itself from one station to the other, and this part of the performance may well be compared with the second stage in the analysis.

The analysis of the patient I am discussing took this course of two stages, but it was not continued beyond the beginning of the second stage. A special constellation of the resistance made it possible, nevertheless, to gain full confirmation of my inferences, and to obtain an adequate insight on broad lines into the way in which her inversion had developed. But before relating the findings of the analysis I must deal with a few points which have either been touched upon already by myself or which will have roused special interest in the reader.

I had made the prognosis partly dependent on how far the girl had succeeded in satisfying her passion. The information I gleaned during the analysis seemed favourable in this respect. With none of the objects of her adoration had the patient enjoyed anything beyond a few kisses and embraces; her genital chastity, if one may use such a phrase, had remained intact. As for the lady who led a double life, and who had roused the girl's most recent and by far her strongest emotions, she had always treated her coldly and had never allowed any greater favour than kissing her hand. Probably the girl was making a virtue of necessity when she kept insisting on the purity of her love and her physical repulsion against the idea of any sexual intercourse. But perhaps she was not altogether wrong when she vaunted of her wonderful beloved that, aristocrat as she was, forced into her present position only by adverse family circumstances, she had preserved, in spite of her situation, a great deal of nobility. For the lady used to recommend the girl every time they met to withdraw her affection from herself and from women in general, and she had persistently rejected the girl's advances up to the time of the attempted suicide.

A second point, which I at once tried to investigate, concerned any possible motives in the girl herself which might serve to support a psycho-analytic treatment. She did not try to deceive me by saying that she felt any urgent need to be freed from her homosexuality. On the contrary, she said she could not conceive of any other way of being in love, but she added that for her parents' sake she would honestly help in the therapeutic endeavour, for it pained her very much to be the cause of so much grief to them. I had to take this as a propitious sign to begin with; I could not divine the unconscious affective attitude that lay behind it. What came to light later in this connection decisively influenced the course taken by the analysis and determined its premature conclusion.

Readers unversed in psycho-analysis will long have been awaiting an answer to two other questions. Did this homosexual girl show physical characteristics plainly belonging to the opposite sex, and did the case prove to be one of congenital or acquired (later developed) homosexuality?

I am aware of the importance attaching to the first of these questions. Only one should not exaggerate it and obscure in its favour the fact that sporadic secondary characteristics of the opposite sex are very often present in normal individuals, and that well-marked physical characteristics of the opposite sex may be found in persons whose choice of object has undergone no change in the direction of inversion; in other words, that in both sexes *the degree of physical hermaphroditism is to a great extent independent of the psychical hermaphroditism*. In modification of this statement it must be added that this independence is more evident in men than women, where bodily and mental traits belonging to the opposite sex are apt to coincide in their incidence. Still I am not in a position to give a satisfactory answer to the first of our questions about my patient; the psycho-analyst customarily forgoes thorough bodily examination of his patients in certain cases. Certainly there was no obvious deviation from the feminine physical type, nor any menstrual disturbance. The beautiful and well-developed girl had, it is true, her father's tall figure, and her facial features were sharp rather than soft and girlish, traits which might be regarded as indicating a physical masculinity. Some of her intellectual attributes also could be connected with masculinity: for instance, her acuteness of comprehension and her lucid objectivity, in so far as she was not dominated by her passion; though these distinctions are conventional rather than scientific. What is certainly of greater importance is that in her behaviour towards her love-object she had throughout assumed the masculine part: that is to say, she displayed the humility and the sublime over-estimation of the sexual object so characteristic of the male lover, the renunciation of all narcissistic satisfaction, and the preference for being lover rather than beloved. She had thus not only chosen a feminine love-object, but had also developed a masculine attitude towards this object.

The second question, whether this was a case of inherited or acquired homosexuality, will be answered by the whole history of the patient's abnormality and its development. The study of this will show how fruitless and inappropriate this question is.

II

After an introduction which digresses in so many directions, the sexual history of the case under consideration can be presented quite concisely. In childhood the girl had passed through the normal attitude characteristic of the feminine Oedipus-complex[2] in a way that was not at all remarkable, and had later also begun to substitute for her father a brother slightly older than herself. She did not remember any sexual traumata in early life, nor were any discovered by the analysis. Comparison of her brother's genital organs and her own, which took place about the beginning of the latency period (at five years old or perhaps a little earlier), left a strong impression on her and had far-reaching after-effects. There were only slight hints pointing to infantile onanism, or else the analysis did not go deep enough to throw light on this point. The birth of a second brother when she was between five and six years old left no special influence upon her development. During the pre-pubertal years at school she gradually became acquainted with the facts of sex, and she received this knowledge with mixed feelings of fascination and frightened aversion, in a way which may be called normal and was not exaggerated in degree. This amount of information about her seems meagre enough, nor can I guarantee that it is complete. It may be that the history of her youth was much richer in experiences; I do not know. As I have already said, the analysis was broken off after a short time, and therefore yielded an anamnesis not much more reliable than the other anamneses of homosexuals, which there is good cause to question. Further, the girl had never been neurotic, and came to the analysis without even one hysterical symptom, so that opportunities for investigating the history of her childhood did not present themselves so readily as usual.

At the age of thirteen to fourteen she displayed a tender and, according to general opinion, exaggeratedly strong affection for a small boy, not quite three years old, whom she used to see regularly in a playground in one of the parks. She took to the child so warmly that in consequence a permanent friendship grew up between herself and his parents. One may infer from this episode that at that time she was possessed of a strong desire to be a mother herself and to have a child. However, after a short time she grew indifferent to the boy, and began to take an interest in mature, but still youthful, women; the manifestations of this in her soon led her father to administer a mortifying chastisement to her.

It was established beyond all doubt that this change occurred simultaneously with a certain event in the family, and one may therefore look to this for some explanation of the change. Before it happened, her libido was focused on motherhood, while afterwards she became a homosexual attracted to mature women, and has remained so ever since. The event which is so significant for our understanding of the case was a new pregnancy of her mother's, and the birth of a third brother when she was about sixteen.

The network of causes and effects that I shall now proceed to lay bare is not a product of my gift for combination; it is based on such trustworthy analytic evidence that I can claim objective validity for it; it was in particular a series of inter-related dreams, easy of interpretation, that proved decisive in this respect.

The analysis revealed beyond all shadow of doubt that the beloved lady was a substitute for – the mother. It is true that she herself was not a mother, but then she was not the girl's first love. The first objects of her affection after the birth of her youngest brother were really mothers, women between thirty and thirty-five whom she had met with their children during summer holidays or in the family circle of acquaintances in town. Motherhood as a 'condition of love' was later on given up, because it was difficult to combine in real life with another one, which grew more and more important. The specially intensive bond with her latest love, the 'Lady', had still another basis which the girl discovered quite easily one day. On account of her slender figure, regular beauty, and off-hand manner, the lady reminded her of her own brother, a little older than herself. Her latest choice corresponded, therefore, not only with her feminine but also with her masculine ideal; it combined gratification of the homosexual tendency with that of the heterosexual one. It is well known that analysis of male homosexuals has in numerous cases revealed the same combination, which should warn us not to form too simple a conception of the nature and genesis of inversion, and to keep in mind the extensive influence of the bisexuality of mankind.[3]

But how are we to understand the fact that it was just the birth of a child who came late in the family, at a time when the girl herself was already mature and had strong wishes of her own, that moved her to bestow her passionate tenderness upon her who gave birth to this child, i.e. her own mother, and to express that feeling towards a substitute for her mother? From all that we know we should have expected just the opposite. In such circumstances mothers with daughters of about a marriageable age usually feel embarrassed in regard to them, while the daughters are apt to feel for their mothers a mixture of compassion, contempt and envy which does nothing to increase their tenderness for them. The girl we are considering, however, had altogether little cause to feel affection for her mother. The latter, still youthful herself, saw in her rapidly developing daughter an inconvenient competitor; she favoured the sons at her expense, limited her independence as much as possible, and kept an especially strict watch against any close relation between the girl and her father. A yearning from the beginning for a kinder mother would, therefore, have been quite intelligible, but why it should have flamed up just then, and in the form of a consuming passion, is not comprehensible.

The explanation is as follows: The girl was just experiencing the revival of the infantile Oedipus-complex at puberty when she suffered a great disappointment. She became keenly conscious of the wish to have a child, and a male one; that it was her father's child and his image that she desired, her consciousness was not allowed to know. And then – it was not she who bore the child, but the unconsciously hated rival, her mother. Furiously resentful and embittered, she turned away from her father, and from men altogether. After this first great reverse she forswore her womanhood and sought another goal for her libido.

In doing so she behaved just as many men do who after a first painful experience turn their backs for ever upon the faithless female sex and become woman-haters. It is related of one of the most attractive and unfortunate princes of our time that he became a homosexual because the lady he was engaged to marry betrayed him with a stranger. I do not know whether this is true historically, but much psychological truth lies behind the rumour. In all of us, throughout life, the libido normally oscillates between male and female objects; the bachelor gives up his men friends when he marries, and returns to club-life when married life has lost its savour. Naturally, when the swing-over is fundamental and final, we suspect some special factor which has definitely favoured one side or the other, and which perhaps only waited for the appropriate moment in order to turn the choice of object finally in its direction.

After her disappointment, therefore, this girl had entirely repudiated her wish for a child, the love of a man, and womanhood altogether. Now it is evident that at this point the developments open to her were very manifold; what actually happened was the most extreme one possible. She changed into a man, and took her mother in place of her father as her love-object.[4] Her relation to her mother had certainly been ambivalent from the beginning, and it proved easy to revive her earlier love for her mother and with its help to bring about an over-compensation for her current hostility towards her. Since there was little to be done with the real mother, there arose from the conversion of feeling described the search for a mother-substitute to whom she could become passionately attached.[5]

In her actual relations with her mother there was a practical motive furthering the change of feeling which might be called an 'advantage through illness'. The mother herself still attached great value to the attentions and the admiration of men. If, then, the girl became homosexual and left men to her mother (in other words, 'retired in favour of' the mother), she removed something which had hitherto been partly responsible for her mother's disfavour.[6]

The attitude of the libido thus adopted was greatly reinforced as soon as the girl perceived how much it displeased her father.

Once she had been punished for an over-affectionate overture made to a woman she realized how she could wound her father and take revenge on him. Henceforth she remained homosexual out of defiance against her father. Nor did she scruple to lie to him and to deceive him in every way. Towards her mother, indeed, she was only so far deceitful as was necessary to prevent her father from knowing things. I had the impression that her behaviour followed the principle of the talion: 'Since you have betrayed me, you must put up with my betraying you'. Nor can I come to any other conclusion about the striking lack of caution displayed by this otherwise ingenious and clever girl. She *wanted* her father to know occasionally of her intercourse with the lady, otherwise she would be deprived of satisfaction of her keenest desire – namely, revenge. So she saw to this by showing herself openly in the company of her adored one, by walking with her in the streets near her father's place of business, and the like. This maladroitness was by no means unintentional. It was remarkable, by the way, that both parents behaved as though they understood the secret psychology of their daughter. The mother was tolerant, as though she appreciated the favour of her daughter's 'retirement' from the arena; the father was furious, as though he realized the deliberate revenge directed against himself.

The girl's inversion, however, received its final reinforcement when she found in her 'Lady' an object which promised to satisfy not only her homosexual tendency, but also that part of her heterosexual libido still attached to her brother.

III

Consecutive presentation is not a very adequate means of describing complicated mental processes going on in different layers of the mind. I am therefore obliged to pause in the discussion of the case and treat more fully and deeply some of the points brought forward above.

I mentioned the fact that in her behaviour to her adored lady the girl had adopted the characteristic masculine type of love. Her humility and her tender lack of pretensions, '*che poco spera e nulla chiede*', her bliss when she was allowed to accompany the lady a little way and to kiss her hand on parting, her joy when she heard her praised as beautiful – while any recognition of her own beauty by another person meant nothing at all to her – her pilgrimages to places once visited by the loved one, the oblivion of all more sensual wishes: all these little traits in her resembled the first passionate adoration of a youth for a celebrated actress whom he regards as far above him, to whom he scarcely dares lift his bashful eyes. The correspondence with the 'type of object-choice in men' that I have described elsewhere, whose special features I traced to the attachment to the mother,[7] held good even to the smallest details. It may seem remarkable that she was not in the least repelled by the evil reputation of her beloved, although her own observations sufficiently confirmed the truth of such rumours. She was after all a well-brought-up and modest girl, who had avoided sexual adventures for herself, and who regarded coarsely sensual gratification as unaesthetic. But already her first passions had been for women who were not celebrated for specially strict propriety. The first protest her father made against her love-choice had been evoked by the pertinacity with which she sought the company of a cinematograph actress at a summer resort. Moreover, in all these affairs it had never been a question of women who had any reputation for homosexuality, and who might, therefore, have offered her some prospect of homosexual gratification; on the contrary, she illogically courted women who were coquettes in the ordinary sense of the word, and she rejected without hesitation the willing advances made by a homosexual friend of her own age. The bad reputation of her 'Lady', however, was positively a 'condition of love' for her, and all that is enigmatical in this attitude vanishes when we remember that in the case of the masculine type of object-choice derived from the mother it is also an essential condition that the loved object should be in some way or other 'of bad repute' sexually, one who really may be called a 'light woman'. When the girl learnt later on how far her adored lady deserved to be called by this title and that she lived simply by giving her bodily favours, her reaction took the form of great compassion and of phantasies and plans for 'rescuing' her beloved from these ignoble circumstances. We have been struck by the same endeavours to 'rescue' in the men of the type referred to above, and in my description of it I have tried to give the analytical derivation of this tendency.

We are led into quite another realm of explanation by the analysis of the attempt at suicide, which I must regard as seriously intended, and which, by the way, considerably improved her position both with her parents and with the lady she loved. She went for a walk with her one day in a part of the town and at an hour at which she was not unlikely to meet her father on his way from his office. So it turned out. Her father passed them in the street and cast a furious look at her and her companion, whom he had by that time come to know. A few moments later she flung herself on to the railway cutting. Now the explanation she gave of the immediate reasons determining her resolution sounded quite plausible. She had confessed to the lady that the man who had given them such an irate glance was her father, and that he had absolutely forbidden their friendship. The lady became incensed at this and ordered the girl to leave her then and there, and never again to wait for her or to address her – the affair must now come to an end. In her despair at having thus lost her loved one for ever, she wanted to put an end to herself. The analysis, however, was able to disclose another and deeper interpretation behind the one she gave, which was confirmed by the evidence of her own dreams. The attempted suicide was, as might have been expected, determined by two other motives besides the one she gave: it was a 'punishment fulfilment' (self-punishment), and a wish-fulfilment. As a wish-fulfilment it signified the attainment of the very wish which, when frustrated, had driven her into homosexuality – namely, the wish to have a child by her father, for now she 'fell'[8] through her father's fault.[9] The fact that at this moment the lady had spoken to the same effect as the father, and had uttered the same prohibition, forms the connecting link between this deeper interpretation and the superficial one of which the girl herself was conscious. From the point of view of self-punishment the girl's action shows us that she had developed in her unconscious strong death-wishes against one or other of her parents: perhaps against her father, out of revenge for impeding her love, but, more likely, also against her mother when she was pregnant with the little brother. For analysis has explained the enigma of suicide in the following way: probably no one finds the mental energy required to kill himself unless, in the first place, he is in doing this at the same time killing an object with whom he has identified himself, and, in the second place, is turning against himself a death-wish which had been directed against someone else. Nor need the regular discovery of these unconscious death-wishes in those who have attempted suicide surprise us as strange (any more than it need make an impression as confirming our deductions), since the unconscious of all human beings is full enough of such death-wishes, even against those we love.[10] The girl's identification of herself with her mother, who ought to have died at the birth of the child denied to herself, makes this 'punishment-fulfilment' itself again into a 'wish-fulfilment'. Lastly, a discovery that several quite different motives, all of great strength, must have co-operated to make such a deed possible is only in accord with what we should expect.

In the girl's account of her conscious motives the father did not figure at all; there was not even any mention of fear of his anger. In the motivation laid bare by the analysis he played the principal part. Her relation to her father had this same decisive importance for the course and outcome of the analytic treatment, or rather, analytic exploration. Behind her pretended consideration for her parents, for whose sake she had been willing to make the attempt to be transformed, lay concealed her attitude of defiance and revenge against her father which held her fast to her homosexuality. Secure under this cover, the resistance allowed a considerable degree of freedom to the analytic investigation. The analysis went forward almost without any signs of resistance, the patient participating actively with her intellect, though absolutely tranquil emotionally. Once when I expounded to her a specially important part of the theory, one touching her nearly, she replied in an inimitable tone, 'How very interesting,' as though she were a *grande dame* being taken over a museum and glancing through her lorgnon at objects to which she was completely indifferent. The impression one had of her analysis was not unlike that of an hypnotic treatment, where the resistance has in the same way withdrawn to a certain limit, beyond which it then proves to be unconquerable. The resistance very often pursues similar tactics – Russian tactics,¹¹ as they might be called – in cases of the obsessional neurosis, which for this reason yield the clearest results for a time and permit of a penetrating inspection of the causation of the symptoms. One begins to wonder how it is that such marked progress in analytic understanding can be unaccompanied by even the slightest change in the patient's compulsions and inhibitions, until at last one perceives that everything accomplished had been admitted only under the mental reservation of doubt,[12] and behind this protective barrier the neurosis may feel secure. 'It would be all very fine,' thinks the patient, often quite consciously, 'if I were obliged to believe what the man says, but there is no question of that, and so long as that is not so I need change nothing.' Then, when one comes to close quarters with the motivation of this doubt, the fight with the resistances breaks forth in earnest.

In the case of our patient, it was not doubt, but the affective factor of revenge against her father that made her cool reserve possible, that divided the analysis into two distinct stages, and rendered the results of the first stage so complete and perspicuous. It seemed, further, as though nothing resembling a transference to the physician had been effected. That, however, is of course absurd, or, at least, is a loose way of expressing it; for some kind of relation to the analyst must come about, and this is usually transferred from an infantile one. In reality she transferred to me the deep antipathy to men which had dominated her ever since the disappointment she had suffered from her father. Bitterness against men is as a rule easy to gratify upon the analyst; it need not evoke any violent emotional manifestations, it simply expresses itself in rendering futile all his endeavours and in clinging to the neurosis. I know from experience how difficult it is to make the patient understand just this mute kind of symptomatic behaviour and to make him aware of this latent, and often exceedingly strong, hostility without endangering the treatment. So as soon as I recognized the girl's attitude to her father, I broke off the treatment and gave the advice that, if it was thought worth while to continue the therapeutic efforts, it should be done by a woman. The girl had in the meanwhile promised her father that at any rate she would not communicate with the 'Lady', and I do not know whether my advice, the motive for which is evident, will be followed.

Only once in the course of this analysis did anything appear which I could regard as a positive transference, a greatly weakened revival of the original passionate love for the father. Even this manifestation was not quite free from other motives, but I mention it because it brings up, in another direction, an interesting problem of analytic technique. At a certain period, not long after the treatment had begun, the girl brought a series of dreams which, distorted as is customary and couched in the usual dream-language, could nevertheless be easily translated with certainty. Their content, when interpreted, was, however, remarkable. They anticipated the cure of the inversion through the treatment, expressed her joy over the prospects in life then opened before her, confessed her longing for a man's love and for children, and so might have been welcomed as a gratifying preparation for the desired change. The contradiction between them and the girl's utterances in waking life at the time was very great. She did not conceal from me that she meant to marry, but only in order to escape from her father's tyranny and to follow her true inclinations undisturbed. As for the husband, she remarked rather contemptuously, she would easily deal with him, and besides, one could have sexual relations with a man and a woman at one and the same time, as the example of the adored lady showed. Warned through some slight impression or other, I told her one day that I did not believe these dreams, that I regarded them as false or hypocritical, and that she intended to deceive me just as she habitually deceived her father. I was right; after this exposition this kind of dream ceased. But I still believe that, beside the intention to mislead me, the dreams partly expressed the wish to win my favour; they were also an attempt to gain my interest and my good opinion – perhaps in order to disappoint me all the more thoroughly later on.

I can imagine that to point out the existence of lying dreams of this kind, destined to please the analyst, will arouse in some readers who call themselves analysts a real storm of helpless indignation. 'What!' they will exclaim, 'so the unconscious, the real centre of our mental life, the part of us that is so much nearer the divine than our poor consciousness, so that too can lie! Then how can we still build on the interpretations of analysis and the accuracy of our findings?' To which one must reply that the recognition of these lying dreams does not constitute an astounding novelty. I know, indeed, that the craving of mankind for mysticism is ineradicable, and that it makes ceaseless efforts to win back for mysticism the playground it has been deprived of by the *Traumdeutung*, but in the case under consideration surely everything is simple enough. A dream is not the 'unconscious' itself; it is the form into which a thought from the preconscious, or even from waking conscious life, can, thanks to the favouring conditions of sleep, be recast. During sleep this thought has been reinforced by unconscious wish-excitations and thus has experienced distortion through the 'dream-work', which is determined by the mechanisms valid for the unconscious. With our dreamer, the intention to mislead me, just as she did her father, certainly emanated from the preconscious, or perhaps even from consciousness; it could come to expression by entering into connection with the unconscious wish-impulse to please the father (or father-substitute), and in this way it created a lying dream. The two intentions, to betray and to please the father, originate in the same complex; the former resulted from the repression of the latter, and the later one was reduced by the dream-work to the earlier one. There can therefore be no question of any devaluation of the unconscious, nor of a shaking of our confidence in the results of our analysis.

I will not miss this opportunity of expressing for once my astonishment that human beings can go through such great and momentous phases of their love-life without heeding them much, sometimes even, indeed, without having the faintest suspicion of them: or else that, when they do become aware of these phases, they deceive themselves so thoroughly in their judgement of them. This happens not only with neurotics, where we are familiar with the phenomenon, but seems also to be common enough in ordinary life. In the present case, for example, a girl develops a devotion for women, which her parents at first find merely vexatious and hardly take seriously; she herself knows quite well that her feelings are greatly engaged, but still she is only slightly aware of the sensations of intense love until a certain disappointment is followed by an absolutely excessive reaction, which shows everyone concerned that they have to do with a consuming passion of elemental strength. Even the girl herself had never perceived anything of the conditions necessary for the outbreak of such a mental upheaval. In other cases we come across girls or women in a state of severe depression, who on being asked for a possible cause of their condition tell us that they have, it is true, had a little feeling for a certain person, but that it was nothing deep and that they soon got over it when they had to give up hope. And yet it was this renunciation, apparently so easily borne, that became the cause of serious mental disturbance. Again, we have to do with men who have passed through casual love-affairs and then realize only from the subsequent effects that they had been passionately in love with someone whom they had apparently regarded lightly. One is also amazed at the unexpected results that may follow an artificial abortion which had been decided upon without remorse and without hesitation. One must agree that the poets are right who are so fond of portraying people in love without knowing it, or uncertain whether they do love, or who think that they hate when in reality they love. It would seem that the knowledge received by our consciousness of what is happening to our love-instincts is especially liable to be incomplete, full of gaps, or falsified. Needless to say, in this discussion I have not omitted to allow for the part played by subsequent failures of memory.

IV

I now come back, after this digression, to the consideration of my patient's case. We have made a survey of the forces which led the girl's libido from the normal Oedipus attitude into that of homosexuality, and of the paths thus traversed by it in the mind. Most important in this respect was the impression made by the birth of her little brother, and we might from this be inclined to classify the case as one of late acquired inversion.

But at this point we become aware of a state of things which also confronts us in many other instances in which light has been thrown by psycho-analysis on a mental process. So long as we trace the development from its final stage backwards, the connection appears continuous, and we feel we have gained an insight which is completely satisfactory or even exhaustive. But if we proceed the reverse way, if we start from the premises inferred from the analysis and try to follow these up to the final result, then we no longer get the impression of an inevitable sequence of events which could not be otherwise determined. We notice at once that there might have been another result, and that we might have been just as well able to understand and explain the latter. The synthesis is thus not so satisfactory as the analysis; in other words, from a knowledge of the premises we could not have foretold the nature of the result.

It is very easy to account for this disturbing state of affairs. Even supposing that we thoroughly know the aetiological factors that decide a given result, still we know them only qualitatively, and not in their relative strength. Some of them are so weak as to become suppressed by others, and therefore do not affect the final result. But we never know beforehand which of the determining factors will prove the weaker or the stronger. We only say at the end that those which succeeded must have been the stronger. Hence it is always possible by analysis to recognize the causation with certainty, whereas a prediction of it by synthesis is impossible.

We do not, therefore, mean to maintain that every girl who experiences a disappointment of this kind, of the longing for love that springs from the Oedipus attitude during puberty, will necessarily on that account fall a victim to homosexuality. On the contrary, other kinds of reaction to this trauma are probably commoner. Then, however, there must have been present in this girl special factors that turned the scale, factors outside the trauma, probably of an internal nature. Nor is there any difficulty in pointing them out.

It is well known that even in the normal person it takes a certain time before a decision in regard to the sex of the love-object is finally achieved. Homosexual enthusiasms, unduly strong friendships tinged with sensuality, are common enough in both sexes during the first years after puberty. This was also so with our patient, but in her these tendencies undoubtedly showed themselves to be stronger, and lasted longer, than with others. In addition, these presages of later homosexuality had always occupied her conscious life, while the attitude arising from the Oedipus-complex had remained unconscious and had appeared only in such signs as her tender fondling of the little boy. As a school-girl she was for a long time in love with a strict and unapproachable mistress, obviously a mother-substitute. A long time before the birth of her brother and still longer before the first reprimand at the hands of her father, she had taken a specially keen interest in various young mothers. From very early years, therefore, her libido had flowed in two streams, the one on the surface being one that we may unhesitatingly designate homosexual. This latter was probably a direct and unchanged continuation of an infantile mother-fixation. Possibly the analysis described here actually revealed nothing more than the process by which, on an appropriate occasion the deeper heterosexual libido-stream was also deflected into the manifest homosexual one.

The analysis showed, further, that the girl had suffered from childhood from a strongly marked 'masculinity complex'. A spirited girl, always ready to fight, she was not at all prepared to be second to her slightly older brother; after inspecting his genital organs she had developed a pronounced envy of the penis, and the thoughts derived from this envy still continued to fill her mind. She was in fact a feminist; she felt it to be unjust that girls should not enjoy the same freedom as boys, and rebelled against the lot of woman in general. At the time of the analysis the idea of pregnancy and child-birth was disagreeable to her, partly, I surmise, on account of the bodily disfigurement connected with them. Her girlish narcissism had betaken itself to this refuge,[13] and ceased to express itself as pride in her good looks. Various clues indicated that she must formerly have taken great pleasure in exhibitionism and scoptophilia. Anyone who is anxious that the claims of environment in aetiology should not come short, as opposed to those of heredity, will call attention to the fact that the girl's behaviour, as described above, was exactly what would follow from the combined effect in a person with a strong mother-fixation of the two influences of her mother's indifference and of her comparison of her genital organs with her brother's. It is possible here to trace back to the impression of an effective external influence in early life something which one would have been ready to regard as a constitutional peculiarity. But a part even of this acquired disposition, if it has really been acquired, has to be ascribed to the inborn constitution. So we see in practice a continual mingling and blending of what in theory we should try to separate into a pair of opposites — namely, inherited and acquired factors.

An earlier, more tentative conclusion of the analysis might have led to the view that this was a case of late-acquired homosexuality, but deeper consideration of the material undertaken later impels us to conclude that it is rather a case of inborn homosexuality which, as usual, became fixed and unmistakably manifest only in the period following puberty. Each of these classifications does justice only to one part of the state of affairs ascertainable by observation, but neglects the other. It would be best not to attach too much value to this way of stating the problem.

Publications on homosexuality usually do not distinguish clearly enough between the questions of the choice of object, on the one hand, and of the sexual characteristics and sexual attitude of the subject, on the other, as though the answer to the former necessarily involved the answers to the latter. Experience, however, proves the contrary: a man with predominantly male characteristics and also masculine in his love-life may still be inverted in respect to his object, loving only men instead of women. A man in whose character feminine attributes evidently predominate, who may, indeed, behave in love like a woman, might be expected, from this feminine attitude, to choose a man for his love-object; but he may nevertheless be heterosexual, and show no more inversion in respect of his object than an average normal man. The same is true of women; here also mental sexual character and object-choice do not necessarily coincide. The mystery of homosexuality is therefore by no means so simple as it is commonly depicted in popular expositions, e.g. a feminine personality, which therefore has to love a man, is unhappily attached to a male body; or a masculine personality, irresistibly attracted by women, is unfortunately cemented to a female body. It is instead a question of three series of characteristics, namely —

Physical sexual characteristics—Mental sexual characteristics
(physical hermaphroditism)   (masculine, or feminine, attitude)
Kind of object-choice

— which, up to a certain point, vary independently of one another, and are met with in different individuals in manifold permutations. Tendentious publications have obscured our view of this inter-relationship by putting into the foreground, for practical reasons, the third feature (the kind of object-choice), which is the only one that strikes the layman, and in addition by exaggerating the closeness of the association between this and the first feature. Moreover, they block the way leading to a deeper insight into all that is uniformly designated homosexuality by rejecting two fundamental facts which have been revealed by psycho-analytic investigation. The first of these is that homosexual men have experienced a specially strong fixation in regard to the mother; the second, that, in addition to their manifest heterosexuality, a very considerable measure of latent or unconscious homosexuality can be detected in all normal people. If these findings are taken into account, then, to be sure, the supposition that nature in a freakish mood created a 'third sex' falls to the ground.

It is not for psycho-analysis to solve the problem of homo-sexuality. It must rest content with disclosing the psychical mechanisms that resulted in determination of the object-choice, and with tracing the paths leading from them to the instinctual basis of the disposition. There its work ends, and it leaves the rest to biological research, which has recently brought to light, through Steinach's experiments,[14] such very important results concerning the influence exerted by the first factor mentioned above on the second and third. Psycho-analysis has a common basis with biology, in that it presupposes an original bisexuality in human beings (as in animals). But psycho-analysis cannot elucidate the intrinsic nature of what in conventional or in biological phraseology is termed 'masculine' and 'feminine': it simply takes over the two concepts and makes them the foundation of its work. When we attempt to reduce them further, we find masculinity vanishing into activity and femininity into passivity, and that does not tell us enough. In what has gone before I have tried to explain how far we may reasonably expect, or how far experience has already proved, that the elucidations yielded by analysis furnish us with the means for altering inversion. When one compares the extent to which we can influence it with the remarkable transformations that Steinach has effected in some cases by his operations, it does not make a very imposing impression. Thus it would be premature, or a harmful exaggeration, if at this stage we were to indulge in hopes of a 'therapy' of inversion that could be generally used. The cases of male homosexuality in which Steinach has been successful fulfilled the condition, which is not always present, of a very patent physical 'hermaphroditism'. Any analogous treatment of female homosexuality is at present quite obscure. If it were to consist in removing the probably hermaphroditic ovaries, and in implanting others, which would, it is hoped, be of a single sex, there would be little prospect of its being applied in practice. A woman who has felt herself to be a man, and has loved in masculine fashion, will hardly let herself be forced into playing the part of a woman when she must pay for this transformation, which is not in every way advantageous, by renouncing all hope of motherhood.

The Economic Problem in Masochism[1]

(1924)

WE HAVE A RIGHT to describe the existence of the masochistic trend in the life of the human instincts as from the economic point of view mysterious. For if mental processes are governed by the pleasure-principle, so that avoidance of 'pain' and obtaining pleasure is their first aim, masochism is incomprehensible. If physical pain and feelings of distress[2] can cease to be signals of danger and be ends in themselves, the pleasure-principle is paralysed, the watchman of our mental life is to all intents and purposes himself drugged and asleep.

In this light, masochism appears to us as a great danger, which is in no way true of sadism, its counterpart. We feel tempted to call the pleasure-principle the watchman of our lives, instead of only the watchman of our mental life. But then the question of the relation of the pleasure-principle to the two varieties of instincts that we have distinguished, the death-instincts and the erotic (libidinal) life-instincts, demands investigation, and we can reach no further conclusion about the problem of masochism till we have answered this call.

As will be remembered,[3] we have conceived the principle which governs all mental processes as a special case of Fechner's *tendency to stability*, and consequently have ascribed to the mental apparatus the aim of extinguishing, or at least of maintaining at as low a level as possible, the quantities of excitation flowing into it. For this tendency that has been presumed by us Barbara Low has suggested the name Nirvana-principle, which we accept. But we have unquestioningly identified the pleasure-pain-principle with this Nirvana-principle. From this it would follow that every 'pain' coincides with a heightening, every pleasure with a lowering, of the stimulus-tension existing in the mind; the Nirvana-principle (and the pleasure-principle which is assumed to be identical with it) would be entirely in the service of the death-instincts (the aim of which is to lead our throbbing existence into the stability of an inorganic state) and would have the function of warning us against the claims of the life-instinct, of the libido, which tries to disturb the course life endeavours to take. Unfortunately, this view cannot be correct. It seems that we experience the ebb and flow of quantities of stimuli directly in perceptions of tension which form a series, and it cannot be doubted that there is such a thing as both pleasurable tension and 'painful' lowering of tension. The condition of sexual excitement is the most striking example of a pleasurable increase in tension of this kind, but it is certainly not the only one. Pleasure and 'pain' cannot, therefore, be referred to a quantitative increase or decrease of something which we call stimulus-tension, although they clearly have a great deal to do with this factor. It seems as though they do not depend on this quantitative factor, but on some peculiarity in it which we can only describe as qualitative. We should be much further on with psychology if we knew what this qualitative peculiarity was. Perhaps it is something rhythmic, the periodical duration of the changes, the risings and fallings of the volume of stimuli; we do not know.

Whatever it is, we must perceive that the Nirvana-principle, which belongs to the death-instincts, underwent a modification in the living organism through which it became the pleasure-principle, and henceforth we shall avoid regarding the two principles as one. It is not difficult to infer what force it was that effected this modification, that is, if one has any interest at all in following this argument. It can only be the life-instinct, the libido, which has thus wrested a place for itself alongside the death-instinct in regulating the processes of life. In this way we obtain a series, a small but an interesting one: the *Nirvana*-principle expresses the tendency of the death-instincts, the *pleasure*-principle represents the claims of the libido and that modification of it, the *reality*-principle, the influence of the outer world.

None of these three principles can actually be put out of action by another. As a rule they know how to tolerate one another, although conflicts must occasionally arise from the various aims towards which each strives — a quantitative reduction of the stimulus-pressure on one side, on another side some qualitative feature in it, and lastly a postponement of the discharge of tension and a temporary acquiescence in 'painful' tension.

The conclusion to be derived from these considerations is that a description of the pleasure-principle as the watchman over our lives cannot be altogether put aside.

Let us return to masochism. It comes under our observation in three shapes: as a condition under which sexual excitation may be roused; as an expression of feminine nature; and as a norm of behaviour. According to this one may distinguish an *erotogenic*, a *feminine*, and a *moral* type of masochism. The first, the erotogenic masochism, the lust of pain, is also to be found at bottom in the other forms; the concept of it can be supported on biological and constitutional grounds; it remains incomprehensible unless one can bring oneself to make certain assumptions about matters that are wrapt in obscurity. The third, in certain respects the most important form in which masochism appears, has only lately, as a sense of guilt that is for the most part unconscious, been properly appreciated by psycho-analysis; it already admits, however, of full explanation and of co-ordination into our previous knowledge. Feminine masochism, on the other hand, is the form most accessible to observation, least mysterious, and is comprehensible in all its relations. We may begin our discussion with it.

In men (to whom for reasons connected with the material

I shall limit my remarks) we know this kind of masochism sufficiently well from the phantasies of masochistic persons, who are often in consequence impotent; their phantasies either terminate in an onanistic act or else themselves constitute the sexual gratification. These phantasies are in complete accord with the real conditions sought by masochistic perverts, whether these situations are enacted as an end in themselves or serve to induce potency and lead up to sexual intercourse. In both cases – for the real situations are in fact only a kind of make-believe performance of the phantasies – the manifest content is of being pinioned, bound, beaten painfully, whipped, in some way mis-handled, forced to obey unconditionally, defiled, degraded. Far more rarely some kind of mutilation is also included in their content, but then only in a very restricted manner. The obvious interpretation, which is easily arrived at, is that the masochist wants to be treated like a little, helpless, dependent child, but especially like a naughty child. It is unnecessary to adduce case-material in this connection, for it is all so very much alike and is accessible to any observer, even to non-analysts. But if one has an opportunity of studying cases in which the maso-chistic phantasies have undergone specially rich elaboration, one easily discovers that in them the subject is placed in a situation characteristic of womanhood, i.e. they mean that he is being castrated, is playing the passive part in coitus, or is giving birth. For this reason I have called this form of masochism *a potiori* feminine, although so many of its features point to childish life.

This stratification in superimposed layers of the infantile and the feminine will later find a simple explanation. Castration, or the blinding which represents it, often leaves a negative trace in these phantasies by the condition that just the genitals or the eyes are not to be injured in any way. (Incidentally, masochistic tortures seldom convey an impression of such seriousness as the brutalities – phantasied or actual – of sadists.) Moreover, in the manifest content of the masochistic phantasies a feeling of guilt comes to expression, it being assumed that the subject has committed some crime (the nature of which is left uncertain) which is to be expiated by his undergoing the pain and torture. This looks like a superficial rationalization of the masochistic content of the phantasy, but behind it there lies a relation to infantile masturbation. On the other hand, this element of guilt takes us to the third, the moral type of masochism.

The feminine type of masochism described is based entirely on the primary erotogenic type, on the 'lust of pain', which cannot be explained without going very far back.

In my *Drei Abhandlungen zur Sexualtheorie*, in the section on the sources of infantile sexuality, I put forward the proposition that sexual excitation arises as an accessory effect of a large series of internal processes as soon as the intensity of these processes has exceeded certain quantitative limits; indeed, that perhaps nothing very important takes place within the organism without contributing a component to the excitation of the sexual instinct. According to this, an excitation of physical pain and feelings of distress would surely also have this effect. This libidinal sympathetic excitation accompanying the tension of physical pain and feelings of distress would be an infantile physiological mechanism which ceases to operate later on. It would reach a varying degree of development in different sexual constitutions; in any case it would provide the physiological foundation on which the structure of erotogenic masochism is subsequently erected in the mind.

The inadequacy of this explanation is seen, however, in that it throws no light on the regular and close connection of masochism with sadism, its counterpart in the life of the instincts. If we go a step further back to our hypothesis of the two varieties of instincts which we believe to be active in animate beings, we come to another conclusion which, however, does not contradict the one just mentioned. In the multicellular living organism the libido meets the death or destruction instinct which holds sway there, and which tries to disintegrate this cellular being and bring each elemental primary organism into a condition of inorganic stability (though this again may be but relative). To the libido falls the task of making this destructive instinct harmless, and it manages to dispose of it by directing it to a great extent and early in life – with the help of a special organic system, the musculature – towards the objects of the outer world. It is then called the instinct of destruction, of mastery, the will to power. A section of this instinct is placed directly in the service of the sexual function, where it has an important part to play: this is true sadism. Another part is not included in this displacement outwards; it remains within the organism and is 'bound' there libidinally with the help of the accompanying sexual excitation mentioned above: this we must recognize as the original erotogenic masochism.

We are entirely without any understanding of the physiological ways and means by which this subjugation of the death-instinct by the libido can be achieved. In the psychoanalytical world of ideas we can only assume that a very extensive coalescence and fusion, varying according to conditions, of the two instincts takes place, so that we never have to deal with pure life-instincts and death-instincts at all, but only with combinations of them in different degrees. Corresponding with the fusion of instincts there may under certain influences occur a '*de*fusion' of them. How large a part of the death-instincts may refuse to be subjugated in this way by becoming attached to libidinal quantities is at present not possible to ascertain.

If one is willing to disregard a certain amount of inexactitude, it might be said that the death-instinct active in the organism – the primal sadism – is identical with masochism. After the chief part of it has been directed outwards towards objects, there remains as a residuum within the organism the true erotogenic masochism, which on the one hand becomes a component of the libido and on the other still has the subject itself for an object. So that this masochism would be a witness and a survival of that phase of development in which the amalgamation, so important for life afterwards, of death-instinct and Eros took place. We should not be astonished to hear that under certain conditions the sadism or destruction instinct which has been directed outwards can be introjected, turned inward again, regressing in this way to its earlier condition. It then provides that secondary masochism which supplements the original one.

The erotogenic type of masochism passes through all the developmental stages of the libido, and from them it takes the changing shapes it wears in the life of the mind. The fear of being devoured by the totem-animal (father) is derived from the primitive oral stage of libido-organization; the desire to be beaten by the father from the next-following sadistic-anal stage; castration, although it is subsequently denied, enters into the content of masochistic phantasies as a residue from the phallic stage[4]; and from the final genital stage are derived of course the situations characteristic of womanhood, namely, the passive part in coitus and the act of giving birth. The part played by the nates in masochism is also easily intelligible, apart from its obvious foundation in reality. The nates are the special erotogenic bodily regions which have preference in the sadistic-anal stage, as the nipple in the oral stage and the penis in the genital stage.

The third form of masochism, the moral type, is chiefly remarkable for having loosened its connection with what we recognize to be sexuality. To all other masochistic sufferings there still clings the condition that it should be administered by the loved person; it is endured at his command; in the moral type of masochism this limitation has been dropped. It is the suffering itself that matters; whether the sentence is cast by a loved or by an indifferent person is of no importance; it may even be caused by impersonal forces or circumstances, but the true masochist always holds out his cheek wherever he sees a chance of receiving a blow. One is much tempted, in explaining this attitude, to leave the libido out of account and to confine oneself to an assumption that here the instinct of destruction is again turned inwards and is now raging against the self; yet there should be some meaning in the usage of speech, which has not ceased to connect this norm of behaviour in life with erotism and calls these maimers of themselves masochists too.

True to a habit which has grown out of our technique, let us first consider the extreme, undeniably pathological form of this masochism. I have described elsewhere[5] how in analytic treatment we come across patients whose behaviour in regard to the effects of the analysis compels us to ascribe to them an 'unconscious' feeling of guilt. I there mentioned the trait by which these people are recognized (the 'negative therapeutic reaction'), and I did not conceal the fact that a strong feeling of this kind amounts to one of the most difficult resistances and the greatest menace to the success of our medical or educative aims. The gratification of this unconscious sense of guilt is perhaps the strongest item in the whole 'advantage through illness' (which is as a rule composed of many different gains), i.e. in the sum-total of the forces which oppose the cure and struggle against relinquishing the neurosis; the suffering that the neurosis involves is the very element which makes it of value to the masochistic trend. It is instructive, too, to find, against all theory and expectation, that a neurosis which has defied every therapeutic effort may vanish when the person has become involved in the misery of an unhappy marriage, has lost his fortune, or has developed a dangerous organic disease. The one form of suffering has then given way to another, and all that mattered, as we see, was that a certain level of suffering should be maintained.

Patients do not easily believe what we tell them about an unconscious sense of guilt. They know well enough by what torments (pangs of conscience) a conscious feeling of guilt, the consciousness of guilt, can express itself, and so they cannot admit that they could harbour entirely analogous feelings in themselves without observing a trace of them. I think we may meet their objection by abandoning the term 'unconscious feeling of guilt', which is in any case an incorrect one psychologically, and substitute for it a 'need for punishment' which describes the state of things observed just as aptly. We cannot, however, let ourselves be prevented from judging and localizing this unconscious feeling of guilt in the same way as we do the conscious variety.

We have ascribed to the super-ego the function of the conscience and have recognized the consciousness of guilt as an expression of a tension between ego and super-ego. The ego reacts with feelings of anxiety (pangs of conscience) to the perception that it has failed to perform the behests of its ideal, the super-ego. Now we want to know how the super-ego came to play this exacting part and why the ego has to fear a difference of opinion with its ideal.

We have said that the function of the ego consists in uniting with one another the claims of the three powers it serves, in reconciling them; and we can add that it has in the super-ego a model for this which it can strive to emulate. This super-ego is in fact just as much a representative of the *id* as of the outer world. It originated through the introjection into the ego of the first objects of the libidinal impulses in the *id*, namely, the two parents, by which process the relation to them was desexualized, that is, underwent a deflection from direct sexual aims. Only in this way was it possible for the child to overcome the Oedipus-complex. Now the super-ego has retained essential features of the introjected persons, namely, their power, their severity, their tendency to watch over and to punish. As has been set forth elsewhere,[6] it is quite conceivable that this severity becomes intensified through the 'defusion' of the instincts which takes place along with this incorporation into the ego. The super-ego, the conscience at work in it, can then become harsh, cruel and inexorable against the ego which is in its charge. The categorical imperative of Kant is thus a direct inheritance from the Oedipus-complex.

These same persons, however, whose effect persists as the

power of conscience after they have ceased to be objects of libidinal impulses in the *id*, belong also to the real outer world. This is where they came from; their power, behind which lie concealed all the influences of the past and of tradition, was one of the most acutely felt manifestations of reality. In virtue of their coincidence the super-ego, which replaces the Oedipus-complex, becomes also a representative of the real outer world and is thus a model for the ego's endeavours.

In this way the Oedipus-complex proves itself, as has already been suggested on an historical basis,[7] to be the origin of morality in each one of us. In the course of development through childhood which brings about an ever-increasing severance from the parents, their personal significance for the super-ego recedes. To the imagos they leave behind are then linked on the influences of teachers, authorities, of self-chosen models and heroes venerated by society; these persons need no longer be introjected by the ego, which has now become much more resistant. The last figure in the series beginning with the parents is that dark supremacy of Fate, which only the fewest among us are able to conceive of impersonally. Little can be said against the Dutch writer, Multatuli,[8] when he substitutes the divine pair Λόγος καὶ Ἀνάγκη for the Μοῖρα of the Greeks; but all those who transfer the guidance of the world to Providence, to God, or to God and Nature, rouse a suspicion that they still look upon these farthest and remotest powers as a parent-couple – mythologically – and imagine themselves linked to them by libidinal bonds. In *Das Ich und das Es* I have made an attempt to derive the objective fear of death in mankind also from the same sort of parental conception of Fate. It seems to be very difficult to free oneself from it.

After these preliminaries we can return to our consideration of the moral type of masochism. We said that the persons in question, by their behaviour – in the treatment and in their lives – make the impression of being morally inhibited to an excessive degree, of being dominated by an especially sensitive conscience, although they are not at all conscious of any such ultra-morality. On close inspection we can surely see the distinction which divides this kind of unconscious development of morality from the moral type of masochism. In the first, the accent falls on the heightened sadism of the super-ego to which the ego subjects itself; in the last, it falls instead on the masochism in the ego itself, which seeks punishment, whether from the super-ego within or from parental authorities without. It may be excused us that we confounded them to begin with, for in both cases it is a question of a relation between the ego and the super-ego or the powers equivalent to it; in both cases there is a craving which is satisfied by punishment and suffering. It is hardly an insignificant detail then that the sadism of the super-ego is for the most part acutely perceived consciously, while the masochistic impulse of the ego as a rule remains hidden from the person and must be inferred from his behaviour.

The unconsciousness of the moral form of masochism guides us to a near clue. We have translated the words 'unconscious feeling of guilt' as meaning a need for punishment by some parental authority. Now we know that the wish to be beaten by the father, which is so common, is closely connected with the other wish, to have some passive (feminine) sexual relations with him, and is only a regressive distortion of the latter. If we introduce this explanation into the content of moral masochism, its hidden meaning becomes clear to us. Conscience and morality arose through overcoming, desexualizing, the Oedipus-complex; in moral masochism morality becomes sexualized afresh, the Oedipus-complex is re-activated, a regression from morality back to the Oedipus-complex is under way. This is to the advantage neither of the person concerned nor of morality. An individual may, it is true, preserve the whole or a certain amount of his morality alongside his masochism, but, on the other hand, a good part of his conscience may become swallowed up by his masochism. Further, the masochism in him creates a temptation to 'sinful acts' which must then be expiated by the reproaches of the sadistic conscience (as in so many Russian character-types) or by chastisement from the great parental authority of Fate. In order to provoke punishment from this last parent-substitute the masochist must do something inexpedient, act against his own interests, ruin the prospects which the real world offers him, and possibly destroy his own existence in the world of reality.

The revulsion of sadism against the self regularly occurs under the condition of civilized suppression of the instincts, which withholds a great part of the destructive instinctual components from being exercised in life. One can imagine that this backward-flowing part of the instinct of destruction comes to expression in the ego as an intensified masochism. The manifestations of conscience allow us to infer, however, that the destructiveness rebounding from the outer world is also absorbed by the super-ego without any such transformation and increases its sadism against the ego. The sadism of the super-ego and the masochism of the ego supplement each other and combine to produce the same effects. In my opinion it is only in this way possible to understand how it is that a feeling of guilt ensues – frequently or even quite generally – from a suppression of instinct and how it is that the more anyone refrains from aggressiveness towards others the more strict and sensitive his conscience becomes. One might expect that a person who knows himself to be in the habit of avoiding aggressions that are regarded as undesirable by civilization would have a good conscience as a result and would therefore watch over his ego less suspiciously. The situation is generally represented as though the requirements of social life came first and the instinctual renunciation were its consequence. The origin of morality remains then unexplained. The actual state of things seems to be a reversal of this: the first renunciation of instinctual gratification is enforced by external powers, and it is this that creates morality, which expresses itself in conscience and exacts a further renunciation of instinct.

Moral masochism thus becomes the classical piece of evidence for the existence of 'instinctual fusion'. Its dangerousness lies in its origin in the death-instinct and represents that part of the latter which escaped deflection on to the outer world in the form of an instinct of destruction. But since, on the other hand, it has the value of an erotic component, even the destruction of anyone by himself cannot occur without gratification of the libido.

Papers on Technique

Observations on 'Wild' Psycho-Analysis[1]

(1910)

A FEW DAYS AGO an elderly lady, under the protection of a female friend, called upon me for a consultation, complaining of anxiety-states. She was in the second half of the forties, fairly well preserved, and had obviously not yet finished with her womanhood. A divorce from her last husband had been the occasion exciting the anxiety-states; but the anxiety had become greatly intensified, according to her account, since she had consulted a young physician in the suburb she lived in, for he had informed her that her sexual desires were the cause of her anxiety. He said that she could not tolerate the loss of intercourse with her husband, and so there were only three ways by which she could recover her health – she must either return to her husband, or take a lover, or satisfy herself. Since then she had been convinced that she was incurable, for she would not return to her husband, and the other two alternatives were repugnant to her moral and religious feelings. She had come to me, however, because the doctor had said that I was responsible for this new opinion, and that she had only to come and ask me to confirm what he said, and I should tell her that this and nothing else was the truth. The friend who was with her, a still older, pinched and unhealthy-looking woman, then implored me to assure the patient that the doctor was mistaken. It could not possibly be true, for she herself had been a widow for many years, and had remained respectable without suffering from anxiety.

I will not dwell on the awkward predicament in which I was placed by this visit, but instead will consider the conduct of the practitioner who sent this lady to me. First, however, it will be as well to adopt a cautious attitude, which may possibly not be superfluous – indeed we will hope so. Long experience has taught me – as it may others – not to accept straight away as true what patients, especially nervous patients, relate about their physician. A neurologist not only easily becomes the object of many of the patient's hostile feelings, whatever method of treatment he employs; he must also sometimes resign himself to accepting responsibility, by a kind of projection, for the buried repressed wishes of his nervous patients. That such accusations then nowhere find more credence than among other physicians is a melancholy but a significant circumstance.

I have some grounds, therefore, for hoping that this lady gave me a tendentiously distorted account of what her physician had said, and that I do a man who is unknown to me an injustice by connecting my remarks about 'wild' psycho-analysis with this incident. But all the same, by doing so I may perhaps prevent others from acting wrongly towards their patients.

Let us suppose, therefore, that her medical practitioner spoke to the patient exactly as she reported of him. Everyone will at once vouchsafe the criticism that if a physician holds it necessary to discuss the question of sexuality with a woman he must do so with tact and consideration. Compliance with this demand, however, coincides with carrying out certain of the *technical* regulations of psycho-analysis; moreover, the physician in question was ignorant of a number of the *scientific* principles of psycho-analysis or had misapprehended them, and thus showed how little understanding of its nature and purposes he had in fact acquired.

We will begin with the second of these, with his scientific errors. His advice to the lady shows clearly in what sense he understands the expression 'sexual life' – in the popular sense, namely, in which by sexual needs nothing is meant but the need for coitus or analogous acts producing orgasm and emission of sexual secretions. The physician cannot have been unaware, however, that psycho-analysis is commonly reproached with having extended the connotation of the term 'sexual' far beyond its usual range. The fact is undisputed; whether it may justly be used as a reproach shall not be discussed here. In psycho-analysis the term 'sexuality' comprises far more; it goes lower and also higher than the popular sense of the word. This extension is justified genetically; we reckon as belonging to 'sexual life' all expressions of tender feeling, which spring from the source of primitive sexual feelings, even when those feelings have become inhibited in regard to their original sexual aim or have exchanged this aim for another which is no longer sexual. For this reason we prefer to speak of *psycho-sexuality*, thus laying stress on the point that the mental factor should not be overlooked or under-estimated. We use the word 'sexuality' in the same comprehensive sense as that in which the German language uses the word *lieben* (to love). And we have long known that a mental lack of satisfaction with all its consequences can exist where there is no lack of normal sexual intercourse; as therapeutists, too, we have constantly to remember that the unsatisfied sexual trends (the substitutive satisfactions of which in the form of nervous symptoms we have to combat) can often find only very inadequate outlet in coitus or other sexual acts.

Anyone not sharing this psycho-analytical point of view has no right to call to his aid psycho-analytical theories concerned with the aetiological significance of sexuality. By emphasizing exclusively the somatic factor in sexuality he certainly simplifies the problem greatly, but he alone must bear the responsibility for what he does.

A second and equally gross misunderstanding is discernible behind the physician's advice.

It is true that psycho-analysis puts forward lack of sexual satisfaction as the cause of nervous disorders. But does it not also go much further than this? Is its teaching to be ignored as too complicated when it declares that nervous symptoms arise from a conflict between two forces – on the one hand, the libido (which is for the most part excessive), and on the other, a too severe aversion from sexuality or a repression? No one who remembers this second factor, which is by no means secondary in importance, can ever believe that sexual satisfaction in itself constitutes a remedy of general reliability for the sufferings of neurotics. A good number of nervous persons are, indeed, either in the actual circumstances or altogether incapable of satisfaction. If they were capable of it, if they were without their inner resistances, the strength of the instinct itself would point the way to satisfaction for them even though no physician recommended it. What is the good, therefore, of advice such as that supposed to have been given to this lady by her physician?

Even if it could be justified scientifically, it is not advice that she can carry out. If she had had no inner resistances against onanism or against a liaison she would of course have adopted one of these measures long before. Or does the physician think that a woman of over forty has never heard of such a thing as taking a lover, or does he over-estimate his influence so much as to think that she could never decide upon such a step without medical recommendation?

All this seems very simple, and yet it must be admitted that there is one factor which often complicates the issue in forming a judgement. Some nervous states which we call the *actual* neuroses, such as typical neurasthenia and pure forms of anxiety-neurosis, obviously depend on the physical factor in sexual life, and we have no certain knowledge of the part played in them by the mental factor and by repression. In such cases it is natural that the physician should first consider some 'actual' therapy, some alteration in the physical sexual way of life, and he does so with perfect justification if his diagnosis is correct. The lady who consulted the young physician complained chiefly of anxiety-states, and so he probably assumed that she was suffering from an *anxiety-neurosis*, and felt justified in recommending an actual therapy to her. Again a convenient misapprehension! A person suffering from anxiety is not for that reason necessarily suffering from anxiety-neurosis; a diagnosis of it cannot be based on its name; one has to know what manifestations are comprised in an anxiety-neurosis, and be able to distinguish it from other pathological states in which anxiety appears. My impression was that the lady in question was suffering from anxiety-hysteria, and the whole value of such nosographical distinctions, one which quite justifies them, lies in the fact that they indicate a different aetiology and a different therapy. No one who took into consideration the possibility of anxiety-hysteria in this case would have fallen into the error of neglecting the mental factors, as this physician did with his three alternatives.

Oddly enough, the three therapeutic alternatives of this would-be psycho-analyst leave no room for – psycho-analysis! This woman can only be cured of her anxiety by returning to her husband, or by satisfying her needs by onanism or with a lover. And where does analytic treatment come in, the treatment which we regard as the first remedy in anxiety-states?

This brings us to the *technical* errors to be remarked in the way that, according to our assumption, this physician proceeded. The idea that a neurotic is suffering from a sort of ignorance, and that if one removes this ignorance by telling him facts (about the causal connection of his illness with his life, about his experiences in childhood, and so on) he must recover, is an idea that has long been superseded, and one derived from superficial appearances. The pathological factor is not his ignorance in itself, but the root of this ignorance in his *inner resistances*; it was they that first called this ignorance into being, and they still maintain it now. In combating these resistances lies the task of the therapy. Telling the patient what he does not know because he has repressed it, is only one of the necessary preliminaries in the therapy. If knowledge about his unconscious were as important for the patient as the inexperienced in psycho-analysis imagine, it would be sufficient to cure him for him to go to lectures or read books. Such measures, however, have as little effect on the symptoms of nervous disease as distributing menu-cards in time of famine has on people's hunger. The analogy goes even further than its obvious application, too; for describing his unconscious to the patient is regularly followed by intensification of the conflict in him and exacerbation of his symptoms.

Since, however, psycho-analysis cannot dispense with making

this disclosure to patients, it prescribes that two conditions are to be fulfilled before it is done. First, by preparatory work, the repressed material must have come very near to the patient's thoughts, and secondly, he must be sufficiently firmly attached by an affective relationship to the physician (transference) to make it impossible for him to take fresh flight again.

Only when these two conditions are fulfilled is it possible to recognize and to overcome the resistances which have led to the repression and the ignorance. Psycho-analytic measures, therefore, cannot possibly dispense with a fairly long period of contact with the patient, and attempts to bully the patient during his first consultation by brusquely telling him the hidden things one infers behind his story are technically reprehensible; they mostly lead to their own doom, too, by inspiring a hearty dislike for the physician in the patient and putting an end to any further influence.

Besides all this, one may sometimes make a false inference, and one is never in a position to discover the whole truth. In psycho-analysis these exact technical precautions take the place of a vague demand, implying a peculiar talent, for 'medical tact'.

It is not enough, therefore, for a physician to know a little of what psycho-analysis has discovered; he must also have familiarized himself with its technique if he wishes his medical practice to be guided by a psycho-analytic point of view. This technique is even today not to be learnt from books, and it is certainly not to be discovered independently without great sacrifices of time, labour and success. It is to be learnt, like other medical measures, from those who are already proficient in it. In forming a judgement on the incident that I took as a starting-point for these remarks, therefore, it is a matter of some significance that I do not know the physician who is said to have given the lady such advice and have never before heard his name.

Neither for myself nor for my friends and co-workers is it pleasant to claim in this way a monopoly in the use of psycho-analytic technique. But in face of the danger to patients and to the cause of psycho-analysis which one foresees in this 'wild' psycho-analysis, we have no other choice. In the spring of 1910 we founded an International Psycho-Analytical Association, in which the members admit their participation by allowing publication of their names, in order to be able to repudiate responsibility for what is done by those who do not belong to us and yet call their methods 'psycho-analysis'. For as a matter of fact 'wild' analysts of this kind do more harm to the cause of psycho-analysis than to individual patients. I have often found that a clumsy feat of a similar kind led to good results in the end, although it first produced an exacerbation of the patient's condition. Not always, but still often. When he has abused the physician enough and feels impervious enough to any further influence of the kind, his symptoms give way, or he decides to take some step leading to recovery. The final improvement then 'comes of itself', or is ascribed to some entirely harmless treatment by another physician to whom the patient turned afterwards. In the case of the lady whose complaint against her doctor we have heard, I should say that, in spite of all, the wild psycho-analyst did more for her than some highly respected authority who might have told her she was suffering from a 'vasomotor neurosis'. He did force her attention to the real cause of her trouble, or in that direction, and in spite of all her struggles that cannot be without some favourable results. But he has done himself harm and helped to intensify the prejudices which patients feel, owing to their natural resistances, against the ways of psycho-analysts. And this can be avoided.

The Dynamics of the Transference[1]

(1912)

THE ALMOST inexhaustible subject of 'transference' has recently been dealt with in this Journal by W. Stekel in a descriptive manner.[2] I wish to add a few remarks in order to make clear how it happens that the transference inevitably arises during the analysis and comes to play its well-known part in the treatment.

Let us bear clearly in mind that every human being has acquired, by the combined operation of inherent disposition and of external influences in childhood, a special individuality in the exercise of his capacity to love – that is, in the conditions which he sets up for loving, in the impulses he gratifies by it, and in the aims he sets out to achieve in it.[3] This forms a *cliché* or stereotype in him, so to speak (or even several), which perpetually repeats and reproduces itself as life goes on, in so far as external circumstances and the nature of the accessible love-objects permit, and is indeed itself to some extent modifiable by later impressions. Now our experience has shown that of these feelings which determine the capacity to love only a part has undergone full psychical development; this part is directed towards reality, and can be made use of by the conscious personality, of which it forms part. The other part of these libidinal impulses has been held up in development, withheld from the conscious personality and from reality, and may either expend itself only in phantasy, or may remain completely buried in the unconscious so that the conscious personality is unaware of its existence. Expectant libidinal impulses will inevitably be roused, in anyone whose need for love is not being satisfactorily gratified in reality, by each new person coming upon the scene, and it is more than probable that both parts of the libido, the conscious and the unconscious, will participate in this attitude.

It is therefore entirely normal and comprehensible that the libido-cathexes, expectant and in readiness as they are in those who have not adequate gratification, should be turned also towards the person of the physician. As we should expect, this accumulation of libido will be attached to prototypes, bound up with one of the *clichés* already established in the mind of the person concerned, or, to put it in another way, the patient will weave the figure of the physician into one of the 'series' already constructed in his mind. If the physician should be specially connected in this way with the father-imago (as Jung has happily named it),[4] it is quite in accordance with his actual relationship to the patient; but the transference is not bound to this prototype;

it can also proceed from the mother- or brother-imago and so on. The peculiarity of the transference to the physician lies in its excess, in both character and degree, over what is rational and justifiable – a peculiarity which becomes comprehensible when we consider that in this situation the transference is effected not merely by the conscious ideas and expectations of the patient, but also by those that are under suppression, or unconscious.

Nothing more would need to be said or would perplex us concerning this characteristic of the transference, if it were not that two points which are of particular interest to psycho-analysts still remain unexplained by it. First, it is not clear why neurotic subjects under analysis develop the transference so much more intensely than those who are not being analysed; and secondly, it remains a mystery why in analysis the transference provides the *strongest resistance* to the cure, whereas in other forms of treatment we recognize it as the vehicle of the healing process, the necessary condition for success. Experience shows, and a test will always confirm it, that when the patient's free associations fail,[5] the obstacle can be removed every time by an assurance that he is now possessed by a thought which concerns the person of the physician or something relating to him. No sooner is this explanation given than the obstacle is removed, or at least the absence of thoughts has been transformed into a refusal to speak.

It appears at the first glance to be an enormous disadvantage in psycho-analysis as compared with other methods that in it the transference, elsewhere such a powerful instrument for success, should become here the most formidable ally of the resistance. On closer consideration, however, the first of these difficulties at least will disappear. It is not the fact that the transference in psycho-analysis develops more intensely and immoderately than outside it. Institutions and homes for the treatment of nervous patients by methods other than analysis provide instances of transference in its most excessive and unworthy forms, extending even to complete subjection, which also show its erotic character unmistakably. A sensitive observer, Gabriele Reuter, depicted these facts at a time when psycho-analysis hardly existed, in a remarkable book[6] which altogether reveals great insight into the nature and causes of the neuroses. This peculiarity of the transference is not, therefore, to be placed to the account of psycho-analysis but is to be ascribed to the neurosis itself. The second problem still remains unexplained.

This problem must now be tackled at close quarters: Why does the transference in analysis confront us as resistance? Let us call to mind the psychological situation in the treatment. One of the invariable and indispensable preliminary conditions in *every* case of psychoneurosis is the process which Jung has aptly named *introversion* of the libido.[7] This means that the quantity of libido which is capable of becoming conscious, and is directed towards reality, has become diminished, while the part which is unconscious and turned away from reality (and, although it may still nourish phantasies in the person concerned, belongs to the unconscious) is by so much increased. The libido (entirely or in part) has found its way back into regression and has re-animated the infantile imagos;[8] and thither we pursue it in the analytic treatment, aiming always at unearthing it, making it accessible to consciousness and at last serviceable to reality. Wherever in our analytic delving we come upon one of the hiding-places of the withdrawn libido, there ensues a battle; all the forces which have brought about the regression of the libido will rise up as 'resistances' against our efforts in order to maintain the new condition. For if the introversion or regression of the libido had not been justified by some relation to the outer world (in the broadest terms, by a frustration of some desired gratification) and at the time been even expedient, it would never have taken place at all. Yet the resistances which have this origin are not the only ones, nor even the most powerful. The libido at the disposal of the personality had always been exposed to the attraction of unconscious complexes (strictly speaking, of that part of those complexes which belongs to the unconscious), and underwent regression because the attraction of reality had weakened. In order to free it, this attraction of the unconscious must now be overcome; that is, the repression of the unconscious impulses and their derivatives, which has subsequently developed in the mind of the person concerned, must be lifted. Here arises by far the greater part of the resistances, which so often succeed in upholding the illness, even though the original grounds for the recoil from reality have now disappeared. From both these sources come the resistances with which the analysis has to struggle.

Every step of the treatment is accompanied by resistance; every single thought, every mental act of the patient's, must pay toll to the resistance, and represents a compromise between the forces urging towards the cure and those gathered to oppose it.

Now as we follow a pathogenic complex from its representative in consciousness (whether this be a conspicuous symptom or something apparently quite harmless) back to its root in the unconscious, we soon come to a place where the resistance makes itself felt so strongly that it affects the next association, which has to appear as a compromise between the demands of this resistance and those of the work of exploration. Experience shows that this is where the transference enters on the scene. When there is anything in the complex-material (the content of the complex) which can at all suitably be transferred on to the person of the physician such a transference will be effected, and from it will arise the next association; it will then manifest itself by the signs of resistance – for instance, a cessation in the flow of associations. We conclude from such experiences that this transferred idea is able to force itself through to consciousness in preference to all other possible associations, just *because* it also satisfies resistance. This type of incident is repeated innumerable times during an analysis. Over and over again, when one draws near to a pathogenic complex, that part of it which is first thrust forward into consciousness will be some aspect of it which can be transferred; having been so, it will then be defended with the utmost obstinacy by the patient.[9]

Once this point is won, the elements of that complex which are still unresolved cause little further difficulty. The longer the analysis lasts, and the more clearly the patient has recognized that distortions of the pathogenic material in themselves offer no protection against disclosure, the more consistently he makes use of that variety of distortion which obviously brings him the greatest advantage, the distortion by transference. These incidents all converge towards a situation in which eventually all the conflicts must be fought out on the field of transference.

Transference in analysis thus always seems at first to be only the strongest weapon of the resistance, and we are entitled to draw the inference that the intensity and duration of the transference are an effect and expression of the resistance. The mechanism of transference is indeed explained by the state of readiness in which the libido that has remained accumulated about the infantile imagos exists, but the part played by it in the process of cure is only intelligible in the light of its relation to the resistance.

How does it come about that the transference is so preeminently suitable as a weapon of resistance? One might think that this could easily be answered. It is surely clear enough that it must become peculiarly difficult to own up to any particular reprehended wish when the confession must be made to the very person with whom that feeling is most concerned. To proceed at all in such situations as this necessity produces would appear hardly possible in real life. This impossibility is precisely what the patient is aiming at when he merges the physician with the object of his emotions. Yet on closer consideration we see that this apparent gain cannot supply the answer to the riddle, for, on the contrary, an attitude of affectionate and devoted attachment can surmount any difficulty in confession; in analogous situations in real life we say: 'I don't feel ashamed with you; I can tell you everything.' The transference to the physician might quite as well relieve the difficulties of confession, and we still do not understand why it aggravates them.

The answer to this reiterated problem will not be found by pondering it any further, but must be sought in the experience gained by examination of individual instances of transference-resistance occurring in the course of an analysis. From these one perceives eventually that the use of the transference for resistance cannot be understood so long as one thinks simply of 'transference'. One is forced to distinguish 'positive' transference from 'negative' transference, the transference of affectionate feeling from that of hostile feeling, and to deal separately with the two varieties of the transference to the physician. Positive transference can then be divided further into such friendly or affectionate feelings as are capable of becoming conscious and the extensions of these in the unconscious. Of these last, analysis shows that they invariably rest ultimately on an erotic basis; so that we have to conclude that all the feelings of sympathy, friendship, trust and so forth which we expend in life are genetically connected with sexuality and have developed out of purely sexual desires by an enfeebling of their sexual aim, however pure and non-sensual they may appear in the forms they take on to our conscious self-perception. To begin with we knew none but sexual objects; psycho-analysis shows us that those persons whom in real life we merely respect or are fond of may be sexual objects to us in our unconscious minds still.

So the answer to the riddle is this, that the transference to the physician is only suited for resistance in so far as it consists in *negative* feeling or in the repressed *erotic* elements of positive feeling. As we 'raise' the transference by making it conscious we detach only these two components of the emotional relationship from the person of the physician; the conscious and unobjectionable component of it remains, and brings about the successful result in psycho-analysis as in all other remedial methods. In so far we readily admit that the results of psycho-analysis rest upon a basis of suggestion; only by suggestion we must be understood to mean that which we, with Ferenczi,[10] find that it consists of – influence on a person through and by means of the transference-manifestations of which he is capable. The eventual independence of the patient is our ultimate object when we use suggestion to bring him to carry out a mental operation that will necessarily result in a lasting improvement in his mental condition.

The next question is, Why do these manifestations of transference-resistance appear only in psycho-analysis and not in other forms of treatment, in institutions, for example? The answer is that they do appear there also, but they need to be recognized for what they are. The outbreak of negative transference is a very common occurrence in institutions; as soon as he is seized by it the patient leaves, uncured or worse. The erotic transference has not such an inhibitory effect in institutions, since there, as otherwise in life, it is decorously glossed over, instead of being exposed; nevertheless, it betrays itself unequivocally as resistance to the cure, not, indeed, by driving the patient out of the place – on the contrary, it binds him to the spot – but just as certainly by keeping him away from real life. Actually it is quite unimportant for his cure whether or not the patient can overcome this or that anxiety or inhibition in the institution; what is of importance, on the contrary, is whether or not he will be free from them in real life.

The negative transference requires a more thorough elucidation than is possible within the limits of this paper. It is found in the curable forms of the psychoneuroses alongside the affectionate transference, often both directed on to the same person at the same time, a condition for which Bleuler has coined the useful term 'ambivalence'.[11] This ambivalence of the feelings appears to be normal up to a point, but a high degree of it is certainly a special peculiarity of neurotics. In the obsessional neurosis an early 'splitting of the pairs of opposites' seems to characterize the instinctual life and to form one of the constitutional conditions of this disease. The ability of neurotics to make the transference a form of resistance is most easily accounted for by ambivalence in the flow of feelings. Where the capacity to transfer feeling has come to be of an essentially negative order, as with paranoids, the possibility of influence or cure ceases.

After all this investigation we have so far considered one aspect only of transference-phenomena; some attention must be given to another side of this question. Those who have formed a true impression of the effect of an extreme transference-resistance on the patient, of the way in which as soon as he comes under its influence he is hurled out of all reality in his relation to the physician – how he then arrogates to himself freedom to ignore the psycho-analytic rule (to communicate without reserve whatever goes through his mind), how all the resolutions with which he entered upon the analysis then become obliterated, and how the logical connections and conclusions which just before had impressed him deeply then become matters of indifference to him – will need some further explanation than that supplied by the factors mentioned above to account for this effect, and these other factors are, indeed, not far to seek; they lie again in the psychological situation in which the analysis has placed the patient.

In following up the libido that is withdrawn from consciousness we penetrate into the region of the unconscious, and this provokes reactions which bring with them to light many of the characteristics of unconscious processes as we have learnt to know them from the study of dreams. The unconscious feelings strive to avoid the recognition which the cure demands; they seek instead for reproduction, with all the power of hallucination and the inappreciation of time characteristic of the unconscious. The patient ascribes, just as in dreams, currency and reality to what results from the awakening of his unconscious feelings; he seeks to discharge his emotions, regardless of the reality of the situation. The physician requires of him that he shall fit these emotions into their place in the treatment and in his life-history, subject them to rational consideration, and appraise them at their true psychical value. This struggle between physician and patient, between intellect and the forces of instinct, between recognition and the striving for discharge, is fought out almost entirely over the transference-manifestations. This is the ground on which the victory must be won, the final expression of which is lasting recovery from the neurosis. It is undeniable that the subjugation of the transference-manifestations provides the greatest difficulties for the psycho-analyst; but it must not be forgotten that they, and they only, render the invaluable service of making the patient's buried and forgotten love-emotions actual and manifest; for in the last resort no one can be slain *in absentia* or *in effigie.*

On Beginning the Treatment:
The Question of the First Communications.
The Dynamics of the Cure[1]

(1913)

HE WHO HOPES to learn the fine art of the game of chess from books will soon discover that only the opening and closing moves of the game admit of exhaustive systematic description, and that the endless variety of the moves which develop from the opening defies description; the gap left in the instructions can only be filled in by the zealous study of games fought out by master-hands. The rules which can be laid down for the practical application of psycho-analysis in treatment are subject to similar limitations.

I intend now to try to collect together for the use of practising analysts some of the rules for the opening of the treatment. Among them there are some which may seem to be mere details, as indeed they are. Their justification is that they are simply rules of the game, acquiring their importance by their connection with the whole plan of the game. I do well, however, to bring them forward as 'recommendations' without claiming any unconditional acceptance for them. The exceptional diversity in the mental constellations concerned, the plasticity of all mental processes, and the great number of the determining factors involved prevent the formulation of a stereotyped technique, and also bring it about that a course of action, ordinarily legitimate, may be at times ineffective, while one which is usually erroneous may occasionally lead to the desired end. These circumstances do not prevent us from establishing a procedure for the physician which will be found most generally efficient.

Some years ago I set forth the considerations of chief importance in the selection of patients, which I shall therefore not repeat here[2]; since that time other psycho-analysts have confirmed their validity. I will add, though, that since then, when I know little of a case, I have formed the practice of first undertaking it only provisionally for one or two weeks. If one breaks off within this period the patient is spared the distress of an unsuccessful attempt at cure; it was only 'taking a sounding' in order to learn more about the case and to decide whether it was a suitable one for psycho-analysis. No other kind of preliminary examination is possible; the most lengthy discussions and questionings in ordinary consultation are no substitute. This experiment, however, is in itself the beginning of an analysis, and must conform to its rules; there may perhaps be this difference in that on the whole one lets the patient talk, and explains nothing more than is absolutely necessary to keep him talking.

For the purposes of diagnosis, also, it is an advantage to begin with a period of a few weeks designed as an experiment. Often enough, when one sees a case of neurosis with hysterical or obsessional symptoms, mild in character and of short duration (just the type of case, that is, which one would regard as suitable for the treatment), a doubt which must not be overlooked arises whether the case may not be one of incipient dementia praecox, so called (schizophrenia, according to Bleuler; paraphrenia, as I prefer to call it), and may not sooner or later develop well-marked signs of this disease. I do not agree that it is always possible to effect the distinction so easily. I know that there are psychiatrists who hesitate less often in their differential diagnosis, but I have been convinced that they are just as often mistaken. For the psycho-analyst, however, the mistake is more serious than for so-called clinical psychiatrists. The latter has little of value to offer either to the one type of case or to the other; he merely runs the risk of a theoretical mistake, and his diagnosis has but an academic interest. In an unsuitable case, however, the psycho-analyst has committed a practical error; he has occasioned useless expense and discredited his method of treatment; he cannot fulfil his promise of cure if the patient is suffering from paraphrenia instead of from hysteria or obsessional neurosis, and therefore he has particularly strong motives for avoiding mistakes in diagnosis. In an experimental course of a few weeks suspicious signs will often be observed which will decide him not to pursue the attempt further. Unfortunately I cannot assert that an attempt of this kind will invariably ensure certainty; it is but one more useful precaution.[3]

Lengthy preliminary discussions before the beginning of the treatment, previous treatment by another method, and also previous acquaintance between physician and patient, have certain disadvantageous consequences for which one must be prepared. They result in the patient entering upon the analysis with a transference already effected, which must then be slowly uncovered by the physician; whereas otherwise he is in a position to observe the growth and development of it from the outset. By this means the patient gains a start upon us which we do not willingly grant him in the treatment.

One must distrust all those who wish to put off beginning the treatment. Experience shows that at the appointed time they fail to return, even though their motive for the delay (that is, their rationalization of the intention) appears to the novice to be above suspicion.

Special difficulties arise when friendship or acquaintance already exists between the physician and the patient, or their families. The psycho-analyst who is asked to undertake treatment of the wife or child of a friend must be prepared for it to cost him the friendship, no matter what the outcome of the treatment; nevertheless he must make the sacrifice unless he can propose a trustworthy substitute.

Both the general public and medical men — still fain to confound psycho-analytic with suggestive treatment — are inclined to attribute great importance to the expectations which the patient brings to the new treatment. They often believe that one patient will not give much trouble because he has a great belief in psycho-analysis and is fully convinced of its truth and curative power; and that another patient will doubtless prove more difficult because he is of a sceptical nature and will not believe until he has experienced good results in his own person. Actually, however, this attitude on the part of the patient has very little importance; his preliminary belief or disbelief is almost negligible compared with the inner resistances which hold the neurosis fast. A blissful trustfulness on the patient's part makes the relationship at first a very pleasant one; one thanks him for it, but warns him that this favourable prepossession will be shattered by the first difficulty arising in the analysis. To the sceptic one says that the analysis requires no faith; that he may be as critical and suspicious as he pleases; that one does not regard his attitude as the effect of his judgement at all, for he is not in a position to form a reliable judgement on the matter; his distrust is but a symptom like his other symptoms and will not interfere if he conscientiously carries out what the rule of the treatment requires of him.

Whoever is familiar with the nature of neurosis will not be astonished to hear that even a man who is very well able to carry out analysis upon others can behave like any other mortal and be capable of producing violent resistances as soon as he himself becomes the object of analytic investigation. When this happens it serves to remind us again of the dimensions which the mind has in regard to its depth, and it does not surprise us to find that a neurosis is rooted in mental strata that were never penetrated by an intellectual study of analysis.

Points of importance for the beginning of the treatment are the arrangements about time and money. In regard to time, I adhere rigidly to the principle of leasing a definite hour. A certain hour of my available working day is appointed to each patient; it is his, and he is liable for it, even if he does not make use of it. This arrangement, which is regarded as a matter of course for teachers of music or languages among our upper classes, perhaps seems too rigorous for a medical man, or even unworthy of the profession. All the many accidents which may prevent the patient from attending every day at the same hour will be referred to, and some allowance will be expected for the numerous intercurrent ailments which may arise in the course of a lengthy analytic treatment. My only answer is: No other way is practicable. Under a less stringent regime the 'occasional' non-attendances accumulate so greatly that the physician's material existence is threatened; whereas strict adherence to the arrangement has the effect that accidental hindrances do not arise at all and intercurrent illnesses but seldom. One is hardly ever put in the position of enjoying a leisure hour which one is paid for and would be ashamed of; the work continues without interruptions, and one is spared the disheartening and bewildering experience that an unexpected pause in the work always occurs just when it promises to be especially important and productive. Nothing brings home to one with such overwhelming conviction the significance of the psychogenic factor in the daily life of mankind, the frequency of fictitious 'indispositions', and the non-existence of chance as the practice of psycho-analysis for some years strictly on the principle of hire by the hour. In cases of indubitable organic illness, the occurrence of which cannot be excluded in spite of interest in the psychical work, I break off the treatment, regard myself as entitled to dispose otherwise of the hour which becomes free, and take the patient back again when he has recovered and I again have a free hour.

I work with my patients every day, except Sundays and public holidays, that is, usually six days a week. For slight cases, or the continuation of a treatment already well advanced, three days in the week will suffice. Otherwise, restriction of the time expended brings no advantage to physician or patient; it is not to be thought of at the beginning. Even short interruptions have a disconcerting effect on the work; we used to speak jokingly of the 'Monday-crust' when we began work again after the rest on Sunday; with more frequent intervals the risk arises that one will not be able to keep pace with the patient's real life, that the analysis will lose contact with the present and be forced into by-paths. Occasionally one meets with patients to whom one must give more than the average time of one hour a day, because the best part of an hour is gone before they begin to open out and to communicate anything at all.

An unwelcome question which the patient asks the physician at the outset is: How long will the treatment last? What length of time will you require to relieve me of my trouble? If one has proposed an experimental course of a few weeks one can avoid a direct reply to this question by undertaking to give a more trustworthy answer later on. The answer is like that of Aesop in the fable of the Wanderer; on being asked the length of the journey he answered 'Go', and gave the explanation that he must know the pilgrim's pace before he could tell the time his journey would take him. This explanation helps one over the difficulty at the start, but the comparison is not a good one, for the neurotic can easily alter his pace and at times make but very slow progress. The question of the probable duration of the treatment is hardly to be answered at all, in fact.

As a result of the lack of insight on the part of patients combined with the lack of straightforwardness on the part of physicians, analysis is expected to realize the most boundless claims in the shortest time. As an example I will give some details from a letter which I received a few days ago from a lady in Russia. Her age is fifty-three; her illness began twenty-three years ago; for the last ten years she has been incapable of continued work; 'various cures in homes' have not succeeded in making an 'active life' possible for her. She hopes to be completely cured by psycho-analysis, of which she has read, but her illness has already cost her family so much that she cannot undertake a visit of more than six weeks or two months to Vienna. In addition to this there is another difficulty: she wishes to 'explain herself' from the beginning in writing, since any discussion of her complexes would excite an attack or render her 'temporarily dumb'. No one would expect a man to lift a heavy table with two fingers as if it were a little stool, or to build a large house in the time it would take to put up a wooden hut, but as soon as it becomes a question of the neuroses (which mankind seems not yet to have fitted into the general scheme of his ideas) even intelligent people forget the necessity for proportion between work, time and success – a comprehensible result, too, of the deep ignorance which prevails concerning the aetiology of neuroses. Thanks to this ignorance a neurosis is generally regarded as a sort of 'maiden from afar'; the world knows not whence it comes, and therefore expects it to vanish away some day.

Medical men support this happy belief; even the experienced among them often fail to estimate properly the severity of nervous disorders. A friend and colleague of mine, to whose credit I account it that after several decades of scientific work on other principles he has betaken himself to the recognition of psycho-analysis, once wrote to me: What we need is a short, convenient form of treatment for out-patients suffering from obsessional neurosis. I could not supply him with it, and felt ashamed; so I tried to excuse myself with the remark that probably physicians would also be very glad of a treatment for consumption or cancer which combined these advantages.

To speak more plainly, psycho-analysis is always a matter of long periods of time, of six months or a year, or more – a longer time than the patient expects. It is therefore a duty to explain this fact to the patient before he finally resolves upon the treatment. I hold it to be altogether more honourable, and also more expedient, to draw his attention, without alarming him unduly but from the very beginning, to the difficulties and sacrifices involved by analytic treatment; thereby depriving him of the right to assert later on that he had been inveigled into a treatment the implications and extent of which he did not realize. The patient who lets himself be dissuaded by these considerations would later on have shown himself unsuitable; it is a good thing to institute a selection in this way before the beginning of the treatment. With the progress of understanding among patients the number of those who stand this first test increases.

I do not bind patients to continue the treatment for a certain length of time; I permit each one to break off whenever he likes, though I do not conceal from him that no success will result from a treatment broken off after only a small amount of work, and that it may easily, like an unfinished operation, leave him in an unsatisfactory condition. In the early years of my practice of psycho-analysis I had the greatest difficulty in prevailing upon patients to continue; this difficulty has long since altered; I must now anxiously exert myself to induce them to give it up.

The shortening of the analytic treatment remains a reasonable wish, the realization of which, as we shall hear, is being sought after in various ways. Unfortunately, it is opposed by a very important element in the situation – namely, the slowness with which profound changes in the mind bring themselves about, fundamentally the same thing as the 'inappreciation of time' characteristic of our unconscious processes. When the patients are confronted with the great expenditure of time required for the analysis they often bethink themselves of suggesting a makeshift way out of the difficulty. They divide up their complaints and describe some as unendurable and others as secondary, saying, 'If only you will relieve me of this (for instance, a headache or a particular fear) I will manage by myself to endure life with the other troubles.' They exaggerate the selective capacity of the analysis in this. The analyst is certainly able to do a great deal, but he cannot determine beforehand exactly what results he will effect. He sets in operation a certain process, the 'loosening' of the existing repressions: he can watch over it, further it, remove difficulties in the way of it, and certainly do much also to vitiate it; but on the whole, once begun, the process goes its own way and does not admit of prescribed direction, either in the course it pursues or in the order in which the various stages to be gone through are taken. The power of the analyst over the symptoms of disease is comparable in a way to sexual potency; the strongest man can beget a whole child, it is true, but he cannot effect the production of a head alone, or an arm, or a leg in the female organ, he cannot even prescribe the sex of the child. He, too, only sets in operation a highly complicated process, determined by foregone events, and ending with the severance of the child from the mother. Again, a neurosis has the character of an organism; its component manifestations are not independent of one another, they each condition and mutually support the others; a man can only suffer from one neurosis, never from several accidentally combined in his person. Suppose one had freed the patient, according to his wish, from the one unendurable symptom, he might then have discovered that a symptom which was previously negligible had increased until it in turn had become intolerable. In general, the analyst who wishes the results to be as independent as possible of the influence of suggestion from himself (that is, of transference) will do best to refrain from using even the fraction of selective influence upon the results of the cure which is perhaps open to him. The patients who are most welcome to the psycho-analyst will be those who desire complete health so far as they are capable of it, and who will place as much time at his disposal for the cure as the process requires. Naturally, such favourable conditions are to be met with only in the minority of cases.

The next point to be decided on beginning the treatment is the money question, the physician's fee. The analyst does not dispute that money is to be regarded first and foremost as the means by which life is supported and power is obtained, but he maintains that, besides this, powerful sexual factors are involved in the value set upon it; he may expect, therefore, that money questions will be treated by cultured people in the same manner as sexual matters, with the same inconsistency, prudishness and hypocrisy. He is therefore determined beforehand not to concur in this attitude, and in his dealings with patients to treat of money matters with the same matter-of-course frankness that he wishes to induce in them towards matters relating to sexual life. By voluntarily introducing the subject of fees and stating the price for which he gives his time, he shows the patient that he himself has cast aside false shame in these matters. Ordinary prudence then demands that the sums to be paid should not be allowed to accumulate until they are very large, but that payment should be made at fairly short regular intervals (every month or so). (It is well known that the value of the treatment is not enhanced in the patient's eyes if a very low fee is asked.) This is of course not the usual practice of neurologists or other physicians in our European cities. But the psycho-analyst may put himself in the position of surgeons, who are both honest and expensive because they deal in measures which can be of aid. In my opinion it is more dignified and ethically less open to objection to acknowledge one's actual claims and needs rather than, as the practice is now among medical men, to act the part of the disinterested philanthropist, while that enviable situation is denied to one and one grumbles in secret, or animadverts loudly, over the lack of consideration or the miserliness shown by patients. In estimating his fee the analyst must allow for the fact that, in spite of strenuous work, he can never earn as much as other medical specialists.

For the same reasons he may refrain from giving treatment gratuitously, making no exceptions to this in favour of his colleagues or their relatives. This last requisition seems to conflict with the claims of professional fellow-feeling; one must consider, however, that gratuitous treatment means much more to a psycho-analyst than to other medical men – namely, the dedication of a considerable portion (an eighth or a seventh part, perhaps) of the time available for his livelihood over a period of several months. Another treatment conducted gratuitously at the same time would rob him of a quarter or a third of his earning capacity, which would be comparable to the effects of some serious accident.

Then the question arises whether the advantage to the patient would not outweigh the physician's sacrifice. I may rely on my own judgement in this matter, since I have given an hour daily, and sometimes two, for ten years to gratuitous treatment, because I wished, for the purpose of studying the neuroses, to work with the fewest possible hindrances. The advantages which I sought in this way were not forthcoming. Gratuitous treatment enormously increases many neurotic resistances, such as the temptations of the transference-relationship for young women, or the opposition to the obligatory gratitude in young men arising from the father-complex, which is one of the most troublesome obstacles to the treatment. The absence of the corrective influence in payment of the professional fee is felt as a serious handicap; the whole relationship recedes into an unreal world; and the patient is deprived of a useful incentive to exert himself to bring the cure to an end.

One may stand quite aloof from the ascetic view of money as a curse and yet regret that analytic therapy is almost unattainable for the poor, both for external and for internal reasons. Little can be done to remedy this. Perhaps there is some truth in the widespread belief that those who are forced by necessity to a life of heavy labour succumb less easily to neurosis. But at all events experience shows without a doubt that, in this class, a neurosis once acquired is only with very great difficulty eradicated. It renders the sufferer too good service in the struggle for existence; the accompanying secondary 'epinosic gain' has here too much importance. The pity which the world has refused to his material distress the sufferer now claims by right of his neurosis and absolves himself from the obligation of combating his poverty by work. Anyone who tries to deal by psychotherapeutic means with a neurosis in a poor person usually makes the discovery that what is really required of him in such a case is a very different, material kind of therapy – the sort of healing which, according to tradition, Emperor Joseph II used to dispense. Naturally, one does occasionally meet with people of worth who are helpless from no fault of their own, in whom unpaid treatment leads to excellent results without exciting any of the difficulties mentioned.

For the middle classes the necessary expense of psycho-analysis is only apparently excessive. Quite apart from the fact that restored health and capacity for life on the one hand, and a moderate outlay in money on the other, cannot be measured in the same category; if one contrasts a computation of the never-ceasing costs of nursing homes and medical treatment with the increase of capacity to live well and earn well after a successful analytic treatment, one may say that the patient has made a good bargain. Nothing in life is so expensive as illness – and foolishness.

Before I conclude these remarks on beginning the analytic treatment a word must be said about a certain ceremonial obser-vance regarding the position in which the treatment is carried out. I adhere firmly to the plan of requiring the patient to recline upon a sofa, while one sits behind him out of his sight. This arrangement has an historic meaning; it is the last ves-tige of the hypnotic method out of which psycho-analysis was evolved; but for many reasons it deserves to be retained. The first is a personal motive, one that others may share with me, however. I cannot bear to be gazed at for eight hours a day (or more). Since, while I listen, I resign myself to the control of my unconscious thoughts I do not wish my expression to give the patient indications which he may interpret or which may influence him in his communications. The patient usually regards being required to take up this position as a hardship and objects to it, especially when scoptophilia plays an important part in the neurosis. I persist in the measure, however, for the intention and result of it are that all imperceptible influence on the patient's associations by the transference may be avoided, so that the transference may be isolated and clearly outlined when it appears as a resistance. I know that many analysts work in a different way, though I do not know whether the main motive of their departure is the ambition to work in a different way or an advantage which they gain thereby.

The conditions of the treatment being now regulated in this manner, the question arises at what point and with what material it shall begin.

What subject-matter the treatment begins with is on the whole immaterial, whether with the patient's life-story, with a history of the illness or with recollections of childhood; but in any case the patient must be left to talk, and the choice of subject left to him. One says to him, therefore, 'Before I can say anything to you, I must know a great deal about you; please tell me what you know about yourself.'

The only exception to this concerns the fundamental rule of the psycho-analytic technique which the patient must observe. This must be imparted to him at the very beginning: 'One thing more, before you begin. Your talk with me must differ in one respect from an ordinary conversation. Whereas usually you rightly try to keep the threads of your story together and to exclude all intruding associations and side-issues, so as not to wander too far from the point, here you must proceed differently.

You will notice that as you relate things various ideas will occur to you which you feel inclined to put aside with certain criticisms and objections. You will be tempted to say to yourself: "This or that has no connection here, or it is quite unimportant, or it is nonsensical, so it cannot be necessary to mention it." Never give in to these objections, but mention it even if you feel a disinclination against it, or indeed just because of this. Later on you will perceive and learn to understand the reason for this injunction, which is really the only one that you have to follow. So say whatever goes through your mind. Act as if you were sitting at the window of a railway train and describing to some one behind you the changing views you see outside. Finally, never forget that you have promised absolute honesty, and never leave anything unsaid because for any reason it is unpleasant to say it.'[4]

Patients who date their illness from a particular time usually concentrate upon the events leading up to it; others who themselves recognize the connection of their neurosis with their childhood often begin with an account of their whole life-story. A consecutive narrative should never be expected and nothing should be done to encourage it. Every detail of the story will later have to be related afresh, and only with this repetition will additional matter appear enabling the significant connections which are unknown to the patient to be traced.

There are patients who from the first hour carefully prepare their communications, ostensibly so as to make better use of the time given to treatment. This appears to be eagerness on their part, but it is resistance. One must disallow this preparation; it is employed to guard against the appearance of unwelcome thoughts; the patient may believe ever so honestly in his praiseworthy intention, but resistance will play its part in this kind of considered preparation and will see to it that in this way the most valuable part of the communication escapes. One will soon find that the patient invents yet other methods by which the required material may be withheld from analysis. He will perhaps talk over the treatment every day with some intimate friend, and in this discussion bring out all the thoughts which should occur to him in the presence of the physician. The treatment then suffers from a leak which lets through just what is most valuable. It will then soon be time to recommend the patient to treat the analysis as a matter between himself and his physician, and to exclude everyone else from sharing in it, no matter how closely bound to him or how inquisitive they may be. In later stages of the treatment the patient is not usually tempted in this way.

Certain patients wish their treatment kept secret, often because they have kept their neurosis secret, and I put no obstacle in the way of this. That in consequence the world hears nothing of some of the most brilliantly successful cures is of course a consideration not to be taken into account. Obviously the patient's decision in favour of secrecy at once reveals one feature of his inner history.

In advising at the beginning of treatment that as few persons as possible shall be informed of it, one protects patients to some extent from the many hostile influences seeking to detach them from the analysis. Such influences may be very mischievous at the outset of the cure; later they are usually immaterial, or even useful in bringing into prominence resistances which are attempting concealment.

If during the course of the analysis the patient requires temporarily some other medical or special treatment, it is far wiser to call in some colleague outside analytic work than to administer this treatment oneself. Analysis combined with other treatment, for neurotic maladies with a strong organic connection, is nearly always impracticable; the patients withdraw their interest from the analysis when there is more than one way leading them to health. Preferably one postpones the organic treatment until after the conclusion of the mental; if the former were tried first, in most cases it would do no good.

To return to the beginning of the treatment. Patients are occasionally met with who begin the treatment with an absolute disclaimer of the existence of any thoughts in their minds which they could utter, although the whole field of their life-history and their neurosis lies before them untrodden. One must accede this first time as little as at any other to their request that one should propose something for them to speak of. One must bear in mind what it is that confronts one in these cases. A formidable resistance has come out into the open in order to defend the neurosis; one takes up its challenge then and there, and grips it by the throat. Emphatic and repeated assurance that the absence of all ideas at the beginning is an impossibility, and that there is some resistance against the analysis, soon brings the expected confessions from the patient or else leads to the first discovery of some part of his complexes. It is ominous if he has to confess that while listening to the rule of the analysis he formed a determination in spite of it not to communicate this or that; not quite so bad if he only has to declare the distrust he has of the treatment or the appalling things he has heard about it. If he denies these and similar possibilities when they are suggested to him, further pressure will constrain him to acknowledge that he has neglected certain thoughts which are occupying his mind. He was thinking of the treatment itself but not in a definite way, or else the appearance of the room he is in occupied him, or he found himself thinking of the objects round him in the consulting-room, or of the fact that he is lying on a sofa; for all of which thoughts he has substituted 'nothing'. These indications are surely intelligible; everything connected with the situation of the moment represents a transference to the physician which proves suitable for use as resistance. It is necessary then to begin by uncovering this transference; thence the way leads rapidly to penetration of the pathogenic material in the case. Women who are prepared by events in their past lives for a sexual overture, or men with unusually strong, repressed homosexuality, are the most prone to exhibit this denial of all ideas at the outset of the analysis.

The first symptoms or chance actions of the patient, like the first resistance, have a special interest and will betray one of the governing complexes of the neurosis. A clever young philosopher, with leanings towards aesthetic exquisiteness, hastens to twitch the crease in his trousers into place before lying down for the first sitting; he reveals himself as an erstwhile coprophiliac of the highest refinement, as was to be expected of the developed aesthete. A young girl on the same occasion hurriedly pulls the hem of her skirt over her exposed ankle; she has betrayed the kernel of what analysis will discover later, her narcissistic pride in her bodily beauty and her tendencies to exhibitionism.

Very many patients object especially to the arrangement of reclining in a position where the physician sits out of sight behind them; they beg to be allowed to undergo analysis in some other position, mostly because they do not wish to be deprived of a view of the physician. Permission is invariably refused; one cannot prevent them, however, from contriving to say a few words before the beginning of the 'sitting itself', and after one has signified its termination and they have risen from the sofa. In this way they make in their own minds a division of the treatment into an official part, in which they behave in a very inhibited manner, and an informal 'friendly' part, in which they really speak freely and say a good deal that they do not themselves regard as belonging to the treatment. The physician does not fall in for long with this division of the time, he makes a note of what is said before or after the sitting, and in bringing it up at the next opportunity he tears down the partition which the patient has tried to erect. It again is a structure formed from the material of a transference-resistance.

So long as the patient continues to utter without obstruction the thoughts and ideas rising to his mind, the theme of the transference should be left untouched. One must wait until the transference, which is the most delicate matter of all to deal with, comes to be employed as resistance.

The next question with which we are confronted is a main one. It runs: When shall we begin our disclosures to the patient? When is it time to unfold to him the hidden meaning of his thoughts and associations, to initiate him into the postulates of analysis and its technical devices?

The answer to this can only be: Not until a dependable transference, a well-developed *rapport*, is established in the patient. The first aim of the treatment consists in attaching him to the treatment and to the person of the physician. To ensure this one need do nothing but allow him time. If one devotes serious interest to him, clears away carefully the first resistances that arise and avoids certain mistakes, such an attachment develops in the patient of itself, and the physician becomes linked up with one of the imagos of those persons from whom he was used to receive kindness. It is certainly possible to forfeit this primary success if one takes up from the start any standpoint other than that of understanding, such as a moralizing attitude, perhaps, or if one behaves as the representative or advocate of some third person, maybe the husband or wife, and so on.

This answer of course involves a condemnation of that mode of procedure which consists in communicating to the patient the interpretation of the symptoms as soon as one perceives it oneself, or of that attitude which would account it a special triumph to hurl these 'solutions' in his face at the first interview. It is not difficult for a skilled analyst to read the patient's hidden wishes plainly between the lines of his complaints and the story of his illness; but what a measure of self-complacency and thoughtlessness must exist in one who can upon the shortest acquaintance inform a stranger, who is entirely ignorant of analytical doctrines, that he is bound by an incestuous love for his mother, that he harbours wishes for the death of the wife he appears to love, that he conceals within himself the intention to deceive his chief, and so forth! I have heard that analysts exist who plume themselves upon these kinds of lightning-diagnoses and 'express'-treatments, but I warn everyone against following such examples. Such conduct brings both the man and the treatment into discredit and arouses the most violent opposition, whether the interpretations be correct or not; yes, and the truer they are actually the more violent is the resistance they arouse. Usually the therapeutic effect at the moment is nothing; the resulting horror of analysis, however, is ineradicable. Even in later stages of the analysis one must be careful not to communicate the meaning of a symptom or the interpretation of a wish until the patient is already close upon it, so that he has only a short step to take in order to grasp the explanation himself. In former years I often found that premature communication of interpretations brought the treatment to an untimely end, both on account of the resistances suddenly aroused thereby and also because of the relief resulting from the insight so obtained.

The following objection will be raised here: Is it then our task to lengthen the treatment, and not rather to bring it to an end as rapidly as possible? Are not the patient's sufferings due to his lack of knowledge and understanding, and is it not a duty to enlighten him as soon as possible, that is, as soon as the physician himself knows the explanations? The answer to this question requires a short digression concerning the significance of knowledge and the mechanism of the cure in psycho-analysis.

In the early days of analytic technique it is true that we regarded the matter intellectually and set a high value on the patient's knowledge of that which had been forgotten, so that we hardly made a distinction between our knowledge and his in these matters. We accounted it specially fortunate if it were possible to obtain information of the forgotten traumas of childhood from external sources, from parents or nurses, for instance, or from the seducer himself, as occurred occasionally; and we hastened to convey the information and proofs of its correctness to the patient, in the certain expectation of bringing the neurosis and the treatment to a rapid end by this means. It was a bitter disappointment when the expected success was not forthcoming. How could it happen that the patient, who now had the knowledge of his traumatic experience, still behaved in spite of it as if he knew no more than before? Not even would the recollection of the repressed trauma come to mind after it had been told and described to him.

In one particular case the mother of an hysterical girl had confided to me the homosexual experience which had greatly influenced the fixation of the attacks. The mother herself had come suddenly upon the scene and had been a witness of it; the girl, however, had totally forgotten it, although it had occurred not long before puberty. Thereupon I made a most instructive observation. Every time that I repeated the mother's story to the girl she reacted to it with an hysterical attack, after which the story was again forgotten. There was no doubt that the patient was expressing a violent resistance against the knowledge which was being forced upon her; at last she simulated imbecility and total loss of memory in order to defend herself against what I told her. After this, there was no alternative but to abandon the previous attribution of importance to knowledge in itself, and to lay the stress upon the resistances which had originally induced the condition of ignorance and were still now prepared to defend it. Conscious knowledge, even if it were not again expelled, was powerless against these resistances.

This disconcerting ability in patients to combine conscious knowledge with ignorance remains unexplained by what is called normal psychology. By reason of the recognition of the unconscious, psycho-analysis finds no difficulty in it; the phenomenon described is, however, one of the best confirmations of the conception by which mental processes are approached as being differentiated topographically. The patients are aware, in thought, of the repressed experience, but the connection between the thought and the point where the repressed recollection is in some way imprisoned is lacking. No change is possible until the conscious thought-process has penetrated to this point and has overcome the resistances of the repression there. It is just as if a decree were promulgated by the Ministry of Justice to the effect that juvenile misdemeanours should be dealt with by certain lenient methods. As long as this concession has not come to the knowledge of the individual magistrates, or in the event of their not choosing to make use of it but preferring to deal justice according to their own lights, nothing will be changed in the treatment accorded to youthful delinquents. For the sake of complete accuracy, though, it may be added that communicating to the patient's consciousness information about what is repressed does not entirely fail of any effect at all. It does not produce the hoped-for result of abolishing the symptoms, but it has other consequences. It first arouses resistances, but when these are overcome it sets a mental process in action, in the course of which the desired influence upon the unconscious memory is eventually effected.

At this point we should review the play of forces brought into action by the treatment. The primary motive-power used in therapy is the patient's suffering and the wish to be cured which arises from it. The volume of this motive-force is diminished in various ways, discoverable only in the course of the analysis, above all by what we call the 'epinosic gain'; the motive-power itself must be maintained until the end of the treatment; every improvement effects a diminution of it. Alone, however, the force of this motive is insufficient to overcome the illness; two things are lacking in it, the knowledge of the paths by which the desired end may be reached, and the amount of energy needed to oppose the resistances. The analytic treatment helps to supply both these deficiencies. The accumulation of energy necessary to overcome the resistances is supplied by analytic utilization of the energies which are always ready to be 'transferred'; and by timely communications to the patient at the right moment analysis points out the direction in which these energies should be employed. The transference alone frequently suffices to bring about a disappearance of the symptoms of the disease, but this is merely temporary and lasts only as long as the transference itself is maintained. The treatment is then nothing more than suggestion, not a psycho-analysis. It deserves the latter name only when the intensity of the transference has been utilized to overcome the resistances; only then does illness become impossible, even though the transference is again dissolved as its function in the treatment requires.

In the course of the treatment another helpful agency is roused – the patient's intellectual interest and understanding.

But this alone is hardly worth consideration by the side of the other forces engaged in the struggle, for it is always in danger of succumbing to the clouding of reasoning power under the influence of resistances. Hence it follows that the new sources of strength for which the sufferer is indebted to the analyst resolve themselves into transference, and instruction (by explanation). The patient only makes use of the instruction, however, in so far as he is induced to do so by the transference; and therefore until a powerful transference is established the first explanation should be withheld; and likewise, we may add, with each subsequent one, we must wait until each disturbance of the transference by the transference-resistances arising in succession has been removed.

Recollection, Repetition,
and Working Through[1]

(1914)

IT SEEMS TO ME not unnecessary constantly to remind students of the far-reaching changes which psychoanalytic technique has undergone since its first beginnings. Its first phase was that of Breuer's catharsis, direct concentration upon the events exciting symptom-formation and persistent efforts on this principle to obtain reproduction of the mental processes involved in that situation, in order to bring about a release of them through conscious operations. The aims pursued at that time, by the help of the hypnotic condition, were 'recollection' and 'abreaction'. Next, after hypnosis had been abandoned, the main task became that of divining from the patient's free associations what he failed to remember. Resistances were to be circumvented by the work of interpretation and by making its results known to the patient; concentration on the situations giving rise to symptom-formation and on those which lay behind the outbreak of illness was retained, while abreaction receded and seemed to be replaced by the work the patient had to do in overcoming his critical objections to his associations, in accordance with the fundamental psycho-analytic rule. Finally, the present-day technique evolved itself, whereby the analyst abandons concentration on any particular element or problem, contents himself with studying whatever is occupying the patient's mind at the moment, and employs the art of interpretation mainly for the purpose of recognizing the resistances which come up in regard to this material and making the patient aware of them. A rearrangement of the division of labour results from this; the physician discovers the resistances which are unknown to the patient; when these are removed the patient often relates the forgotten situations and connections without any difficulty. The aim of these different procedures has of course remained the same throughout: descriptively, to recover the lost memories; dynamically, to conquer the resistances caused by repression.

One is bound to be grateful still to the old hypnotic technique for the way in which it unrolled before us certain of the mental processes of analysis in an isolated and schematic form. Only this could have given us the courage to create complicated situations ourselves in the analytic process and to keep them perspicuous.

Now in those days of hypnotic treatment 'recollection' took a very simple form. The patient put himself back into an earlier situation, which he seemed never to confound with the present, gave an account of the mental processes belonging to it, in so far as they were normal, and appended to this whatever conclusions arose from making conscious what had before been unconscious.

I will here interpolate a few observations which every analyst has found confirmed in his experience. The forgetting of impressions, scenes, events, nearly always reduces itself to 'dissociation' of them. When the patient talks about these 'forgotten' matters he seldom fails to add: 'In a way I have always known that, only I never thought of it.' He often expresses himself as disappointed that not enough things come into his mind which he can hail as 'forgotten', which he has never thought of since they happened. Even this desire on his part is fulfilled, however, particularly in cases of conversion-hysteria. The 'forgotten' material is still further circumscribed when we estimate at their true value the screen-memories which are so generally present. In many cases I have had the impression that the familiar childhood-amnesia, which is theoretically so important to us, is entirely outweighed by the screen-memories. Not merely is much that is essential in childhood preserved in them, but actually all that is essential. Only one must understand how to extract it from them by analysis. They represent the forgotten years of childhood just as adequately as the manifest content represents the dream-thoughts.

The other group of mental processes, the purely internal mental activities, such as phantasies, relations between ideas, impulses, feelings, connections, may be contrasted with impressions and events experienced, and must be considered apart from them in its relation to forgetting and remembering. With these processes it particularly often happens that something is 'remembered' which never could have been 'forgotten', because it was never at any time noticed, never was conscious; as regards the fate of any such 'connection' in the mind, moreover, it seems to make no difference whatever whether it was conscious and then was forgotten or whether it never reached consciousness at all. The conviction which a patient obtains in the course of analysis is quite independent of remembering it in that way.

In the manifold forms of obsessional neurosis particularly, 'forgetting' consists mostly of a falling away of the links between various ideas, a failure to draw conclusions, an isolating of certain memories.

No memory of one special kind of highly important experience can usually be recovered: these are experiences which took place in very early childhood, before they could be comprehended, but which were *subsequently* interpreted and understood. One gains a knowledge of them from dreams, and is compelled to believe in them on irresistible evidence in the structure of the neurosis; moreover, one can convince oneself that after his resistances have been overcome the patient no longer invokes the absence of any memory of them (sensation of familiarity) as a ground for refusing to accept them. This matter, however, is one demanding so much critical caution and introducing so much that is novel and startling that I will reserve it for special discussion in connection with suitable material.[2]

To return to the comparison between the old and the new techniques; in the latter there remains very little, often nothing, of this smooth and pleasing course of events belonging to the former. There are cases which, under the new technique, conduct themselves up to a point like those under the hypnotic technique and only later abandon this behaviour; but others behave differently from the beginning. If we examine the latter class in order to define this difference, we may say that here the patient *remembers* nothing of what is forgotten and repressed, but that he expresses it in *action*. He reproduces it not in his memory but in his behaviour; he *repeats* it, without of course knowing that he is repeating it.

For instance, the patient does not say that he remembers how defiant and critical he used to be in regard to the authority of his parents, but he behaves in that way towards the physician. He does not remember how he came to a helpless and hopeless deadlock in his infantile searchings after the truth of sexual matters, but he produces a mass of confused dreams and associations, complains that he never succeeds at anything, and describes it as his fate never to be able to carry anything through. He does not remember that he was intensely ashamed of certain sexual activities, but he makes it clear that he is ashamed of the treatment to which he has submitted himself, and does his utmost to keep it a secret; and so on.

Above all, the beginning of the treatment sets in with a repetition of this kind. When one announces the fundamental psycho-analytical rule to a patient with an eventful life-history and a long illness behind him, and then waits for him to pour forth a flood of information, the first thing that happens often is that he has nothing to say. He is silent and declares that nothing comes into his mind. That is of course nothing but the repetition of a homosexual attitude, which comes up as a resistance against remembering anything. As long as he is under treatment he never escapes from this compulsion to repeat; at last one understands that it is his way of remembering.

The relation between this compulsion to repeat and the transference and resistance is naturally what will interest us most of all. We soon perceive that the transference is itself only a bit of repetition, and that the repetition is the transference of the forgotten past not only on to the physician, but also on to all the other aspects of the current situation. We must be prepared to find, therefore, that the patient abandons himself to the compulsion to repeat, which is now replacing the impulse to remember, not only in his relation with the analyst but also in all other matters occupying and interesting him at the time, for instance, when he falls in love or sets about any project during the treatment. Moreover, the part played by resistance is easily recognized. The greater the resistance the more extensively will expressing in action (repetition) be substituted for recollecting. The ideal kind of recollection of the past which belongs to hypnosis is indeed a condition in which resistance is completely abrogated. If the treatment begins under the auspices of a mild and unpronounced positive transference, it makes an unearthing of memories like that in hypnosis possible to begin with, while the symptoms themselves are for the time quiescent; if then, as the analysis proceeds, this transference becomes hostile or unduly intense, consequently necessitating repression, remembering immediately gives way to expression in action. From then onward the resistances determine the succession of the various repetitions. The past is the patient's armoury out of which he fetches his weapons for defending himself against the progress of the analysis, weapons which we must wrest from him one by one.

The patient reproduces instead of remembering, and he reproduces according to the conditions of the resistance; we may now ask what it is exactly that he reproduces or expresses in action. The answer is that he reproduces everything in the reservoirs of repressed material that has already permeated his general character – his inhibitions and disadvantageous attitudes of mind, his pathological traits of character. He also repeats during the treatment all his symptoms. And now we can see that our special insistence upon the compulsion to repeat has not yielded any new fact, but is only a more comprehensive point of view. We are only making it clear to ourselves that the patient's condition of illness does not cease when his analysis begins, that we have to treat his illness as an actual force, active at the moment, and not as an event in his past life. This condition of present illness is shifted bit by bit within the range and field of operation of the treatment, and while the patient lives it through as something real and actual, we have to accomplish the therapeutic task, which consists chiefly in translating it back again into terms of the past.

Causing memories to be revived under hypnosis gives the impression of an experiment in the laboratory. Allowing 'repetition' during analytic treatment, which is the latest form of technique, constitutes a conjuring into existence of a piece of real life, and can therefore not always be harmless and indifferent in its effects on all cases. The whole question of 'exacerbation of symptoms during treatment', so often unavoidable, is linked up with this.

The very beginning of the treatment above all brings about a change in the patient's conscious attitude towards his illness. He has contented himself usually with complaining of it, with regarding it as nonsense, and with under-estimating its importance; for the rest, he has extended the ostrich-like conduct of repression which he adopted towards the sources of his illness on to its manifestations. Thus it happens that he does not rightly know what are the conditions under which his phobia breaks out, has not properly heard the actual words of his obsessive idea or not really grasped exactly what it is his obsessive impulse is impelling him to do. The treatment of course cannot allow this. He must find the courage to pay attention to the details of his illness. His illness itself must no longer seem to him contemptible, but must become an enemy worthy of his mettle, a part of his personality, kept up by good motives, out of which things of value for his future life have to be derived. The way to reconciliation with the repressed part of himself which is coming to expression in his symptoms is thus prepared from the beginning; yet a certain tolerance towards the illness itself is induced. Now if this new attitude towards the illness intensifies the conflicts and brings to the fore symptoms which till then had been indistinct, one can easily console the patient for this by pointing out that these are only necessary and temporary aggravations, and that one cannot overcome an enemy who is absent or not within range. The resistance, however, may try to exploit the situation to its own ends, and abuse the permission to be ill. It seems to say: 'See what happens when I really let myself go in these things! Haven't I been right to relegate them all to repression?' Young and childish persons in particular are inclined to make the necessity for paying attention to their illness a welcome excuse for luxuriating in their symptoms.

There is another danger, that in the course of the analysis, other, deeper-lying instinctual trends which had not yet become part of the personality may come to be 'reproduced'. Finally, it is possible that the patient's behaviour outside the transference may involve him in temporary disasters in life, or even be so designed as permanently to rob the health he is seeking of all its value.

The tactics adopted by the physician are easily justified. For him recollection in the old style, reproduction in the mind, remains the goal of his endeavours, even when he knows that it is not to be obtained by the newer method. He sets about a perpetual struggle with the patient to keep all the impulses which he would like to carry into action within the boundaries of his mind, and when it is possible to divert into the work of recollection any impulse which the patient wants to discharge in action, he celebrates it as a special triumph for the analysis. When the transference has developed to a sufficiently strong attachment, the treatment is in a position to prevent all the more important of the patient's repetition-actions and to make use of his intentions alone, *in statu nascendi*, as material for the therapeutic work. One best protects the patient from disasters brought about by carrying his impulses into action by making him promise to form no important decisions affecting his life during the course of the treatment, for instance, choice of a profession or of a permanent love-object, but to postpone all such projects until after recovery.

At the same time one willingly accords the patient all the freedom that is compatible with these restrictions, nor does one hinder him from carrying out projects which, though foolish, are not of special significance; one remembers that it is only by dire experience that mankind ever learns sense. There are no doubt persons whom one cannot prevent from plunging into some quite undesirable project during the treatment and who become amenable and willing to submit the impulse to analysis only afterwards. Occasionally, too, it is bound to happen that the untamed instincts assert themselves before there is time for the curbing-rein of the transference to be placed on them, or that an act of reproduction causes the patient to break the bond that holds him to the treatment. As an extreme example of this, I might take the case of an elderly lady who had repeatedly fled from her house and her husband in a twilight state, and gone no one knew where, without having any idea of a motive for this 'elopement'. Her treatment with me began with a marked positive transference of affectionate feeling, which intensified itself with uncanny rapidity in the first few days, and by the end of a week she had 'eloped' again from me, before I had time to say anything to her which might have prevented this repetition.

The main instrument, however, for curbing the patient's compulsion to repeat and for turning it into a motive for remembering consists in the handling of the transference. We render it harmless, and even make use of it, by according it the right to assert itself within certain limits. We admit it into the transference as to a playground, in which it is allowed to let itself go in almost complete freedom and is required to display before us all the pathogenic impulses hidden in the depths of the patient's mind. If the patient does but show compliance enough to respect the necessary conditions of the analysis we can regularly succeed in giving all the symptoms of the neurosis a new transference-colouring, and in replacing his whole ordinary neurosis by a 'transference-neurosis' of which he can be cured by the therapeutic work. The transference thus forms a kind of intermediary realm between illness and real life, through which the journey from the one to the other must be made. The new state of mind has absorbed all the features of the illness; it represents, however, an artificial illness which is at every point accessible to our interventions. It is at the same time a piece of real life, but adapted to our purposes by specially favourable conditions, and it is of a provisional character. From the repetition-reactions which are exhibited in the transference the familiar paths lead back to the awakening of the memories, which yield themselves without difficulty after the resistances have been overcome.

I might break off at this point but for the title of this paper, which requires me to discuss a further point in analytic technique. The first step in overcoming the resistance is made, as we know, by the analyst's discovering the resistance, which is never recognized by the patient, and acquainting him with it. Now it seems that beginners in analytic practice are inclined to look upon this as the end of the work. I have often been asked to advise upon cases in which the physician complained that he had pointed out his resistance to the patient and that all the same no change had set in; in fact, the resistance had only then become really pronounced and the whole situation had become more obscure than ever. The treatment seemed to make no progress. This gloomy foreboding always proved mistaken. The treatment was as a rule progressing quite satisfactorily; only the analyst had forgotten that naming the resistance could not result in its immediate suspension. One must allow the patient time to get to know this resistance of which he is ignorant, to 'work through' it, to overcome it, by continuing the work according to the analytic rule in defiance of it. Only when it has come to its height can one, with the patient's co-operation, discover the repressed instinctual trends which are feeding the resistance; and only by living then through in this way will the patient be convinced of their existence and their power. The physician has nothing more to do than to wait and let things take their course, a course which cannot be avoided nor always be hastened. If he holds fast to this principle, he will often be spared the disappointment of failure in cases where all the time he has conducted the treatment quite correctly.

This 'working through' of the resistances may in practice amount to an arduous task for the patient and a trial of patience for the analyst. Nevertheless, it is the part of the work that effects the greatest changes in the patient and that distinguishes analytic treatment from every kind of suggestive treatment. Theoretically one may correlate it with the 'abreaction' of quantities of affect pent-up by repression, without which the hypnotic treatment remained ineffective.

Observations on Transference-Love[1]

(1915)

EVERY BEGINNER in psycho-analysis probably feels alarmed at first at the difficulties in store for him when he comes to interpret the patient's associations and deal with the reproduction of repressed material. When the time comes, however, he soon learns to look upon these difficulties as insignificant and instead becomes convinced that the only serious difficulties are encountered in handling the transference.

Among the situations to which the transference gives rise, one is very sharply outlined, and I will select this, partly because it occurs so often and is so important in reality and partly because of its theoretical interest. The case I mean is that in which a woman or girl patient shows by unmistakable allusions or openly avows that she has fallen in love, like any other mortal woman, with the physician who is analysing her. This situation has its distressing and its comical aspects as well as its serious ones;

it is so complicated, and conditioned by so many factors, so unavoidable and so difficult to dissolve, that discussion of it has long been a pressing need of analytic technique. But since those who mock at the failings of others are not always themselves free from them, we have hardly been inclined to rush in to the fulfilment of this task. The obligation of professional discretion, which cannot be disregarded in life but which is useless in our science, makes itself felt here again and again. In so far as psycho-analytical publications are a part of life, we have here an insoluble conflict. I have recently disregarded this matter of discretion for once[2] and shown how this same transference situation at first retarded the development of psycho-analytic therapy for ten years.

To a cultivated layman – and in their relation to psychoanalysis the attitude of such men is the best we encounter – matters concerned with love cannot be measured by the same standards as other things: it is as though they were written on a page by themselves which would not take any other script. If a patient falls in love with her doctor, then, such a man will think only two outcomes are possible – one comparatively rare, in which all the circumstances allow of a permanent legal union between them, and the other much commoner, in which physician and patient part, and abandon the work begun which should have led to her recovery, as though it had been prevented by some elemental phenomenon. There is certainly a third conceivable way out, which even appears compatible with continuing the treatment, and that is a love-relationship between them of an illicit character, not intended to last permanently; but both conventional morality and professional dignity surely make this impossible. In any event our layman would beg the analyst to reassure him as unambiguously as possible that this third alternative is out of the question.

It is clear that the analyst's point of view must be different from this.

Let us take the case of the second possible alternative. After the patient has fallen in love with the physician, they part; the treatment is given up. But very soon the patient's condition necessitates her making another attempt at cure with another physician; the next thing that happens is that she feels she has fallen in love with the second physician, and just the same again when she had broken off and begun again with a third, and so on. This phenomenon, which occurs with such regularity and is one of the foundations of psycho-analytical theory, may be regarded from two points of view, that of the physician analysing and that of the patient in need of analysis.

To the physician it represents an invaluable explanation and a useful warning against any tendency to counter-transference which may be lurking in his own mind. He must recognize that the patient's falling in love is induced by the analytic situation and is not to be ascribed to the charms of his person, that he has no reason whatever therefore to be proud of such a 'conquest', as it would be called outside analysis. And it is always well to be reminded of this. For the patient, however, there are two alternatives: either she must abandon her analytic treatment or she must make up her mind to being in love with physicians as to an inevitable destiny.[3]

I have no doubt that the patient's relatives and friends would decide as emphatically in favour of the first of the two alternatives as the analyst would for the second. In my opinion, however, this is a case in which the decision cannot be left to the tender – or rather, the jealous egoistic – mercies of the relatives and friends. The patient's welfare alone should decide. The love of her relatives cannot cure her neurosis. It is not necessary for the psycho-analyst to force himself upon anyone, but he may take up the stand that for certain purposes he is indispensable. Anyone who takes up Tolstoy's attitude to this problem can remain in undisputed possession of his wife or daughter, but must try to put up with her retaining her neurosis and with the disturbance it involves in her capacity for love. After all, it is the same situation as that of a gynaecological treatment. Incidentally, the jealous father or husband makes a great mistake if he thinks the patient will escape falling in love with the physician if he hands her over to some other kind of treatment than that of analysis in order to get rid of her neurosis. The difference will be, on the contrary, that her falling in love in a way which is bound to remain unexpressed and unanalysed can never render that aid to her recovery which analysis would have extracted from it.

It has come to my knowledge that certain physicians who

practise analysis frequently prepare their patients for the advent of a love-transference or even instruct them to 'go ahead and fall in love with the analyst so that the treatment may make progress'. I can hardly imagine a more nonsensical proceeding. It robs the phenomenon itself of the element of spontaneity which is so convincing and it lays up obstacles ahead which are extremely difficult to overcome.

At the first glance it certainly does not look as if any advantage to the treatment could result from the patient's falling in love in the transference. No matter how amenable she has been up till then, she now suddenly loses all understanding of and interest in the treatment, and will not hear or speak of anything but her love, the return of which she demands; she has either given up her symptoms or else she ignores them; she even declares herself well. A complete transformation ensues in the scene – it is as though some make-believe had been interrupted by a real emergency, just as when the cry of fire is raised in a theatre. Any physician experiencing this for the first time will not find it easy to keep a grasp of the analytic situation and not to succumb to the illusion that the treatment is really at an end.

On reflection one realizes the true state of things. One remembers above all the suspicion that everything impeding the progress of the treatment may be an expression of resistance. It certainly plays a great part in the outbreak of passionate demands for love. One has long noticed in the patient the signs of an affectionate transference on to the physician and could with certainty ascribe to this attitude her docility, her acceptance of the analytic explanations, her remarkable comprehension and the high degree of intelligence which she displayed during this period. This is now all swept away; she has become completely lacking in understanding and seems to be swallowed up in her love; and this change always came over her just as one had to bring her to the point of confessing or remembering one of the particularly painful or heavily repressed vicissitudes in her life-history. She had been in love, that is to say, for a long time; but now the resistance is beginning to make use of it in order to hinder the progress of the treatment, to distract her interest from the work and to put the analyst into a painful and embarrassing position.

If one looks into the situation more closely one can recognize that more complicated motives are also at work, of which some are connected with the falling in love, and others are particular expressions of resistance. To the first belong the patient's efforts to reassure herself of her irresistibility, to destroy the physician's authority by bringing him down to the level of a lover, and to gain all the other advantages which she foresees as incidental to gratification of her love. With regard to the resistance, one may presume that at times it uses the declarations of love as a test for the strait-laced analyst, so that compliance on his part would call down on him a reprimand. But above all one obtains the impression that the resistance acts as an *agent provateur*, intensifying the love of the patient and exaggerating her readiness for the sexual surrender, in order thereby to vindicate the action of her repression more emphatically by pointing to the dangers of such licentiousness. All this by-play, which in less complicated cases may not be present at all, has as we know been regarded by A. Adler as the essential element in the whole process.

But how is the analyst to behave in this situation if he is not to come to grief and yet believes that the treatment should be continued through this love-transference and in spite of it?

It would be very simple for me now, on the score of conventional morality, emphatically to insist that the analyst must never in any circumstances accept or return the tender passion proffered him – that instead he must watch for his chance to urge the infatuated woman to take the moral path and see the necessity of renunciation, and induce her to overcome the animal side of her nature and subdue her passion, so as to continue the analytic work.

I shall not fulfil these expectations, however – neither the first nor the second. Not the first, because I am writing not for patients, but for physicians who have serious difficulties to contend with, and also because in this instance I can go behind moral prescriptions to the source of them, namely, to utility. I am on this occasion in the happy position of being able to put the requirements of analytic technique in the place of a moral decree without any alteration in the results.

Even more emphatically, however, do I decline to fulfil the second of the expectations suggested above. To urge the patient to suppress, to renounce and to sublimate the promptings of her instincts, as soon as she has confessed her love-transference, would be not an analytic way of dealing with them, but a senseless way. It would be the same thing as to conjure up a spirit from the underworld by means of a crafty spell and then to dispatch him back again without a question. One would have brought the repressed impulses out into consciousness only in terror to send them back into repression once more. Nor should one deceive oneself about the success of any such proceeding. When levelled at the passions, lofty language achieves very little, as we all know. The patient will only feel the humiliation, and will not fail to revenge herself for it.

Just as little can I advocate a middle course which would recommend itself to some as especially ingenious; this would consist in averring one's response to the patient's feelings of affection, but in refraining from all the physical accompaniments of these tender feelings, until one could guide the situation along calmer channels and raise it on to a higher level. Against this expedient I have to object that the psycho-analytic treatment is founded on truthfulness. A great part of its educative effect and its ethical value lies in this very fact. It is dangerous to depart from this sure foundation. When a man's life has become bound up with the analytic technique, he finds himself at a loss altogether for the lies and the guile which are otherwise so indispensable to a physician, and if for once with the best intentions he attempts to use them he is likely to betray himself. Since we demand strict truthfulness from our patients, we jeopardize our whole authority if we let ourselves be caught by them in a departure from the truth. And besides, this experimental adoption of tender feeling for the patient is by no means without danger. One cannot keep such complete control of oneself as not one day suddenly to go further than was intended. In my opinion, therefore, it is not permissible to disavow the indifference one has developed by keeping the counter-transference in check.

I have already let it be seen that the analytic technique requires the physician to deny the patient who is longing for love the satisfaction she craves. The treatment must be carried through in a state of abstinence; I do not mean merely corporal abstinence, nor yet deprivation of everything desired, for this could perhaps not be tolerated by any sick person. But I would state as a fundamental principle that the patient's desire and longing are to be allowed to remain, to serve as driving forces for the work and for the changes to be wrought, and that one must beware of granting this source of strength some discharge by surrogates. Indeed, one could not offer the patient anything but surrogates, for until the repressions are lifted her condition makes her incapable of true satisfaction.

Let us admit that this principle – of carrying through the analytic treatment in a state of renunciation – extends far beyond the case we are discussing, and that it needs close consideration in order to define the limits of its possible application. But we will refrain from going into this question now and will keep as closely as possible to the situation we started from. What would happen if the physician were to behave differently, and avail himself of a freedom perhaps available to them both to return the love of the patient and to appease her longing for tenderness from him?

If he had been guided in his decision by the argument that compliance on his part would strengthen his power over the patient so that he could influence her to perform the tasks required by the treatment, that is, could achieve a permanent cure of her neurosis by this means, experience would teach him that he had miscalculated. The patient would achieve her aim, but he would never achieve his. There is an amusing story about a pastor and an insurance agent which describes what would happen. An ungodly insurance agent lay at the point of death and his relatives fetched the holy man to convert him before he died. The interview lasted so long that those outside began to have some hope. At last the door of the sick chamber opened. The free-thinker had not been converted – but the pastor went away insured.

If her advances were returned, it would be a great triumph for the patient, but a complete overthrow for the cure. She would have succeeded in what all patients struggle for, in expressing in action, in reproducing in real life, what she ought only to remember, to reproduce as the content of her mind and to retain within the mental sphere.[4] In the further course of the love-relationship all the inhibitions and pathological reactions of her love-development would come out yet there would be no possibility of correcting them, and the painful episode would end in remorse and a strengthening of her tendency to repression. The love-relationship actually destroys the influence of the analytic treatment on the patient; a combination of the two would be an inconceivable thing.

It is therefore just as disastrous for the analysis if the patient's craving for love prevails as if it is suppressed. The way the analyst must take is neither of these; it is one for which there is no prototype in real life. He must guard against ignoring the transference-love, scaring it away or making the patient disgusted with it; and just as resolutely must he withhold any response to it. He must face the transference-love boldly but treat it like something unreal, as a condition which must be gone through during the treatment and traced back to its unconscious origins, so that it shall assist in bringing to light all that is most hidden in the development of the patient's erotic life, and help her to learn to control it. The more plainly the analyst lets it be seen that he is proof against every temptation, the sooner will the advantage from the situation accrue to the analysis. The patient, whose sexual repressions are of course not yet removed but merely pushed into the background, will then feel safe enough to allow all her conditions for loving, all the phantasies of her sexual desires, all the individual details of her way of being in love to come to light, and then will herself open up the way back from them to the infantile roots of her love.

With one type of woman, to be sure, this attempt to preserve the love-transference for the purposes of analytic work without gratifying it will not succeed. These are women of an elemental passionateness; they tolerate no surrogates; they are children of nature who refuse to accept the spiritual instead of the material; to use the poet's words, they are amenable only to the 'logic of gruel and the argument of dumplings'. With such people one has the choice: either to return their love or else to bring down upon oneself the full force of the mortified woman's fury. In neither event can one safeguard the interests of the treatment. One must acknowledge failure and withdraw; and may at leisure study the problem how the capacity for neurosis can be combined with such an intractable craving for love.

Many analysts must have discovered the way in which other women, less violent in their love, can be brought round gradually to the analytic point of view. Above all, the unmistakable element of resistance in their 'love' must be insisted upon. Genuine love would make the patient docile and intensify her readiness to solve the problems of her case, simply because the man she loved expected it. A woman who was really in love would gladly choose the road to completion of the cure, in order to give herself a value in the physician's eyes and to prepare herself for real life where her feelings of love could find their proper outlet. Instead of this, she is showing a stubborn and rebellious spirit, has thrown up all interest in her treatment, and clearly too all respect for the physician's well-founded judgement. She is bringing out a resistance, therefore, under the guise of being in love; and in addition to this, she has no compunction about trying to lead him into a cleft stick. For if he refuses her love, as duty and his understanding compel him to do, she can take up the attitude that she has been humiliated and, out of revenge and resentment, make herself inaccessible to cure by him, just as she is now doing ostensibly out of love.

As a second argument against the genuineness of this love one advances the fact that it shows not a single new feature connecting it with the present situation, but is entirely composed of repetitions and 'rechauffés' of earlier reactions, including childish ones. One then sets about proving this by detailed analysis of the patient's behaviour in love.

When the necessary amount of patience is added to these arguments it is usually possible to overcome the difficult situation and to continue the work, the patient having either moderated her love or transformed it; the aim of the work then becomes the discovery of the infantile object-choice and of the phantasies woven round it. I will now, however, examine these arguments critically and put the question whether they really represent the truth or whether by employing them we are not in our desperation resorting to prevarication and misrepresentation. In other words: can the love which is manifested in analytic treatment not truly be called real?

I think that we have told the patient the truth, but not the whole truth without regard for consequences. Of our two arguments the first is the stronger. The part taken by resistance in the transference-love is unquestionable and very considerable. But this love was not created by the resistance; the latter finds it ready to hand, exploits it and aggravates the manifestations of it. Nor is its genuineness impugned by the resistance. The second argument is far weaker; it is true that the love consists of new editions of old traces and that it repeats infantile reactions. But this is the essential character of every love. There is no love that does not reproduce infantile prototypes. The infantile conditioning factor in it is just what gives it its compulsive character which verges on the pathological. The transference-love has perhaps a degree less of freedom than the love which appears in ordinary life and is called normal; it displays its dependence on the infantile pattern more clearly, is less adaptable and capable of modification, but that is all and that is nothing essential.

By what other signs can the genuineness of a love be recognized? By its power to achieve results, its capacity to accomplish its aim? In this respect the transference-love seems to give place to none; one has the impression that one could achieve anything by its means.

Let us resume, therefore: One has no right to dispute the 'genuine' nature of the love which makes its appearance in the course of analytic treatment. However lacking in normality it may seem to be, this quality is sufficiently explained when we remember that the condition of being in love in ordinary life outside analysis is also more like abnormal than normal mental phenomena. The transference-love is characterized, nevertheless, by certain features which ensure it a special position. In the first place, it is provoked by the analytic situation; secondly, it is greatly intensified by the resistance which dominates this situation; and thirdly, it is to a high degree lacking in regard for reality, is less sensible, less concerned about consequences, more blind in its estimation of the person loved, than we are willing to admit of normal love. We should not forget, however, that it is precisely these departures from the norm that make up the essential element in the condition of being in love.

The first of these three characteristics of the transference-love is what determines the physician's course of action. He has evoked this love by undertaking analytic treatment in order to cure the neurosis; for him it is an unavoidable consequence of the medical situation, as inevitable as the exposure of a patient's body or being told some life-and-death secret. It is therefore plain to him that he is not to derive any personal advantage from it. The patient's willingness makes no difference whatever; it merely throws the whole responsibility on him. Indeed, as he must know, the patient had from the beginning entertained hopes of this way of being cured. After all the difficulties are overcome she will often confess to a phantasy, an expectation that she had had as she began the treatment – 'if she behaved well, she would be rewarded in the end by the doctor's love for her'.

For the physician there are ethical motives which combine with the technical reasons to hinder him from according the patient his love. The aim that he has to keep in view is that this woman, whose capacity for love is disabled by infantile fixations, should attain complete access over this function which is so inestimably important for her in life, not that she should fritter it away in the treatment, but preserve it for real life, if so be that after her cure life makes that demand on her. He must not let the scene of the race between the dogs be enacted, in which the prize was a chaplet of sausages and which a funny fellow spoilt by throwing one sausage on to the course; the dogs fell upon it and forgot about the race and the chaplet in the distance luring them on to win. I do not mean to say that it is always easy for the physician to keep within the bounds prescribed by technique and ethics. Younger men especially, who are not yet bound by a permanent tie, may find it a hard task. The love between the sexes is undoubtedly one of the first things in life, and the combination of mental and bodily satisfaction attained in the enjoyment of love is literally one of life's culminations. Apart from a few perverse fanatics, all the world knows this and conducts life accordingly; only science is too refined to confess it. Again, when a woman sues for love, to reject and refuse is a painful part for a man to play; and in spite of neurosis and resistance there is an incomparable fascination about a noble woman who confesses her passion. It is not the grossly sensual desires of the patient that constitute the temptation. These are more likely to repel and to demand the exercise of toleration in order to regard them as a natural phenomenon. It is perhaps the finer impulses, those 'inhibited in their aim', which lead a man into the danger of forgetting the rules of technique and the physician's task for the sake of a wonderful experience.

And yet the analyst is absolutely debarred from giving way. However highly he may prize love, he must prize even more highly the opportunity to help his patient over a decisive moment in her life. She has to learn from him to overcome the pleasure-principle, to give up a gratification which lies to hand but is not sanctioned by the world she lives in, in favour of a distant and perhaps altogether doubtful one, which is, however, socially and psychologically unimpeachable. To achieve this mastery of herself she must be taken through the primordial era of her mental development and in this way reach that greater freedom within the mind which distinguishes conscious mental activity – in the systematic sense – from unconscious.

The analytic psychotherapist thus has a threefold battle to wage – in his own mind against the forces which would draw him down below the level of analysis; outside analysis against the opponents who dispute the importance he attaches to the sexual instinctual forces and hinder him from making use of them in his scientific method; and in the analysis against his patients, who at first behave like his critics but later on disclose the over-estimation of sexual life which has them in thrall, and who try to take him captive in the net of their socially ungovernable passions.

The lay public, of whose attitude to psycho-analysis I spoke at the outset, will certainly seize the opportunity given it by this discussion of the transference-love to direct the attention of the world to the dangers of this therapeutic method. The psycho-analyst knows that the forces he works with are of the most explosive kind and that he needs as much caution and conscientiousness as a chemist. But when has it ever been forbidden to a chemist, on account of its danger, to occupy himself with the explosives which, just because of their effectiveness, are so indispensable? It is remarkable that psycho-analysis has to win for itself afresh all the liberties which have long been accorded to other medical work. I certainly do not advocate that the harmless methods of treatment should be abandoned. For many cases they suffice, and when all is said, the *furor sanandi* is no more use to human society than any other kind of fanaticism. But it is grossly to undervalue both the origins and the practical significance of the psychoneuroses to suppose that these disorders are to be removed by pottering about with a few harmless remedies. No; in medical practice there will always be room for the '*ferrum*' and the '*ignis*' as well as for the '*medicina*', and there a strictly regular, unmodified psycho-analysis, which is not afraid to handle the most dangerous forces in the mind and set them to work for the benefit of the patient, will be found indispensable.

Papers on Metapsychology

Formulations regarding the Two Principles in Mental Functioning[1]

(1911)

WE HAVE LONG observed that every neurosis has the result, and therefore probably the purpose, of forcing the patient out of real life, of alienating him from actuality. Nor could a fact such as this escape the observation of Pierre Janet; he spoke of a loss of '*la fonction du réel*' as being a special characteristic of the neurotic, but without discovering the connection of this disturbance with the fundamental conditions of neurosis.[2] By introducing the concept of repression into the genesis of the neuroses we have been able to gain some insight into this connection. The neurotic turns away from reality because he finds it unbearable – either the whole or parts of it. The most extreme type of this alienation from reality is shown in certain cases of hallucinatory psychosis which aim at denying the existence of the particular event that occasioned the outbreak of insanity

(Griesinger). But actually every neurotic does the same with some fragment of reality.[3] And now we are confronted with the task of investigating the development of the relation of the neurotic and of mankind in general to reality, and of so bringing the psychological significance of the real outer world into the structure of our theory.

In the psychology which is founded on psycho-analysis we have accustomed ourselves to take as our starting-point the unconscious mental processes, with the peculiarities of which we have become acquainted through analysis. These we consider to be the older, primary processes, the residues of a phase of development in which they were the only kind of mental processes. The sovereign tendency obeyed by these primary processes is easy of recognition; it is called the pleasure-pain (*Lust-Unlust*) principle, or more shortly the pleasure-principle. These processes strive towards gaining pleasure; from any operation which might arouse unpleasantness ('pain') mental activity draws back (repression). Our nocturnal dreams, our waking tendency to shut out painful impressions, are remnants of the supremacy of this principle and proofs of its power.

In presupposing that the state of mental equilibrium was originally disturbed by the peremptory demands of inner needs, I am returning to lines of thought which I have developed in another place.[4] In the situation I am considering, whatever was thought of (desired) was simply imagined in an hallucinatory form, as still happens today with our dream-thoughts every night.[5] This attempt at satisfaction by means of hallucination was abandoned only in consequence of the absence of the expected gratification, because of the disappointment experienced. Instead, the mental apparatus had to decide to form a conception of the real circumstances in the outer world and to exert itself to alter them. A new principle of mental functioning was thus introduced; what was conceived of was no longer that which was pleasant, but that which was real, even if it should be unpleasant.[6] This institution of the *reality-principle* proved a momentous step.

1. In the first place the new demands made a succession of adaptations necessary in the mental apparatus, which, on account of insufficient or uncertain knowledge, we can only detail very cursorily.

The increased significance of external reality heightened the significance also of the sense-organs directed towards that outer world, and of the *consciousness* attached to them; the latter now learnt to comprehend the qualities of sense in addition to the qualities of pleasure and 'pain' which hitherto had alone been of interest to it. A special function was instituted which had periodically to search the outer world, in order that its data might be already familiar if an urgent inner need should arise; this function was *attention*. Its activity meets the sense-impressions halfway, instead of awaiting their appearance. At the same time there was probably introduced a system of *notation*, whose task was to deposit the results of this periodical activity of consciousness — a part of that which we call *memory*.

In place of repression, which excluded from cathexis as productive of 'pain' some of the emerging ideas, there developed an impartial *passing of judgement*, which had to decide whether a particular idea was true or false, that is, was in agreement with reality or not; decision was determined by comparison with the memory-traces of reality.

A new function was now entrusted to motor discharge, which under the supremacy of the pleasure-principle had served to unburden the mental apparatus of accretions of stimuli, and in carrying out this task had sent innervations into the interior of the body (mien, expressions of affect); it was now employed in the appropriate alteration of reality. It was converted into *action*.

Restraint of motor discharge (of action) had now become necessary, and was provided by means of the process of *thought*, which was developed from ideation. Thought was endowed with qualities which made it possible for the mental apparatus to support increased tension during a delay in the process of discharge. It is essentially an experimental way of acting, accompanied by displacement of smaller quantities of cathexis together with less expenditure (discharge) of them. For this purpose conversion of free cathexis into 'bound' cathexes was imperative, and this was brought about by means of raising the level of the whole cathectic process. It is probable that thinking was originally unconscious, in so far as it rose above mere ideation and turned to the relations between the object-impressions, and that it became endowed with further qualities which were perceptible to consciousness only through its connection with the memory-traces of words.

2. There is a general tendency of our mental apparatus which we can trace back to the economic principle of saving in expenditure; it seems to find expression in the tenacity with which we hold on to the sources of pleasure at our disposal, and in the difficulty with which we renounce them. With the introduction of the reality-principle one mode of thought-activity was split off; it was kept free from reality-testing and remained subordinated to the pleasure-principle alone.[7] This is the act of *phantasy-making*, which begins already in the games of children, and later, continued as *day-dreaming*, abandons its dependence on real objects.

3. The supersession of the pleasure-principle by the reality-principle with all the mental consequences of this, which is here schematically condensed in a single sentence, is not in reality accomplished all at once; nor does it take place simultaneously along the whole line. For while this development is going on in the ego-instincts, the sexual instincts become detached from them in very significant ways. The sexual instincts at first behave auto-erotically; they find their satisfaction in the child's own body and therefore do not come into the situation of frustration which enforces the installation of the reality-principle. Then when later on they begin to find an object, this development undergoes a long interruption in the latency period, which postpones sexual development until puberty. These two factors – auto-erotism and

latency period – bring about the result that the mental development of the sexual instincts is delayed and remains far longer under the supremacy of the pleasure-principle, from which in many people it is never able to withdraw itself at all.

In consequence of these conditions there arises a closer connection, on the one hand, between the sexual instincts and phantasy, and on the other hand, between the ego-instincts and the activities of consciousness. Both in healthy and in neurotic people this connection strikes us as very intimate, although the considerations of genetic psychology put forward above lead us to recognize it as *secondary*. The perpetuated activity of auto-erotism makes possible a long retention of the easier momentary and phantastic satisfaction in regard to the sexual object, in place of real satisfaction in regard to it, the latter requiring effort and delay. In the realm of phantasy, repression remains all-powerful; it brings about the inhibition of ideas *in statu nascendi* before they can be consciously noticed, should cathexis of them be likely to occasion the release of 'pain'. This is the weak place of our mental organization, which can be utilized to bring back under the supremacy of the pleasure-principle thought-processes which had already become rational. An essential part of the mental predisposition to neurosis thus lies in the delayed training of the sexual instincts in the observance of reality and, further, in the conditions which make this delay possible.

4. Just as the pleasure-ego can do nothing but *wish*, work

towards gaining pleasure, and avoiding 'pain', so the reality-ego need do nothing but strive for what is *useful* and guard itself against damage.[8] Actually, the substitution of the reality-principle for the pleasure-principle denotes no dethronement of the pleasure-principle, but only a safeguarding of it. A momentary pleasure, uncertain in its results, is given up, but only in order to gain in the new way an assured pleasure coming later. But the end psychic impression made by this substitution has been so powerful that it is mirrored in a special religious myth. The doctrine of reward in a future life for the — voluntary or enforced — renunciation of earthly lusts is nothing but a mythical projection of this revolution in the mind. In logical pursuit of this prototype, *religions* have been able to effect absolute renunciation of pleasure in this life by means of the promise of compensation in a future life; they have not, however, achieved a conquest of the pleasure-principle in this way. It is *science* which comes nearest to succeeding in this conquest; science, however, also offers intellectual pleasure during its work and promises practical gain at the end.

5. *Education* can without further hesitation be described as an incitement to the conquest of the pleasure-principle, and to its replacement by the reality-principle; it offers its aid, that is, to that process of development which concerns the ego; to this end it makes use of rewards of love from those in charge, and thus it fails if the spoilt child thinks it will possess this love whatever happens and can in no circumstances lose it.

6. *Art* brings about a reconciliation of the two principles in a peculiar way. The artist is originally a man who turns from reality because he cannot come to terms with the demand for the renunciation of instinctual satisfaction as it is first made, and who then in phantasy-life allows full play to his erotic and ambitious wishes. But he finds a way of return from this world of phantasy back to reality; with his special gifts he moulds his phantasies into a new kind of reality, and men concede them a justification as valuable reflections of actual life. Thus by a certain path he actually becomes the hero, king, creator, favourite he desired to be, without pursuing the circuitous path of creating real alterations in the outer world. But this he can only attain because other men feel the same dissatisfaction as he with the renunciation demanded by reality, and because this dissatisfaction, resulting from the displacement of the pleasure-principle by the reality-principle, is itself a part of reality.[9]

7. While the ego goes through its transformation from a *pleasure-ego* into a *reality-ego*, the sexual instincts undergo the changes that lead them from their original auto-erotism through various intermediate phases to object-love in the service of procreation. If it is correct that every step of these two processes of development may become the seat of a predisposition to later neurotic illness, it seems to follow that the decision as regards the form of the subsequent illness (election of neurosis) will depend on the particular phase of ego-development and libido-development in which the inhibition of development has

occurred. The chronological characteristics of the two developments, as yet unstudied, their possible variations in speed with respect to each other, thus receive unexpected significance.

8. There is a most surprising characteristic of unconscious (repressed) processes to which every investigator accustoms himself only by exercising great self-control; it results from their entire disregard of the reality-test; thought-reality is placed on an equality with external actuality, wishes with fulfilment and occurrence, just as happens without more ado under the supremacy of the old pleasure-principle. Hence also the difficulty of distinguishing unconscious phantasies from memories which have become unconscious. One must, however, never allow oneself to be misled into applying to the repressed creations of the mind the standards of reality; this might result in undervaluing the importance of phantasies in symptom-formation on the ground that they are not actualities; or in deriving a neurotic sense of guilt from another source because there is no proof of actual committal of any crime. One is bound to employ the currency that prevails in the country one is exploring; in our case it is the neurotic currency. For example, one may try to solve such a dream as the following. A man who had at one time looked after his father through a long and painful illness up to his death, informed me that in the months following his father's decease he had repeatedly dreamt as follows: *his father was again alive and he was talking to him as of old. But as he did so he felt it exceedingly painful that his father was nevertheless dead, only not aware of the*

fact. No other way leads to the understanding of this seemingly senseless dream than the addition of 'as the dreamer wished', or 'as a result of his wish', after the words 'that his father was nevertheless dead'; and the further addition of 'that he wished it' to the last words. The dream-thought then runs: it was a painful memory for him that he must have desired his father's death (as a release) while he still lived, and how terrible it would have been had his father had any suspicion of it. It is thus a matter of the familiar case of self-reproaches after the loss of a loved person, and in this case the reproach goes back to the infantile significance of the death-wish against the father.

The deficiencies of this short paper, which is rather introductory than expository, are perhaps only to a slight extent excused if I acknowledge them to be unavoidable. In the meagre sentences on the mental consequences of adaptation to the reality-principle I was obliged to intimate opinions which I should have preferred to withhold, the vindication of which will certainly require no small exertion. But I hope that benevolent readers will not fail to observe how even in this work the sway of the reality-principle is beginning.

On Narcissism: An Introduction[1]

(1914)

I

THE WORD 'narcissism' is taken from clinical terminology and was chosen by P. Näcke[2] in 1899 to denote the attitude of a person who treats his own body in the same way as otherwise the body of a sexual object is treated; that is to say, he experiences sexual pleasure in gazing at, caressing and fondling his body, till complete gratification ensues upon these activities. Developed to this degree, narcissism has the significance of a perversion, which has absorbed the whole sexual life of the subject; consequently, in dealing with it we may expect to meet with phenomena similar to those for which we look in the study of all perversions.

Now those engaged in psycho-analytic observation were struck by the fact that isolated features of the narcissistic attitude are found in many people who are characterized by other aberrations – for instance, as Sadger states, in homosexuals – and at last it seemed that a disposition of the libido which must be described as narcissistic might have to be reckoned with in a much wider field, and that it might claim a place in the regular sexual development of human beings.[3] Difficulties in psycho-analytic work upon neurotics led to the same supposition, for it seemed as though this kind of narcissistic attitude in them was one of the factors limiting their susceptibility to influence. Narcissism in this sense would not be a perversion, but the libidinal complement to the egoism of the instinct of self-preservation, a measure of which may justifiably be attributed to every living creature.

A pressing motive for occupying ourselves with the conception of a primary and normal narcissism arose when the attempt was made to bring our knowledge of dementia praecox (Kraepelin), or schizophrenia (Bleuler), into line with the hypothesis upon which the libido-theory is based. Such patients, whom I propose to term paraphrenics, display two fundamental characteristics: they suffer from megalomania and they have withdrawn their interest from the external world (people and things). In consequence of this latter change in them, they are inaccessible to the influence of psycho-analysis and cannot be cured by our endeavours. But this turning away of the paraphrenic from the outer world needs to be more precisely characterized. A patient suffering from hysteria or obsessional neurosis has also, as far as the influence of his illness goes, abandoned his relation to reality. But analysis shows that he has by no means broken off his erotic relations to persons and things. He still retains them in phantasy; i.e. he has, on the one hand, substituted for actual objects imaginary objects founded on memories, or has blended the two; while, on the other hand, he has ceased to direct his motor activities to the attainment of his aims in connection with real objects. It is only to this condition of the libido that we may legitimately apply the term *introversion* of the libido which is used by Jung indiscriminately. It is otherwise with the paraphrenic. He seems really to have withdrawn his libido from persons and things in the outer world, without replacing them by others in his phantasy. When this does happen, the process seems to be a secondary one, part of an effort towards recovery, designed to lead the libido back towards an object.[4]

The question arises: What is the fate of the libido when withdrawn from external objects in schizophrenia? The megalomania characteristic of these conditions affords a clue here. It has doubtless come into being at the expense of the object-libido. The libido withdrawn from the outer world has been directed on to the ego, giving rise to a state which we may call narcissism. But the megalomania itself is no new phenomenon; on the contrary, it is, as we know, an exaggeration and plainer manifestation of a condition which had already existed previously. This leads us to the conclusion that the narcissism which arises when libidinal cathexes are called in away from external objects must be conceived of as a secondary form, superimposed upon a primary one that is obscured by manifold influences.

Let me expressly state that I am not attempting here to explain or penetrate further into the problem of schizophrenia, but am merely putting together what has been said elsewhere, in order that I may justify this introduction of the concept of narcissism.

This development of the libido-theory – in my opinion, a legitimate development – receives reinforcement from a third quarter, namely, from the observations we make and the conceptions we form of the mental life of primitive peoples and of children. In the former we find characteristics which, if they occurred singly, might be put down to megalomania: an over-estimation of the power of wishes and mental processes, the 'omnipotence of thoughts', a belief in the magical virtue of words, and a method of dealing with the outer world – the art of 'magic' – which appears to be a logical application of these grandiose premises.[5] In the child of our own day, whose development is much more obscure to us, we expect a perfectly analogous attitude towards the external world.[6] Thus we form a conception of an original libidinal cathexis of the ego, part of which cathexis is later yielded up to objects, but which fundamentally persists and is related to the object-cathexes much as the body of a protoplasmic animalcule is related to the pseudopodia which it puts out. In our researches, taking, as they did, neurotic symptoms for their starting-point, this part of the disposition of the libido necessarily remained hidden from us at the outset. We were struck only by the emanations from this libido – the object-cathexes, which can be put forth and drawn back again.

We perceive also, broadly speaking, a certain reciprocity between ego-libido and object-libido. The more that is absorbed by the one, the more impoverished does the other become. The highest form of development of which object-libido is capable is seen in the state of being in love, when the subject seems to yield up his whole personality in favour of object-cathexis; while we have the opposite condition in the paranoiac's phantasy (or self-perception) of the 'end of the world'.[7] Finally, with reference to the differentiation of the energies operating in the mind, we infer that at first in the narcissistic state they exist side by side and that our analysis is not a fine enough instrument to distinguish them; only where there is object-cathexis is it possible to discriminate a sexual energy – the libido – from an energy pertaining to the ego-instincts.

Before going any further I must touch on two questions which lead us to the heart of the difficulties of our subject. In the first place: what is the relation of the narcissism of which we are now speaking to auto-erotism, which we have described as an early state of the libido? And secondly: if we concede to the ego a primary cathexis of libido, why is there any necessity for further distinguishing a sexual libido from a non-sexual energy pertaining to the ego-instincts? Would not the assumption of a uniform mental energy save us all the difficulties of differentiating the energy of the ego-instincts from ego-libido, and ego-libido from object-libido? On the first point I would comment as follows: it is impossible to suppose that a unity comparable to the ego can exist in the individual from the very start; the ego has to develop. But the auto-erotic instincts are primordial; so there must be something added to auto-erotism – some new operation in the mind – in order that narcissism may come into being.

To be required to give a definite answer to the second question must occasion perceptible uneasiness in every psycho-analyst. One dislikes the thought of abandoning observation for barren theoretical discussions, but all the same we must not shirk an attempt at explanation. Conceptions such as that of an ego-libido, an energy pertaining to the ego-instincts, and so on, are certainly neither very easy to grasp nor is their content sufficiently rich; a speculative theory of these relations of which we are speaking would in the first place require as its basis a sharply defined concept. But I am of opinion that that is just the difference between a speculative theory and a science founded upon constructions arrived at empirically. The latter will not begrudge to speculation its privilege of a smooth, logically unassailable structure, but will itself be gladly content with nebulous, scarcely imaginable conceptions, which it hopes to apprehend more clearly in the course of its development, or which it is even prepared to replace by others. For these ideas are not the basis of the science upon which everything rests: that, on the contrary, is observation alone. They are not the foundation-stone, but the coping of the whole structure, and they can be replaced and discarded without damaging it. The same thing is happening in our day in the science of physics, the fundamental notions of which as regards matter, centres of force, attraction, etc., are scarcely less debatable than the corresponding ideas in psycho-analysis.

The value of the concepts 'ego-libido' and 'object-libido' is that they are derived from the study of the essential characteristics of neurotic and psychotic processes. The differentiation of the libido into that which is proper to the ego and that which attaches itself to objects is a necessary extension of an original hypothesis which discriminated between ego-instincts and sexual instincts. At any rate, analysis of the pure transference neuroses (hysteria and the obsessional neurosis) compelled me so to discriminate, and I only know that all attempts to account for these phenomena by other means have been completely unsuccessful.

In the complete absence of any theory of the instincts which would help us to find our bearings, we may be permitted, or rather, it is incumbent upon us, in the first place to work out any hypothesis to its logical conclusion, until it either fails or becomes confirmed. There are various points in favour of the hypothesis of a primordial differentiation between sexual instincts and other instincts, ego-instincts, besides the usefulness of such an assumption in the analysis of the transference neuroses. I admit that this latter consideration alone would not be decisive, for it might be a question of an indifferent energy operating in the mind which was converted into libido only by the act of object-cathexis. But, in the first place, this differentiation of concepts corresponds to the distinction between hunger and love, so widely current. And, in the second place, there are biological considerations in its favour. The individual does actually carry on a double existence: one designed to serve his own purposes and another as a link in a chain, in which he serves against, or at any rate without, any volition of his own. The individual himself regards sexuality as one of his own ends; while from another point of view he is only an appendage to his germ-plasm, to which he lends his energies, taking in return his toll of pleasure – the mortal vehicle of a (possibly) immortal substance – like the inheritor of an entailed property who is only the temporary holder of an estate which survives him. The differentiation of the sexual instincts from the ego-instincts would simply reflect this double function of the individual. Thirdly, we must recollect that all our provisional ideas in psychology will some day be based on an organic substructure. This makes it probable that special substances and special chemical processes control the operation of sexuality and provide for the continuation of the individual life in that of the species. We take this probability into account when we substitute special forces in the mind for special chemical substances.

Just because I try in general to keep apart from psychology everything that is not strictly within its scope, even biological thought, I wish at this point expressly to admit that the hypothesis of separate ego-instincts and sexual instincts (that is to say, the libido-theory) rests scarcely at all upon a psychological basis, but is essentially supported upon the facts of biology. So I shall also be consistent enough to drop this hypothesis if psycho-analytic work itself should suggest as more valuable another hypothesis about the instincts. So far, this has not happened. It may then be that – when we penetrate deepest and furthest – sexual energy, the libido, will be found to be only the product of a differentiation in the energy at work generally in the mind. But such a statement is of no importance. It has reference to matters so remote from the problems of our observation and so empty of available knowledge, that to dispute it is as idle as to affirm it; it is possible that this primordial identity has as little to do with our analytical interests as the primordial kinship of all human races has to do with the proof of kinship with a testator required by the Probate Court. All these speculations lead nowhere; since we cannot wait for another science to present us with a theory of the instincts ready-made, it is far more to the purpose that we should try to see what light may be thrown upon this basic problem of biology by a synthesis of psychological phenomena. Let us be fully aware of the possibility of error; but do not let us be deterred from carrying to its logical conclusion the hypothesis we first adopted of an antithesis between ego-instincts and sexual instincts (an hypothesis to which we were impelled by analysis of the transference neuroses), and so from seeing whether it turns out to be consistent and fruitful, and whether it may be applied to other affections also, e.g. to schizophrenia.

Of course, it would be a very different matter if it were proved that the libido-theory had already come to grief in the attempt to explain the last-named disease. That this is so has been maintained by C. G. Jung,[8] and so I have been obliged to enter upon this last disquisition, which I would gladly have been spared. I should have preferred, without any discussion of the premises, to follow out the course embarked upon in the analysis of the Schreber case. But Jung's assertion is, to say the least of it, premature. The grounds he gives for it are scanty. At the outset, he quotes me as saying that I myself have been obliged, owing to the difficulties of the Schreber analysis, to extend the conception of the libido, i.e. to give up its sexual content and to identify libido with psychic 'interest' in general. Ferenczi, in an exhaustive criticism of Jung's work, has already said all that is necessary in correction of this erroneous interpretation.[9] I can only corroborate this critic and repeat that I have never thus retracted the libido-theory. Another argument of Jung's, namely, that we must not assume that the loss of the normal function of appreciating reality can be brought about only by the withdrawal of the libido, is no argument but a dictum. It begs the question, it anticipates the decision and waives discussion; for whether and how this is possible is just what has to be investigated. In his next large work,[10] Jung just misses the solution which I had long since indicated: 'At the same time there is this to be taken into consideration, a point to which Freud refers in his work on the Schreber case, that the introversion of the *libido sexualis* leads to a cathexis of the "ego", and that possibly it is this that produces the effect of a loss of reality. It is indeed a tempting possibility to explain the psychology of the loss of reality in this fashion.' But Jung discusses this possibility very little further. A few pages later he dismisses it with the remark that from this conditioning factor 'would result, not dementia praecox, but the psychology of an ascetic anchorite'. How little this inept comparison can help us to a conclusion may be learnt from the reflection that an anchorite who 'tries to erase every trace of sexual interest' (but only in the popular sense of the word 'sexual') does not even necessarily display any pathogenic disposition of the libido. He may have turned away his interest from human beings entirely, and yet may have sublimated it to a heightened interest in the divine, in nature, or in the animal kingdom, without his libido having undergone introversion to his phantasies or retrogression to his ego. This comparison would seem to rule out in advance the possibility of differentiating between interest emanating from erotic or that from other sources. Further, when we remember that the researches of the Swiss school, however meritorious, have elucidated only two features in the picture of dementia praecox – the existence of complexes common to healthy and neurotic persons alike, and the similarity of the phantasy-formations of that disease to popular myths – but have not been able to throw any further light on the pathogenic mechanism, we may repudiate Jung's assertion that the libido-theory has broken down in the attempt to understand dementia praecox, and is therefore rendered invalid for the other neuroses also.

II

It seems to me that certain peculiar difficulties lie in the way of a direct study of narcissism. Our chief means of access to an understanding of this condition will probably remain the analysis of paraphrenics. As the transference neuroses have enabled us to trace the libidinal instinctual impulses, so dementia praecox and paranoia will give us insight into the psychology of the ego. Once more, in order to arrive at what is normal and apparently so simple, we shall have to study the pathological with its distortions and exaggerations. At the same time, there are other sources from which we may derive a knowledge of narcissism, which I will now mention in their order – namely, the study of organic disease, of hypochondria, and of love between the sexes.

In estimating the influence of organic disease upon the distribution of the libido, I follow a suggestion of S. Ferenczi's, which he made to me in conversation. It is universally known, and seems to us a matter of course, that a person suffering organic pain and discomfort relinquishes his interest in the things of the outside world, in so far as they do not concern his suffering. Closer observation teaches us that at the same time he withdraws libidinal interest from his love-objects: so long as he suffers, he ceases to love. The banality of this fact is no reason why we should be deterred from translating it into terms of the libido-theory. We should then say: the sick man withdraws his libidinal cathexes back upon his own ego, and sends them forth again when he recovers. 'Concentrated is his soul,' says W. Busch, of the poet suffering from toothache, 'in his jaw-tooth's aching hole.' Here libido and ego-interest share the same fate and have once more become indistinguishable from each other. The familiar egoism of the sick person covers them both. We find it so natural because we are certain that in the same situation we should behave in just the same way. The way in which the readiness to love, however great, is banished by bodily ailments, and suddenly replaced by complete indifference, is a theme which has been sufficiently exploited by comic writers.

The condition of sleep, like illness, implies a narcissistic withdrawal of the libido away from its attachments back to the subject's own person, or, more precisely, to the single desire for sleep. The egoism of dreams fits in very well in this connection. In both states we have, if nothing else, examples of changes in the distribution of the libido which are consequent upon a change in the ego.

Hypochondria, like organic disease, manifests itself in distressing and painful bodily sensations and also concurs with organic disease in its effect upon the distribution of the libido. The hypochondriac withdraws both interest and libido – the latter specially markedly – from the objects of the outer world and concentrates both upon the organ which engages his attention. A difference between hypochondria and organic disease now becomes evident: in the latter, the distressing sensations are based upon demonstrable organic changes; in the former, this is not so. But it would be entirely in keeping with our general conception of the processes of neurosis if we decided to say that hypochondria must be right; organic changes cannot be absent in it either. Now in what could such changes consist?

Here we may fall back upon our experience, which shows that bodily sensations of a painful nature, comparable to those of hypochondria, are not lacking in the other neuroses. I have said once before that I am inclined to class hypochondria with neurasthenia and anxiety-neurosis as a third 'actual neurosis'. Probably it would not be going too far to put it in this way: that in the other neuroses too there is regularly present some small admixture of hypochondria. Perhaps we have the best example of this in the anxiety-neurosis and in the hysteria superimposed upon it. Now the familiar prototype of an organ sensitive to pain, in some way changed and yet not diseased in the ordinary sense, is that of the genital organ in a state of excitation. It becomes congested with blood, swollen, moist, and is the seat of manifold sensations. If we apply to that activity of a given bodily area which consists in conveying sexually exciting stimuli to the mind the term *erotogenicity*, and if we reflect that the conclusions of our theory of sexuality have long accustomed us to the notion that certain other areas of the body – the *erotogenic* zones – may act as substitutes for the genitals and behave analogously to them, we then have only one step further to venture here. We can make up our minds to regard erotogenicity as a property common to all organs and are then justified in speaking of an increase or decrease in the degree of it in any given part of the body. It is possible that for every such change in the erotogenicity of the organs there is a parallel change in the libidinal cathexis in the ego. In such factors may lie the explanation of what is at the bottom of hypochondria and what it is that can have upon the distribution of the libido the same effect as actual organic disease.

We see that, if we follow out this line of thought, we encounter the problem not only of hypochondria, but of the other 'actual neuroses' – neurasthenia and anxiety-neurosis. Let us therefore stop at this point. It is not within the scope of a purely psychological inquiry to penetrate so far behind the frontiers of physiological research. Let us only mention that from this point of view we may surmise that the relation of hypochondria to paraphrenia is similar to that of the other actual neuroses to hysteria and the obsessional neurosis: which is as much as to say that it is dependent on the ego-libido as the others are on the object-libido, and that hypochondriacal anxiety, emanating from the ego-libido, is the counterpart to neurotic anxiety. Further: since we are already familiar with the idea that the mechanism of disease and symptom-formation in the transference neuroses, the passage from introversion to regression, is to be connected with a damming-up of the object-libido,[11] we may come to closer quarters with the conception of a damming-up of the ego-libido also and may bring this conception into relation with the phenomena of hypochondria and paraphrenia.

Of course curiosity will here suggest the question why such a damming-up of libido in the ego should be experienced as 'painful'. There I shall content myself with the answer that 'pain' is in general the expression of increased tension, and thus a *quantity* of the material event is, here as elsewhere, transformed into the *quality* of 'pain' in the mind; nevertheless, it may be not the absolute amount of the physical process which is decisive for the development of pain, but rather a certain function of this absolute amount. At this point we may even venture to touch on the question: whence does that necessity arise that urges our mental life to pass on beyond the limits of narcissism and to attach the libido to objects? The answer which would follow from our line of thought would once more be that we are so impelled when the cathexis of the ego with libido exceeds a certain degree. A strong egoism is a protection against disease, but in the last resort we must begin to love in order that we may not fall ill, and must fall ill if, in consequence of frustration, we cannot love. Somewhat after this fashion does Heine conceive of the psychogenesis of the Creation:

> *Krankheit ist wohl der letzte Grund*
> *Des ganzen Schöpferdrangs gewesen;*
> *Erschaffend konnte ich genesen,*
> *Erschaffend wurde ich gesund.*[12]

We have recognized our mental apparatus above all as a device for mastering excitations which would otherwise be felt as unpleasant or would have pathogenic effects. The 'working-over' of stimuli in the mind accomplishes wonders for the internal discharge of excitations which are incapable of direct discharge outwards, or for which such a discharge is, for the moment, undesirable. Now it is in the first instance a matter of indifference whether the objects of this internal process of 'working-over' are real or imaginary. The difference does not appear till later, when the turning of the libido towards unreal objects (introversion) has led to a damming-up. The megalomania of paraphrenics permits a similar internal working-over of the libido which has returned to the ego to be made; perhaps it is only when this process fails that the damming-up of the libido in the ego becomes pathogenic and starts the process of recovery which impresses us as being the disease itself.

I shall try here to penetrate a little further into the mechanism of paraphrenia and to put together those conceptions which today seem to me worthy of consideration. The difference between paraphrenic affections and the transference neuroses appears to me to lie in the circumstance that, in the former, the libido that is liberated by frustration does not remain attached to objects in phantasy, but returns to the ego; the megalomania then represents the mastery of this volume of libido, and thus corresponds with the introversion on to the phantasy-creations that is found in the transference neuroses; the hypochondria of paraphrenia, which is homologous to the anxiety of the transference neuroses, arises from a failure of this effort in the mental apparatus. We know that the anxiety of the neuroses can be relieved by further mental 'working-over', e.g. by conversion, reaction-formation or defence-formation (phobia). The corresponding process in paraphrenics is the effort towards recovery, to which the striking phenomena of the disease are due. Since frequently, if not usually, an only partial detachment of the libido from objects accompanies paraphrenia, we can distinguish in the clinical picture three groups of phenomena: (1) those representing such remains as there may be of a normal state or of neurosis (phenomena of a residual nature); (2) those representing the morbid process (the detachment of the libido from its objects and, further, megalomania, hypochondria, affective disturbance and every kind of regression); (3) those representing an attempt at recovery. In (3) the libido is once more attached to objects, after the manner of an hysteria (in dementia praecox or paraphrenia proper), or of an obsessional neurosis (in paranoia). This fresh libidinal cathexis takes place from another level and under other conditions than the primary one. The difference between the transference neuroses arising in this way and the corresponding formations where the ego is normal would afford us the deepest insight into the structure of our mental apparatus.

A third way in which we may study narcissism is by observing the behaviour of human beings in love, with its manifold differentiation in man and woman. In much the same way as the object-libido at first concealed from us the ego-libido, so in considering the object-choice of the child (and the adolescent) we first noticed that the sources from which he takes his sexual objects are his experiences of gratification. The first auto-erotic sexual gratifications are experienced in connection with vital functions in the service of self-preservation. The sexual instincts are at the outset supported upon the ego-instincts; only later do they become independent of these, and even then we have an indication of that original dependence in the fact that those persons who have to do with the feeding, care, and protection of the child become his earliest sexual objects: that is to say, in the first instance the mother or her substitute. Side by side with this type and source of object-choice, which may be called the *anaclitic* type,[13] a second type, the existence of which we had not suspected, has been revealed by psycho-analytic investigation. We have found, especially in persons whose libidinal development has suffered some disturbance, as in perverts and homosexuals, that in the choice of their love-object they have taken as their model not the mother but their own selves. They are plainly seeking themselves as a love-object and their type of object-choice may be termed *narcissistic*. This observation provides us with our strongest motive for regarding the hypothesis of narcissism as a necessary one.

Now this does not mean that human beings are to be divided into two sharply differentiated groups, according as their object-choice conforms to the anaclitic or to the narcissistic type; we rather assume that both kinds of object-choice are open to each individual, though he may show a preference for one or the other. We say that the human being has originally two sexual objects: himself and the woman who tends him, and thereby we postulate a primary narcissism in everyone, which may in the long run manifest itself as dominating his object-choice.

Further, the comparison of man and woman shows that there are fundamental differences between the two in respect of the type of object-choice, although these differences are of course not universal. Complete object-love of the anaclitic type is, properly speaking, characteristic of the man. It displays the marked sexual over-estimation which is doubtless derived from the original narcissism of the child, now transferred to the sexual object. This sexual over-estimation is the origin of the peculiar state of being in love, a state suggestive of a neurotic compulsion, which is thus traceable to an impoverishment of the ego in respect of libido in favour of the love-object. A different course is followed in the type most frequently met with in women, which is probably the purest and truest feminine type. With the development of puberty the maturing of the female sexual organs, which up till then have been in a condition of latency, seems to bring about an intensification of the original narcissism, and this is unfavourable to the development of a true object-love with its accompanying sexual over-estimation; there arises in the woman a certain self-sufficiency (especially when there is a ripening into beauty) which compensates her for the social restrictions upon her object-choice. Strictly speaking, such women love only themselves with an intensity comparable to that of the man's love for them. Nor does their need lie in the direction of loving, but of being loved; and that man finds favour with them who fulfils this condition. The importance of this type of woman for the erotic life of mankind must be recognized as very great. Such women have the greatest fascination for men, not only for aesthetic reasons, since as a rule they are the most beautiful, but also because of certain interesting psychological constellations. It seems very evident that one person's narcissism has a great attraction for those others who have renounced part of their own narcissism and are seeking after object-love; the charm of a child lies to a great extent in his narcissism, his self-sufficiency and inaccessibility, just as does the charm of certain animals which seem not to concern themselves about us, such as cats and the large beasts of prey. In literature, indeed, even the great criminal and the humorist compel our interest by the narcissistic self-importance with which they manage to keep at arm's length everything which would diminish the importance of their ego. It is as if we envied them their power of retaining a blissful state of mind – an unassailable libido-position which we ourselves have since abandoned. The great charm of the narcissistic woman has, however, its reverse side; a large part of the dissatisfaction of the lover, of his doubts of the woman's love, of his complaints of her enigmatic nature, have their root in this incongruity between the types of object-choice.

Perhaps it is not superfluous to give an assurance that, in this description of the feminine form of erotic life, no tendency to depreciate woman has any part. Apart from the fact that tendentiousness is alien to me, I also know that these different lines of development correspond to the differentiation of functions in a highly complicated biological connection; further, I am ready to admit that there are countless women who love according to the masculine type and who develop the over-estimation of the sexual object so characteristic of that type.

Even for women whose attitude towards the man remains cool and narcissistic there is a way which leads to complete object-love. In the child to whom they give birth, a part of their own body comes to them as an object other than themselves, upon which they can lavish out of their narcissism complete object-love. Other women again do not need to wait for a child in order to take the step in development from (secondary) narcissism to object-love. Before puberty they have had feelings of a likeness to men and have developed to some extent on masculine lines; after this tendency has been cut short when feminine maturity is reached, they still retain the capacity of longing for a masculine ideal which is really a survival of the boyish nature that they themselves once owned.

We may conclude these suggestions with a short survey of the paths leading to object-choice.

A person may love:

(1) According to the narcissistic type:

 (*a*) What he is himself (actually himself).

 (*b*) What he once was.

(*c*) What he would like to be.

(*d*) Someone who was once part of himself.

(2) According to the anaclitic type:

(*a*) The woman who tends.

(*b*) The man who protects;

and those substitutes which succeed them one after another. The justification for inserting case (*c*) of the first type has yet to be demonstrated later on in our discussion.

The significance of narcissistic object-choice for homosexuality in men must be appraised in another connection.

The primary narcissism of the child assumed by us, which forms one of the hypotheses in our theories of the libido, is less easy to grasp by direct observation than to confirm by deduction from another consideration. If we look at the attitude of fond parents towards their children, we cannot but perceive it as a revival and reproduction of their own, long since abandoned narcissism. Their feeling, as is well known, is characterized by over-estimation, that sure indication of a narcissistic feature in object-choice which we have already appreciated. Thus they are impelled to ascribe to the child all manner of perfections which sober observation would not confirm, to gloss over and forget all his shortcomings – a tendency with which, indeed, the denial of childish sexuality is connected. Moreover, they are inclined to suspend in the child's favour the operation of all those cultural acquirements which their own narcissism has been forced to respect, and to renew in his person the claims for privileges which were long ago given up by themselves. The child shall have things better than his parents; he shall not be subject to the necessities which they have recognized as dominating life. Illness, death, renunciation of enjoyment, restrictions on his own will, are not to touch him; the laws of nature, like those of society, are to be abrogated in his favour; he is really to be the centre and heart of creation, 'His Majesty the Baby', as once we fancied ourselves to be. He is to fulfil those dreams and wishes of his parents which they never carried out, to become a great man and a hero in his father's stead, or to marry a prince as a tardy compensation to the mother. At the weakest point of all in the narcissistic position, the immortality of the ego which is so relentlessly assailed by reality, security is achieved by fleeing to the child. Parental love, which is so touching and at bottom so childish, is nothing but parental narcissism born again and, transformed though it be into object-love, it reveals its former character infallibly.

III

The disturbances to which the original narcissism of the child is exposed, the reactions with which he seeks to protect himself from them, the paths into which he is thereby forced – these are themes which I shall leave on one side, as an important field for work which still awaits exploration; the most important of these matters, however, can be isolated from the rest and, as the 'castration complex' (in the boy, anxiety concerning the penis; in the girl, envy of the penis), be treated in connection with the effect of early sexual intimidation. Elsewhere, psycho-analytic research leads us to vicissitudes undergone by the libidinal instincts in which they are isolated from, and in opposition to, the ego-instincts; but where the castration complex is in question, our researches permit us to infer the existence of an epoch and a mental state in which the two groups of instincts are acting in harmony with each other, inseparably blent, as narcissistic interests. It is from this state of things that A. Adler has derived his conception of the 'masculine protest', which he has exalted almost to the position of the sole motive power concerned in the formation of neurosis and also of character, and which he conceives of as having its origin, not in a narcissistic, and therefore still libidinal, trend, but in a social valuation. Psycho-analytic research has, from the very beginning, recognized the existence and significance of the 'masculine protest', but has always regarded it, in opposition to Adler, as narcissistic in nature and derived from the castration complex. It appertains to the formation of character, into the genesis of which it enters along with many other factors, and it is completely inadequate to explain the problems of the neuroses, in which Adler will take account of nothing but the manner in which they serve the interests of the ego. I find it quite impossible to base the genesis of neurosis upon so narrow a foundation as the castration complex, however pre-eminent a part this may play in men amongst the resistances to the cure of a neurosis. Lastly, I know also of cases of neurosis in which the 'masculine protest', or in our sense the castration complex, plays no pathogenic part, or does not appear at all.

Observation of normal adults shows that their former megalomania has been subdued and that the mental characteristics from which we inferred their infantile narcissism have vanished. What has become of their ego-libido? Are we to assume that the whole of it has passed over into object-cathexes? Such a possibility is plainly contrary to the whole trend of our argument; but in the psychology of repression we may find a clue to another answer to the question.

We have learnt that libidinal impulses are fated to undergo pathogenic repression if they come into conflict with the subject's cultural and ethical ideas. By this we do not ever mean: if the individual in question has a merely intellectual knowledge of the existence of these ideas; we always mean: if he recognizes them as constituting a standard for himself and acknowledges the claims they make on him. Repression, as we have said, proceeds from the ego; we might say with greater precision: from the self-respect of the ego. The very impressions, experiences, impulses and desires that one man indulges or at least consciously elaborates in his mind will be rejected with the utmost indignation by another, or stifled at once even before they enter consciousness. The difference between the two, however – and here we have the conditioning factor in repression – can easily be expressed in terms of the libido-theory. We may say that the one man has set up an *ideal* in himself by which he measures his actual ego, while the other is without this formation of an ideal. From the point of view of the ego this formation of an ideal would be the condition of repression.

To this ideal ego is now directed the self-love which the real ego enjoyed in childhood. The narcissism seems to be now displaced on to this new ideal ego, which, like the infantile ego, deems itself the possessor of all perfections. As always where the libido is concerned, here again man has shown himself incapable of giving up a gratification he has once enjoyed. He is not willing to forgo his narcissistic perfection in his childhood; and if, as he develops, he is disturbed by the admonitions of others and his own critical judgement is awakened, he seeks to recover the early perfection, thus wrested from him, in the new form of an ego-ideal. That which he projects ahead of him as his ideal is merely his substitute for the lost narcissism of his childhood – the time when he was his own ideal.

This suggests that we should examine the relation between this forming of ideals and sublimation. Sublimation is a process that concerns the object-libido and consists in the instinct's directing itself towards an aim other than, and remote from, that of sexual gratification; in this process the accent falls upon the deflection from the sexual aim. Idealization is a process that concerns the *object*; by it that object, without any alteration in its nature, is aggrandized and exalted in the mind. Idealization is possible in the sphere of the ego-libido as well as in that of the object-libido. For example, the sexual over-estimation of an object is an idealization of it. In so far as sublimation is a process that concerns the instinct and idealization one that concerns the object, the two concepts are to be distinguished one from the other.

The formation of the ego-ideal is often confounded with sublimation, to the detriment of clear comprehension. A man who has exchanged his narcissism for the worship of a high ego-ideal has not necessarily on that account succeeded in sublimating his libidinal instincts. It is true that the ego-ideal requires such sublimation, but it cannot enforce it; sublimation remains a special process which may be prompted by the ideal but the execution of which is entirely independent of any such incitement. It is just in neurotics that we find the highest degrees of tension between the development of their ego-ideal and the measure of their sublimation of primitive libidinal instincts, and in general it is far harder to convince the idealist of the inexpediency of the hiding-place found by his libido than the plain man whose demands in this respect are only moderate. Further, the formation of an ego-ideal and sublimation are quite differently related to the causation of neurosis. As we have learnt, the formation of the ideal increases the demands of the ego and is the most powerful factor favouring repression; sublimation is a way out, a way by which the claims of the ego can be met without involving repression.

It would not surprise us if we were to find a special institution in the mind which performs the task of seeing that narcissistic gratification is secured from the ego-ideal and that, with this end in view, it constantly watches the real ego and measures it by that ideal. If such an institution does exist, it cannot possibly be something which we have not yet discovered; we only need to recognize it, and we may say that what we call our *conscience* has the required characteristics. Recognition of this institution enables us to understand the so-called 'delusions of observation' or, more correctly, of *being watched*, which are such striking symptoms in the paranoid diseases and may perhaps also occur as an isolated form of illness, or intercalated in a transference neurosis. Patients of this sort complain that all their thoughts are known and their actions watched and overlooked; they are informed of the functioning of this mental institution by voices which characteristically speak to them in the third person ('Now she is thinking of that again' . . . 'Now he is going out'). This complaint is justified – it describes the truth; a power of this kind, watching, discovering and criticizing all our intentions, does really exist; indeed, it exists with every one of us in normal life. The delusion of being watched presents it in a regressive form, thereby revealing the genesis of this function and the reason why the patient is in revolt against it.

For that which prompted the person to form an ego-ideal, over which his conscience keeps guard, was the influence of parental criticism (conveyed to him by the medium of the voice), reinforced, as time went on, by those who trained and taught the child and by all the other persons of his environment – an indefinite host, too numerous to reckon (fellow-men, public opinion).

Large quantities of libido which is essentially homosexual are in this way drawn into the formation of the narcissistic ego-ideal and find outlet and gratification in maintaining it. The institution of conscience was at bottom an embodiment, first of parental criticism, and subsequently of that of society; a similar process takes place when a tendency towards repression develops out of a command or prohibition imposed in the first instance from without. The voices, as well as the indefinite number of speakers, are brought into the foreground again by the disease, and so the evolution of conscience is regressively reproduced. But the revolt against this *censorial institution* springs from the person's desire (in accordance with the fundamental character of his illness) to liberate himself from all these influences, beginning with that of his parents, and from his withdrawal of homosexual libido from those influences. His conscience then encounters him in a regressive form as a hostile influence from without.

The lament of the paranoiac shows also that at bottom the self-criticism of conscience is identical with, and based upon, self-observation. That activity of the mind which took over the function of conscience has also enlisted itself in the service of introspection, which furnishes philosophy with the material for its intellectual operations. This must have something to do with the characteristic tendency of paranoiacs to form speculative systems.[14]

It will certainly be of importance to us if we can see in other fields evidence of the activity of this critically watching faculty, which becomes heightened into conscience and philosophic introspection. I would refer here to what Herbert Silberer has called the 'functional phenomenon', one of the few indisputably valuable additions to the theory of dreams. Silberer, as is well known, has shown that in the states between sleeping and waking we can directly observe the translation of thoughts into visual images, but that in these circumstances we frequently have a presentation, not of a thought-content, but of the actual state of the mind (readiness, fatigue, etc.) of the person who is struggling with sleep. Similarly, Silberer has shown that often the end of a dream or some section of the dream-content signifies merely the dreamer's own perception of his sleeping and waking. He has thus demonstrated that self-observation – in the sense of the paranoiac's delusion of being watched – plays a part in dream-formation. This part is not invariable; probably I overlooked it because it does not appear in my own dreams to any great extent; in persons who are gifted philosophically and therefore accustomed to introspection it may become very clear.

We may here recall our discovery that dream-formation takes place under the sway of a censorship which compels distortion of the dream-thoughts. We did not picture this censorship as a special force, an entity, but we chose the term to designate a particular aspect of the repressive tendencies which control the ego: namely, their attitude towards the dream-thoughts. Penetrating further into the structure of the ego, we may recognize the *dream-censor* again in the ego-ideal and in the dynamic utterances of conscience. If this censor is to some extent on the alert even during sleep, we can understand that the necessary condition of its activity – self-observation and self-criticism – should contribute to the dream-content some such thoughts as these: 'Now he is too sleepy to think . . . now he is waking up.'[15]

At this point we may enter upon a discussion of the self-regarding attitude in normal persons and in neurotics.

First of all, the feeling of self-regard appears to us a measure of the ego; what various components go to make up that measure is irrelevant. Everything we possess or achieve, every remnant of the primitive feeling of omnipotence that experience has corroborated, helps to exalt the self-regard.

Applying our distinction between sexual and ego-instincts, we must recognize that the self-regard has a very intimate connection with the narcissistic libido. Here we are supported by two fundamental facts: that in paraphrenics the self-regard is exalted, while in the transference neuroses it is abased, and that where the erotic life is concerned not being loved lowers the self-regarding feelings, while being loved raises them. We have stated that to be loved is the aim and the satisfaction in a narcissistic object-choice.

Further, it is easy to observe that libidinal object-cathexis does not raise the self-regard. The effect of the dependence upon the loved object is to lower that feeling: the lover is humble. He who loves has, so to speak, forfeited a part of his narcissism, which can only be replaced by his being loved. In all these respects the self-regarding feelings seem to remain in a relation to the narcissistic element in the erotic life.

The realization of impotence, of one's own inability to love in consequence of mental or physical disorder, has an exceedingly lowering effect upon the self-regard. Here, as I judge, we shall find one of the sources of the feelings of inferiority of which patients suffering from the transference neuroses so readily complain to us. The main source of these feelings is, however, the impoverishment of the ego, due to the withdrawal from it of extraordinarily large libidinal cathexes — due, that is to say, to the injury sustained by the ego through the sexual trends which are no longer subject to control.

A. Adler is right in maintaining that a person's realization of organic inferiorities in himself acts as a spur upon an active mental life, and produces by way of over-compensation a higher degree of ability. But it would be altogether an exaggeration if, following this lead of Adler's, we tried to prove that every fine achievement was conditioned by an original organic inferiority. Not all artists are handicapped with bad eyesight, nor did all orators originally stammer. And there are plenty of instances of excellent achievements springing from superior organic endowment. In the aetiology of neurosis organic inferiority and imperfect development play an insignificant part, much the same as that played by actual perceptual material in the formation of dreams. The neurosis makes use of such inferiorities as a pretext, just as it does of all other suitable factors. So surely as we credit the assertion of one neurotic patient that it was inevitable that she should fall ill, since she is ugly, deformed or lacking in charm and so no one could love her, the very next neurotic will convince us of our error; for she remains the victim of her neurosis and her aversion to sexuality, although she seems to be desirable, and indeed more desired than the average woman. The majority of hysterical women are among the attractive and even beautiful representatives of their sex, while, on the other hand, the frequency of ugliness, organic infirmities and defects in the lower classes of society does not increase the incidence of neurotic illness amongst them.

The relations existing between self-regard and erotism (libidinal object-cathexes) may be expressed in the following formula: two cases must be distinguished – in the first, the erotic cathexes are 'ego-syntonic', *in accordance with the ego-tendencies*; in the second, on the contrary, those cathexes have suffered repression. In the former case (where the path taken by the libido is acceptable to the ego), love takes its place among all the other activities of the ego. Love in itself, in the form of longing and deprivation, lowers the self-regard; whereas to be loved, to have love returned, and to possess the beloved object, exalts it again. When the libido is repressed the erotic cathexis is felt as a severe depletion of the ego, the satisfaction of love is impossible, and the re-enrichment of the ego can be effected only by a withdrawal of the libido from its objects. The return of the libido from the object to the ego and its transformation into narcissism represents, as it were, the restoration of a happy love, and, conversely, an actual happy love corresponds to the primal condition in which object-libido and ego-libido cannot be distinguished.

Perhaps the importance of the subject, and the difficulty in surveying it, may be my excuse for adding a few remarks that are rather loosely strung together.

The development of the ego consists in a departure from the primary narcissism and results in a vigorous attempt to recover it. This departure is brought about by means of the displacement of libido to an ego-ideal imposed from without, while gratification is derived from the attainment of this ideal.

At the same time the ego has put forth its libidinal object-cathexes. It becomes impoverished in consequence both of these cathexes and of the formation of the ego-ideal, and it enriches itself again both by gratification of its object-love and by fulfilling its ideal.

Part of the self-regard is primary – the residue of childish narcissism; another part arises out of such omnipotence as experience corroborates (the fulfilment of the ego-ideal), whilst a third part proceeds from gratification of object-libido.

The ego-ideal has imposed severe conditions upon the

gratification of libido through objects, for, by means of its censorship, it rejects some of them as incompatible with itself. Where no such ideal has been formed, the sexual trend in question makes its appearance unchanged in the personality in the form of a perversion. As in childhood, to be his own ideal once more, also where sexual tendencies are concerned, is the happiness that man strives to attain.

The state of being in love consists in a flowing-over of ego-libido to the object. This state has the power to remove repressions and to restore perversions. It exalts the sexual object to the position of sexual ideal. Since, in cases where the love is of the anaclitic or object type, this state results from the fulfilment of infantile conditions of love, we may say that whatever fulfils this condition of love becomes idealized.

The sexual ideal may enter into an interesting auxiliary relation to the ego-ideal. Where narcissistic gratification encounters actual hindrances, the sexual ideal may be used as a substitutive gratification. In such a case a person loves (in conformity with the narcissistic type of object-choice) someone whom he once was and no longer is, or else someone who possesses excellences which he never had at all (cf. (c) *supra*). The parallel formula to that given above runs thus: whoever possesses an excellence which the ego lacks for the attainment of its ideal, becomes loved. This expedient is of special importance for the neurotic, whose ego is depleted by his excessive object-cathexes and who on that account is unable to attain to his ego-ideal. He then seeks a way back to narcissism from his prodigal expenditure of libido upon objects, by choosing a sexual ideal after the narcissistic type which shall possess the excellences to which he cannot attain. This is the cure by love, which he generally prefers to cure by analysis. Indeed, he cannot believe in any other curative mechanism; he usually brings expectations of this sort with him to the treatment and then directs them towards the person of the physician. The patient's incapacity for love, an incapacity resulting from his extensive repressions, naturally stands in the way of such a method of cure. When, by means of the treatment, he has been partially freed from his repressions, we are frequently met by the unintended result that he withdraws from further treatment in order to choose a love-object, hoping that life with the beloved person will complete his recovery. We might be satisfied with this result, if it did not bring with it all the dangers of an overwhelming dependence upon this helper in his need.

The ego-ideal is of great importance for the understanding of group psychology. Besides its individual side, this ideal has a social side; it is also the common ideal of a family, a class or a nation. It not only binds the narcissistic libido, but also a considerable amount of the person's homosexual libido, which in this way becomes turned back into the ego. The dissatisfaction due to the non-fulfilment of this ideal liberates homosexual libido, which is transformed into sense of guilt (dread of the community). Originally this was a fear of punishment by the parents, or, more correctly, the dread of losing their love; later the parents are replaced by an indefinite number of fellow-men. This helps us to understand why it is that paranoia is frequently caused by a wounding of the ego, by a frustration of the gratification desired within the sphere of the ego-ideal, and also to understand the coincidence of ideal-formation and sublimation in the ego-ideal, as well as the demolition of sublimations and possible transformation of ideals in paraphrenic disorders.

Instincts and their Vicissitudes[1]

(1915)

THE VIEW IS OFTEN defended that sciences should be built up on clear and sharply defined basal concepts. In actual fact no science, not even the most exact, begins with such definitions. The true beginning of scientific activity consists rather in describing phenomena and then in proceeding to group, classify and correlate them. Even at the stage of description it is not possible to avoid applying certain abstract ideas to the material in hand, ideas derived from various sources and certainly not the fruit of the new experience only. Still more indispensable are such ideas – which will later become the basal concepts of the science – as the material is further elaborated. They must at first necessarily possess some measure of uncertainty; there can be no question of any clear delimitation of their content. So long as they remain in this condition, we come to an understanding about their meaning by repeated references to the material of observation, from which we seem to have deduced our abstract ideas, but which is in point of fact subject to them. Thus, strictly speaking, they are in the nature of conventions; although everything depends on their being chosen in no arbitrary manner, but determined by the important relations they have to the empirical material – relations that we seem to divine before we can clearly recognize and demonstrate them. It is only after more searching investigation of the field in question that we are able to formulate with increased clarity the scientific concepts underlying it, and progressively so to modify these concepts that they become widely applicable and at the same time consistent logically. Then, indeed, it may be time to immure them in definitions. The progress of science, however, demands a certain elasticity even in these definitions. The science of physics furnishes an excellent illustration of the way in which even those 'basal concepts' that are firmly established in the form of definitions are constantly being altered in their content.

A conventional but still rather obscure basal concept of this kind, which is nevertheless indispensable to us in psychology, is that of an *instinct*. Let us try to ascertain what is comprised in this conception by approaching it from different angles.

First, from the side of physiology. This has given us the concept of *stimuli* and the scheme of the reflex arc, according to which a stimulus applied *from the outer world* to living tissue (nervous substance) is discharged by action *towards the outer world*. The action answers the purpose of withdrawing the substance affected from the operation of the stimulus, removing it out of range of the stimulus.

Now what is the relation between 'instinct' and 'stimulus'? There is nothing to prevent our including the concept of 'instinct' under that of 'stimulus' and saying that an instinct is a stimulus to the mind. But we are immediately set on our guard against treating instinct and mental stimulus as one and the same thing. Obviously, besides those of instinctual origin, there are other stimuli to the mind which behave far more like physiological stimuli. For example, a strong light striking upon the eye is not a stimulus of instinctual origin; it is one, however, when the mucous membrane of the oesophagus becomes parched or when a gnawing makes itself felt in the stomach.[2]

We have now obtained material necessary for discriminating between stimuli of instinctual origin and the other (physiological) stimuli which operate on our minds. First, a stimulus of instinctual origin does not arise in the outside world but from within the organism itself. For this reason it has a different mental effect and different actions are necessary in order to remove it. Further, all that is essential in an external stimulus is contained in the assumption that it acts as a single impact, so that it can be discharged by a single appropriate action – a typical instance being that of motor flight from the source of stimulation. Of course these impacts may be repeated and their force may be cumulative, but that makes no difference to our notion of the process and to the conditions necessary in order that the stimulus may be dispelled. An instinct, on the other hand, never acts as a momentary impact but always as a constant force. As it makes its attack not from without but from within the organism, it follows that no flight can avail against it. A better term for a stimulus of instinctual origin is a 'need'; that which does away with this need is 'satisfaction'. This can be attained only by a suitable (adequate) alteration of the inner source of stimulation.

Let us imagine ourselves in the position of an almost entirely helpless living organism, as yet unorientated in the world and with stimuli impinging on its nervous tissue. This organism will soon become capable of making a first discrimination and a first orientation. On the one hand, it will detect certain stimuli which can be avoided by an action of the muscles (flight) – these it ascribes to an outside world; on the other hand, it will also be aware of stimuli against which such action is of no avail and whose urgency is in no way diminished by it – these stimuli are the tokens of an inner world, the proof of instinctual needs. The apperceptive substance of the living organism will thus have found in the efficacy of its muscular activity a means for discriminating between 'outer' and 'inner'.

We thus find our first conception of the essential nature of an instinct by considering its main characteristics, its origin in sources of stimulation within the organism and its appearance as a constant force, and thence we deduce one of its further distinguishing features, namely, that no actions of flight avail against it. Now, in making these remarks, we cannot fail to be struck by a fact which compels us to a further admission. We do not merely accept as basal concepts certain conventions which we apply to the material we have acquired empirically, but we also make use of various complicated postulates to guide us in dealing with psychological phenomena. We have already cited the most important of these postulates; it remains for us expressly to lay stress upon it. It is of a biological nature, and makes use of the concept of 'purpose' (one might say, of adaptation of the means to the end) and runs as follows: the nervous system is an apparatus having the function of abolishing stimuli which reach it, or of reducing excitation to the lowest possible level: an apparatus which would even, if this were feasible, maintain itself in an altogether unstimulated condition. Let us for the present not take exception to the indefiniteness of this idea and let us grant that the task of the nervous system is – broadly speaking – *to master stimuli*. We see then how greatly the simple physiological reflex scheme is complicated by the introduction of instincts. External stimuli impose upon the organism the single task of withdrawing itself from their action: this is accomplished by muscular movements, one of which reaches the goal aimed at and, being the most appropriate to the end in view, is thenceforward transmitted as an hereditary disposition. These instinctual stimuli which emanate from within the organism cannot be dealt with by this mechanism. Consequently, they make far higher demands upon the nervous system and compel it to complicated and interdependent activities, which effect such changes in the outer world as enable it to offer satisfaction to the internal source of stimulation; above all, instinctual stimuli oblige the nervous system to renounce its ideal intention of warding off stimuli, for they maintain an incessant and unavoidable afflux of stimulation. So we may probably conclude that instincts and not external stimuli are the true motive forces in the progress that has raised the nervous system, with all its incomparable efficiency, to its present high level of development. Of course there is nothing to prevent our assuming that the instincts themselves are, at least in part, the precipitates of different forms of external stimulation, which in the course of phylogenesis have effected modifications in the organism.

Then when we find further that the activity of even the most highly developed mental apparatus is subject to the pleasure-principle, i.e. is automatically regulated by feelings belonging to the pleasure-'pain' series, we can hardly reject the further postulate that these feelings reflect the manner in which the process of mastering stimuli takes place. This is certainly so in the sense that 'painful' feelings are connected with an increase and pleasurable feelings with a decrease in stimulation. Let us, however, be careful to preserve this assumption in its present highly indefinite form, until we succeed, if that is possible, in discovering what sort of relation exists between pleasure and 'pain', on the one hand, and fluctuations in the quantities of stimuli affecting mental life, on the other. It is certain that many kinds of these relations are possible, some of them by no means simple.

If now we apply ourselves to considering mental life from a biological point of view, an 'instinct' appears to us as a borderland concept between the mental and the physical, being both the mental representative of the stimuli emanating from within the organism and penetrating to the mind, and at the same time a measure of the demand made upon the energy of the latter in consequence of its connection with the body.

We are now in a position to discuss certain terms used in reference to the concept of an instinct, for example, its impetus, its aim, its object and its source.

By the *impetus* of an instinct we understand its motor element, the amount of force or the measure of the demand upon energy which it represents. The characteristic of impulsion is common to all instincts, is in fact the very essence of them. Every instinct is a form of activity; if we speak loosely of passive instincts, we can only mean those whose aim is passive.

The *aim* of an instinct is in every instance satisfaction, which can only be obtained by abolishing the condition of stimulation in the source of the instinct. But although this remains invariably the final goal of every instinct, there may yet be different ways leading to the same goal, so that an instinct may be found to have various nearer or intermediate aims, capable of combination or interchange. Experience permits us also to speak of instincts which are *inhibited in respect of their aim*, in cases where a certain advance has been permitted in the direction of satisfaction and then an inhibition or deflection has occurred. We may suppose that even in such cases a partial satisfaction is achieved.

The *object* of an instinct is that in or through which it can achieve its aim. It is the most variable thing about an instinct and is not originally connected with it, but becomes attached to it only in consequence of being peculiarly fitted to provide satisfaction. The object is not necessarily an extraneous one: it may be part of the subject's own body. It may be changed any number of times in the course of the vicissitudes the instinct undergoes during life; a highly important part is played by this capacity for displacement in the instinct. It may happen that the same object may serve for the satisfaction of several instincts simultaneously, a phenomenon which Adler calls a 'confluence' of instincts. A particularly close attachment of the instinct to its object is distinguished by the term *fixation*: this frequently occurs in very early stages of the instinct's development and so puts an end to its mobility, through the vigorous resistance it sets up against detachment.

By the *source* of an instinct is meant that somatic process in an organ or part of the body from which there results a stimulus represented in mental life by an instinct. We do not know whether this process is regularly of a chemical nature or whether it may also correspond with the release of other, e.g. mechanical, forces. The study of the sources of instinct is outside the scope of psychology; although its source in the body is what gives the instinct its distinct and essential character, yet in mental life we know it merely by its aims. A more exact knowledge of the sources of instincts is not strictly necessary for purposes of psychological investigation; often the source may be with certainty inferred from the aims.

Are we to suppose that the different instincts which operate upon the mind but of which the origin is somatic are also distinguished by different qualities and act in the mental life in a manner qualitatively different? This supposition does not seem to be justified; we are much more likely to find the simpler assumption sufficient – namely, that the instincts are all qualitatively alike and owe the effect they produce only to the quantities of excitation accompanying them, or perhaps further to certain functions of this quantity. The difference in the mental effects produced by the different instincts may be traced to the difference in their sources. In any event, it is only in a later connection that we shall be able to make plain what the problem of the quality of instincts signifies.

Now what instincts and how many should be postulated? There is obviously a great opportunity here for arbitrary choice. No objection can be made to anyone's employing the concept of an instinct of play or of destruction, or that of a social instinct, when the subject demands it and the limitations of psychological analysis allow of it. Nevertheless, we should not neglect to ask whether such instinctual motives, which are in one direction so highly specialized, do not admit of further analysis in respect of their sources, so that only those primal instincts which are not to be resolved further could really lay claim to the name.

I have proposed that two groups of such primal instincts should be distinguished: the *self-preservative* or ego-instincts and the *sexual* instincts. But this proposition has not the weight of a necessary postulate, such as, for instance, our assumption about the biological 'purpose' in the mental apparatus (*vide supra*); it is merely an auxiliary construction, to be retained only so long as it proves useful, and it will make little difference to the results of our work of description and classification if we replace it by another. The occasion for it arose in the course of the evolution of psycho-analysis, which was first employed upon the psychoneuroses, actually upon the group designated transference neuroses (hysteria and obsessional neurosis); through them it became plain that at the root of all such affections there lies a conflict between the claims of sexuality and those of the ego. It is always possible that an exhaustive study of the other neurotic affections (especially of the narcissistic psychoneuroses, the schizophrenias) may oblige us to alter this formula and therewith to make a different classification of the primal instincts. But for the present we do not know what this new formula may be, nor have we met with any argument which seems likely to be prejudicial to the contrast between sexual and ego-instincts.

I am altogether doubtful whether work upon psychological material will afford any decisive indication for the distinction and classification of instincts. Rather it would seem necessary to apply to this material certain definite assumptions in order to work upon it, and we could wish that these assumptions might be taken from some other branch of knowledge and transferred to psychology. The contribution of biology on this point certainly does not run counter to the distinction between sexual and ego-instincts. Biology teaches that sexuality is not on a level with the other functions of the individual, for its 'purposes' go beyond the individual, their content being the production of new individuals and the preservation of the species. It shows, further, that the relation existing between the ego and sexuality may be conceived of in two ways, apparently equally well justified: in the one, the individual is regarded as of prime importance, sexuality as one of his activities and sexual satisfaction as one of his needs; while in the other the individual organism is looked upon as a transitory and perishable appendage to the quasi-immortal germ-plasm bequeathed to him by the race. The assumption that the sexual function differs from other bodily processes in virtue of special chemical processes is, I understand, also a postulate of the Ehrlich school of biological research.

Since a study of the instincts from the side of consciousness presents almost insuperable difficulties, psycho-analytic investigation of mental disturbances remains the principal source of our knowledge. The development of this line of investigation, however, has necessarily produced hitherto information of a more or less definite nature only in regard to the sexual instincts, for it is this group in particular which can be observed in isolation, as it were, in the psychoneuroses. With the extension of psycho-analysis to other neurotic affections we may be sure that we shall find a basis for our knowledge of the ego-instincts also, though it would be optimistic to expect equally favourable conditions for observation in this further field of research.

An attempt to formulate the general characteristics of the sexual instincts would run as follows: they are numerous, emanate from manifold organic sources, act in the first instance independently of one another and only at a late stage achieve a more or less complete synthesis. The aim which each strives to attain is 'organ-pleasure'; only when the synthesis is complete do they enter the service of the function of reproduction, becoming thereby generally recognizable as sexual instincts. At their first appearance they support themselves upon the instincts of self-preservation, from which they only gradually detach themselves; in their choice of object also they follow paths indicated by the ego-instincts. Some of them remain throughout life associated with these latter and furnish them with libidinal components, which with normal functioning easily escape notice and are clearly recognizable only when disease is present. They have this distinctive characteristic – that they have in a high degree the capacity to act vicariously for one another and that they can readily change their objects. In consequence of the last-mentioned properties they are capable of activities widely removed from their original modes of attaining their aims (sublimation).

Our inquiry into the various vicissitudes which instincts

undergo in the process of development and in the course of life must be confined to the sexual instincts, for these are the more familiar to us. Observation shows us that an instinct may undergo the following vicissitudes:

Reversal into its opposite;
Turning round upon the subject;
Repression;
Sublimation.

Since I do not intend to treat of sublimation here and since repression requires a special chapter to itself, it only remains for us to describe and discuss the two first points. Bearing in mind that there are tendencies which are opposed to the instincts pursuing a straightforward course, we may regard these vicissitudes as modes of defence against the instincts.

The *reversal* of an instinct *into its opposite* may on closer scrutiny be resolved into two different processes: a change from active to passive, and a reversal of the content. The two processes, being essentially distinct, must be treated separately.

Examples of the first process are met with in the two pairs of opposites: sadism-masochism and scoptophilia-exhibitionism. The reversal here concerns only the aims of the instincts. The passive aim (to be tortured, or looked at) has been substituted for the active aim (to torture, to look at). Reversal of content is found in the single instance of the change of love into hate.

The *turning round* of an instinct *upon the subject* is suggested to us by the reflection that masochism is actually sadism turned round upon the subject's own ego, and that exhibitionism includes the love of gazing at the subject's own body. Further, analytic observation leaves us in no doubt that the masochist also enjoys the *act* of torturing when this is being applied to himself, and the exhibitionist the exposing of someone in being exposed himself. So the essence of the process is the change of the object, while the aim remains unchanged.

We cannot fail to note, however, that in these examples turning round upon the subject's self and transformation from active to passive coincide or occur in one process. To elucidate the relation between the two processes, a more thorough investigation must be undertaken.

With the pair of opposites sadism-masochism, the process may be represented as follows:

(*a*) Sadism consists in the exercise of violence or power upon some other person as its object.

(*b*) This object is abandoned and replaced by the subject's self. Together with the turning round upon the self the change from an active to a passive aim in the instinct is also brought about.

(*c*) Again another person is sought as object; this person, in consequence of the alteration which has taken place in the aim of the instinct, has to take over the original role of the subject.

Case (*c*) is the condition commonly termed masochism.

Satisfaction follows in this case also by way of the original sadism, the passive ego placing itself in phantasy back in its former situation, which, however, has now been given up to another subject outside the self. Whether there is, besides this, a more direct masochistic satisfaction is highly doubtful. A primary masochism not derived in the manner I have described from sadism, does not appear to be met with.[3] That it is not superfluous to make the assumption of stage (*b*) is quite clear when we observe the behaviour of the sadistic impulse in cases of obsessional neurosis. In these we have the turning upon the subject's self, without the attitude of passivity towards another: the reversal has only reached the second stage. Self-torment and self-punishment have arisen from the desire to torture, but not masochism. The active voice is changed, not into the passive, but into the reflexive middle voice.

The conception of sadism is made more complicated by the circumstance that this instinct, side by side with its general aim (or perhaps rather, within it), seems to press towards a quite special aim: the infliction of pain, in addition to subjection and mastery of the object. Now psycho-analysis would seem to show that the infliction of pain plays no part in the original aims sought by the instinct: the sadistic child takes no notice of whether or not it inflicts pain, nor is it part of its purpose to do so. But when once the transformation into masochism has taken place, the experience of pain is very well adapted to serve as a passive masochistic aim, for we have every reason to believe that sensations of pain, like other unpleasant sensations, extend into sexual excitation and produce a condition which is pleasurable, for the sake of which the subject will even willingly experience the unpleasantness of pain. Where once the suffering of pain has been experienced as a masochistic aim, it can be carried back into the sadistic situation and result in a sadistic aim of *inflicting pain*, which will then be masochistically enjoyed by the subject while inflicting pain upon others, through his identification of himself with the suffering object. Of course, in either case it is not the pain itself which is enjoyed, but the accompanying sexual excitement, and this is especially easy for the sadist. The enjoyment of pain would thus be a primary masochistic aim, which, however, can then also become the aim of the originally sadistic instinct.

In order to complete my exposition I would add that pity cannot be described as a result of the reversal of the sadistic instinct, but necessitates the conception of a *reaction-formation* against that instinct (for the difference, *vide infra*).

Rather different and simpler results are afforded by the investigation of another pair of opposites, namely, those instincts whose aim is sexual gazing (scoptophilia) and self-display (the 'voyeur' and exhibitionist tendencies as they are called in the language of the perversions). Here again we may postulate the same stages as in the previous instance: (*a*) scoptophilia as an activity directed towards an extraneous object; (*b*) abandonment of the object and a turning of the scoptophilic instinct towards a part of the subject's own person; therewith a transformation to passivity and the setting up of a new aim – that of being looked at; (*c*) the institution of a new subject to whom one displays oneself in order to be looked at. Here too, it is hardly possible to doubt that the active aim appears before the passive, that scoptophilia precedes exhibitionism. But there is an important divergence from what happens in the case of sadism, in that we can recognize in the scoptophilic instinct a yet earlier stage than that described as (*a*). That is to say, that at the beginning of its activity the scoptophilic instinct is auto-erotic: it has indeed an object, but that object is the subject's own body. It is only later that the instinct comes (by the way of comparison) to exchange this object for the analogous one of the body of another (stage (*a*)). Now this preliminary stage is interesting because it is the source of both the situations represented in the resulting pair of opposites, according to which element in the original situation is reversed. The following might serve as a scheme for the scoptophilic instinct:

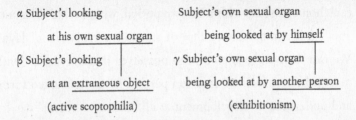

α Subject's looking
    at his own sexual organ
β Subject's looking
    at an extraneous object
    (active scoptophilia)

Subject's own sexual organ
    being looked at by himself
γ Subject's own sexual organ
    being looked at by another person
    (exhibitionism)

A preliminary stage of this kind is absent in sadism, which from the outset is directed upon an extraneous object, although it might not be altogether unreasonable to regard as such a stage the child's efforts to gain control of his own limbs.[4]

With regard to both these instincts just examined as examples, it must be said that transformation of them by a reversal from active to passive and by a turning round upon the subject never in fact concerns the whole amount of impelling force pertaining to the instinct. To some extent its earlier active direction always persists side by side with the later passive direction, even when the transformation is very extensive. The only correct description of the scoptophilic instinct would be that all phases of its development, the auto-erotic, preliminary phase as well as its final active or passive form, co-exist alongside one another; and the truth of this statement becomes manifest if we base our opinion, not upon the actions which are prompted by the instinct, but upon the mechanism of its satisfaction. Perhaps yet another way of conceiving and representing the matter may be justified. We may split up the life of each instinct into a series of 'thrusts', distinct from one another in the time of their occurrence but each homogeneous within its own period, whose relation to one another is comparable to that of successive eruptions of lava. We can then perhaps picture to ourselves that the earliest and most primitive instinct-eruption persists in an unchanged form and undergoes no development at all. The next 'thrust' would then from the outset have undergone a change of form, being turned, for instance, from active to passive, and it would then, with this new characteristic, be superimposed upon the earlier layer, and so on. So that, if we take a survey of the instinctual tendency from its beginning up to any given stopping-point, the succession of 'thrusts' which we have described would present the picture of a definite development of the instinct.

The fact that, at that later period of development, the instinct in its primary form may be observed side by side with its (passive) opposite deserves to be distinguished by the highly appropriate name introduced by Bleuler: *ambivalence*.

These considerations regarding the developmental history of an instinct and the permanent character of the intermediate stages in it should make instinct-development more comprehensible to us. Experience shows that the degree of demonstrable ambivalence varies greatly in individuals, groups and races. Marked ambivalence of an instinct in a human being at the present day may be regarded as an archaic inheritance, for we have reason to suppose that the part played in the life of the instincts by the active impulses in their original form was greater in primitive times than it is on an average today.

We have become accustomed to call the early phase of the development of the ego, during which its sexual instincts find auto-erotic satisfaction, *narcissism*, without having so far entered into any discussion of the relation between auto-erotism and narcissism. It follows that, in considering the preliminary phase of the scoptophilic instinct, when the subject's own body is the object of the scoptophilia, we must place it under the heading of narcissism; it is a narcissistic formation. From this phase the active scoptophilic instinct, which has left narcissism behind, is developed, while the passive scoptophilic instinct, on the contrary, holds fast to the narcissistic object. Similarly, the transformation from sadism to masochism betokens a reversion to the narcissistic object, while in both cases the narcissistic (active) subject is exchanged by identification for another, extraneous ego. Taking into consideration the preliminary narcissistic stage of sadism constructed by us, we approach the more general view that those vicissitudes which consist in the instinct being turned round upon the subject's own ego and undergoing reversal from activity to passivity are dependent upon the narcissistic organization of the ego and bear the stamp of that phase. Perhaps they represent attempts at defence which at higher stages of the development of the ego are effected by other means.

At this point we may remember that so far we have discussed only two pairs of instincts and their opposites: sadism-masochism and scoptophilia-exhibitionism. These are the best-known sexual instincts which appear in ambivalent forms. The other components of the later sexual function are at present too inaccessible to analysis for us to be able to discuss them in a similar way. In general we can assert of them that their activities are auto-erotic, i.e. their object becomes negligible in comparison with the organ which is their source, and as a rule the two coincide. The object of the scoptophilic instinct, although it also in the first instance is a part of the subject's own body, nevertheless is not the eye itself; and with sadism the organic source, probably the musculature with its capacity for action, directly presupposes an object other than itself, even though that object be part of the subject's own body. In the auto-erotic instincts, the part played by the organic source is so decisive that, according to a plausible supposition of P. Federn and L. Jekels,[1] the form and function of the organ determine the activity or passivity of the instinct's aim.

The transformation of the 'content' of an instinct into its opposite is observed in a single instance only – the changing of *love into hate*. It is particularly common to find both these directed simultaneously towards the same object, and this phenomenon of their co-existence furnishes the most important example of ambivalence of feeling.

The case of love and hate acquires a special interest from the circumstance that it resists classification in our scheme of the instincts. It is impossible to doubt the existence of a most intimate relation between these two contrary feelings and sexual life, but one is naturally unwilling to conceive of love as being a kind of special component-instinct of sexuality in the same way as are the others just discussed. One would prefer to regard loving rather as the expression of the whole sexual current of feeling, but this idea does not clear up our difficulties and we are at a loss how to conceive of an essential opposite to this striving.

Loving admits of not merely one, but of three antitheses. First there is the antithesis of loving–hating; secondly, there is loving–being loved; and, in addition to these, loving and hating together are the opposite of the condition of neutrality or indifference. The second of these two antitheses, loving–being loved, corresponds exactly to the transformation from active to passive and may be traced to a primal situation in the same way as the scoptophilic instinct. This situation is that of *loving oneself*, which for us is the characteristic of narcissism. Then, according to whether the self as object or subject is exchanged for an extraneous one, there results the active aim of loving or the passive one of being loved, the latter remaining nearly related to narcissism.

Perhaps we shall come to a better understanding of the manifold opposites of loving if we reflect that our mental life as a whole is governed by *three polarities*, namely, the following antitheses:

> Subject (ego)—Object (external world);
> Pleasure—Pain;
> Active—Passive.

The antithesis of ego–non-ego (outer), i.e. subject–object, is, as we have already said, thrust upon the individual being at an early stage, by the experience that it can abolish external stimuli by means of muscular action but is defenceless against those stimuli that originate in instinct. This antithesis remains sovereign above all in our intellectual activity and provides research with a fundamental situation which no amount of effort can alter. The polarity of pleasure–pain depends upon a feeling-series, the significance of which in determining our actions (will) is paramount and has already been emphasized. The antithesis of active and passive must not be confounded with that of ego-subject–external object. The relation of the ego to the outer world is passive in so far as it receives stimuli from it, active when it reacts to these. Its instincts compel it to a quite special degree of activity towards the outside world, so that, if we wished to emphasize the essence of the matter, we might say that the ego-subject is passive in respect of external stimuli, active in virtue of its own instincts. The antithesis of active–passive coalesces later with that of masculine–feminine, which, until this has taken place, has no psychological significance. The fusion of activity with masculinity and passivity with femininity confronts us, indeed, as a biological fact, but it is by no means so invariably complete and exclusive as we are inclined to assume.

The three polarities within the mind are connected with one another in various highly significant ways. There is a certain primal psychic situation in which two of them coincide. Originally, at the very beginning of mental life, the ego's instincts are directed to itself and it is to some extent capable of deriving satisfaction for them on itself. This condition is known as narcissism and this potentiality for satisfaction is termed auto-erotic.[6] The outside world is at this time, generally speaking, not cathected with any interest and is indifferent for purposes of satisfaction. At this period, therefore, the ego-subject coincides with what is pleasurable and the outside world with what is indifferent (or even painful as being a source of stimulation). Let us for the moment define loving as the relation of the ego to its sources of pleasure: then the situation in which the ego loves itself only and is indifferent to the outside world illustrates the first of the polarities in which 'loving' appeared.

In so far as it is auto-erotic, the ego has no need of the outside world, but, in consequence of experiences undergone by the instincts of self-preservation, it tends to find objects there and doubtless it cannot but for a time perceive inner instinctual stimuli as painful. Under the sway of the pleasure-principle there now takes place a further development. The objects presenting themselves, in so far as they are sources of pleasure, are absorbed by the ego into itself, 'introjected' (according to an expression coined by Ferenczi); while, on the other hand, the ego thrusts forth upon the external world whatever within itself gives rise to pain (*vide infra*: the mechanism of projection).

Thus the original *reality-ego*, which distinguished outer and inner by means of a sound objective criterion, changes into a purified *pleasure-ego*, which prizes above all else the quality of pleasure. For this pleasure-ego the outside world is divided into a part that is pleasurable, which it has incorporated into itself, and a remainder that is alien to it. A part of itself it has separated off, and this it projects into the external world and regards as hostile. According to this new arrangement the congruence of the two polarities –

ego-subject with pleasure;

outside world with pain (or earlier with neutrality)

– is once more established.

When the stage of primary narcissism is invaded by the object, the second contrary attitude to that of love, namely, hate, attains to development.

As we have heard, the ego's objects are presented to it from the outside world in the first instance by the instincts of self-preservation, and it is undeniable also that hate originally betokens the relation of the ego to the alien external world with its afflux of stimuli. Neutrality may be classified as a special case of hate or rejection, after having made its appearance first as the forerunner of hate. Thus at the very beginning, the external world, objects and that which was hated were one and the same thing. When later on an object manifests itself as a source of pleasure, it becomes loved, but also incorporated into the ego, so that for the purified pleasure-ego the object once again coincides with what is extraneous and hated.

Now, however, we note that just as the antithesis love–indifference reflects the polarity ego–external world, so the second antithesis, love–hate, reproduces the polarity pleasure–pain, which is bound up with the former. When the purely narcissistic stage gives place to the object-stage, pleasure and pain denote the relations of the ego to the object. When the object becomes a source of pleasurable feelings, a motor tendency is set up which strives to bring the object near to and incorporate it into the ego; we then speak of the 'attraction' exercised by the pleasure-giving object, and say that we 'love' that object. Conversely, when the object is the source of painful feelings, there is a tendency which endeavours to increase the distance between object and ego and to repeat in relation to the former the primordial attempt at flight from the external world with its flow of stimuli. We feel a 'repulsion' from the object, and hate it; this hate can then be intensified to the point of an aggressive tendency towards the object, with the intention of destroying it.

We might at a pinch say of an instinct that it 'loves' the objects after which it strives for purposes of satisfaction, but to say that it 'hates' an object strikes us as odd; so we become aware that the attitudes of love and hate cannot be said to characterize the relations of instincts to their objects, but are reserved for the relations of the ego as a whole to objects. But, if we consider a colloquial usage which is certainly full of meaning, we see that there is yet another limitation to the significance of love and hate. We do not say of those objects which serve the interests of self-preservation that we love them; rather we emphasize the fact that we need them, and perhaps add an element of a different kind in our relation to them by words which denote a much lesser degree of love – for example, to be fond of, to like, to find agreeable.

So the word 'to love' becomes shifted ever further into the

sphere of the pure pleasure-relation existing between the ego and its object and finally attaches itself to sexual objects in the narrower sense and to those which satisfy the needs of sublimated sexual instincts. The discrimination of the ego-instincts from the sexual, a discrimination which we have imposed upon our psychology, is seen, therefore, to be in conformity with the spirit of our speech. Since we do not customarily say that the single sexual component-instinct loves its object, but see the most appropriate case in which to apply the word 'love' in the relation of the ego to its sexual object, we learn from this fact that the applicability of the word in this relation begins only with the synthesis of all the component-instincts under the primacy of the genitals and in the service of the function of reproduction.

It is noteworthy that in the use of the word 'hate' no such intimate relation to sexual pleasure and the sexual function appears: on the contrary, the painful character of the relation seems to be the sole decisive feature. The ego hates, abhors and pursues with intent to destroy all objects which are for it a source of painful feelings, without taking into account whether they mean to it frustration of sexual satisfaction or of gratification of the needs of self-preservation. Indeed, it may be asserted that the true prototypes of the hate-relation are derived not from sexual life, but from the struggle of the ego for self-preservation and self-maintenance.

So we see that love and hate, which present themselves to us as essentially antithetical, stand in no simple relation to each other. They did not originate in a cleavage of any common primal element, but sprang from different sources and underwent each its own development before the influence of the pleasure-pain relation constituted them antitheses to each other. At this point we are confronted with the task of putting together what we know of the genesis of love and hate.

Love originates in the capacity of the ego to satisfy some of its instincts auto-erotically through the obtaining of 'organ-pleasure'. It is primarily narcissistic, is then transferred to those objects which have been incorporated in the ego, now much extended, and expresses the motor striving of the ego after these objects as sources of pleasure. It is intimately connected with the activity of the later sexual instincts and, when these have been completely synthetized, coincides with the sexual trend as a whole. The preliminary stages of love reveal themselves as temporary sexual aims, while the sexual instincts are passing through their complicated development. First amongst these we recognize the phase of incorporating or devouring, a type of love which is compatible with abolition of any separate existence on the part of the object, and which may therefore be designated ambivalent. At the higher stage of the pregenital sadistic-anal organization, the striving after the object appears in the form of an impulsion to mastery, in which injury or annihilation of the object is a matter of indifference. This form and preliminary stage of love is hardly to be distinguished from hate in its behaviour towards the object. Only when the genital organization is established does love become the antithesis of hate.

The relation of hate to objects is older than that of love. It is derived from the primal repudiation by the narcissistic ego of the external world whence flows the stream of stimuli. As an expression of the pain-reaction induced by objects, it remains in constant intimate relation with the instincts of self-preservation, so that sexual and ego-instincts readily develop an antithesis which repeats that of love and hate. When the sexual function is governed by the ego-instincts, as at the stage of the sadistic-anal organization, they impart the qualities of hate to the instinct's aim as well.

The history of the origin and relations of love makes us understand how it is that love so constantly manifests itself as 'ambivalent', i.e. accompanied by feelings of hate against the same object. This admixture of hate in love is to be traced in part to those preliminary stages of love which have not been wholly outgrown, and in part is based upon reactions of aversion and repudiation on the part of the ego-instincts which, in the frequent conflicts between the interests of the ego and those of love, can claim to be supported by real and actual motives. In both cases, therefore, the admixture of hate may be traced to the source of the self-preservative instincts. When a love-relationship with a given object is broken off, it is not infrequently succeeded by hate, so that we receive the impression of a transformation of love into hate. This descriptive characterization is amplified by the view that, when this happens, the hate which is motivated by considerations of reality is reinforced by a regression of the love to the sadistic preliminary stage, so that the hate acquires an erotic character and the continuity of a love-relation is ensured.

The third antithesis of love, the transformation of loving into being loved, represents the operation of the polarity of active and passive, and is to be judged in the same way as in scoptophilia and sadism. We may sum up by saying that the essential feature in the vicissitudes undergone by instincts is *their subjection to the influences of the three great polarities that govern mental life*. Of these three polarities we might describe that of activity–passivity as the *biological*, that of ego–external world as the *real*, and finally that of pleasure–pain as the *economic* respectively.

That possible vicissitude undergone by an instinct which we call *repression* will form the subject of a further inquiry.

Repression[1]

(1915)

ONE OF THE vicissitudes an instinctual impulse may undergo is to meet with resistances the aim of which is to make the impulse inoperative. Under certain conditions, which we shall presently investigate more closely, the impulse then passes into the state of *repression*. If it were a question of the operation of an external stimulus, obviously flight would be the appropriate remedy; with an instinct, flight is of no avail, for the ego cannot escape from itself. Later on, rejection based on judgement (*condemnation*) will be found to be a good weapon against the impulse. Repression is a preliminary phase of condemnation, something between flight and condemnation; it is a concept which could not have been formulated before the time of psycho-analytic research.

It is not easy in theory to deduce the possibility of such a thing as repression. Why should an instinctual impulse suffer such a fate? For this to happen, obviously a necessary condition must be that attainment of its aim by the instinct should produce 'pain' instead of pleasure. But we cannot well imagine such a contingency. There are no such instincts; satisfaction of an instinct is always pleasurable. We should have to assume certain peculiar circumstances, some sort of process which changes the pleasure of satisfaction into 'pain'.

In order the better to define repression we may discuss some other situations in which instincts are concerned. It may happen that an external stimulus becomes internal, for example, by eating into and destroying a bodily organ, so that a new source of constant excitation and increase of tension is formed. The stimulus thereby acquires a far-reaching similarity to an instinct. We know that a case of this sort is experienced by us as *physical pain*. The aim of this pseudo-instinct, however, is simply the cessation of the change in the organ and of the pain accompanying it. There is no other direct pleasure to be attained by cessation of the pain. Further, pain is imperative; the only things which can subdue it are the effect of some toxic agent in removing it and the influence of some mental distraction.

The case of physical pain is too obscure to help us much in our purpose. Let us suppose that an instinctual stimulus such as hunger remains unsatisfied. It then becomes imperative and can be allayed by nothing but the appropriate action for satisfying it; it keeps up a constant tension of need. Anything like a repression seems in this case to be utterly out of the question.

So repression is certainly not an essential result of the tension produced by lack of satisfaction of an impulse being raised to an unbearable degree. The weapons of defence of which the organism avails itself to guard against that situation must be discussed in another connection.

Let us instead confine ourselves to the clinical experience we meet with in the practice of psycho-analysis. We then see that the satisfaction of an instinct under repression is quite possible; further, that in every instance such a satisfaction is pleasurable in itself, but is irreconcilable with other claims and purposes; it therefore causes pleasure in one part of the mind and 'pain' in another. We see then that it is a condition of repression that the element of avoiding 'pain' shall have acquired more strength than the pleasure of gratification. Psycho-analytic experience of the transference neuroses, moreover, forces us to the conclusion that repression is not a defence-mechanism present from the very beginning, and that it cannot occur until a sharp distinction has been established between what is conscious and what is unconscious: that *the essence of repression lies simply in the function of rejecting and keeping something out of consciousness*. This conception of repression would be supplemented by assuming that, before the mental organization reaches this phase, the other vicissitudes which may befall instincts, e.g. reversal into the opposite or turning round upon the subject, deal with the task of mastering the instinctual impulses.

It seems to us now that in view of the very great extent to which repression and the unconscious are correlated, we must defer probing more deeply into the nature of repression until we have learnt more about the structure of the various institutions in the mind – and about what differentiates consciousness from the unconscious. Till we have done this, all we can do is to put together in purely descriptive fashion some characteristics of repression noted in clinical practice, even though we run the risk of having to repeat unchanged much that has been said elsewhere.

Now we have reason for assuming *a primal repression*, a first phase of repression, which consists in a denial of entry into consciousness to the mental (ideational) presentation of the instinct. This is accompanied by a *fixation*; the ideational presentation in question persists unaltered from then onwards and the instinct remains attached to it. This is due to certain properties of unconscious processes of which we shall speak later.

The second phase of repression, *repression proper*, concerns mental derivatives of the repressed instinct-presentation, or such trains of thought as, originating elsewhere, have come into associative connection with it. On account of this association, these ideas experience the same fate as that which underwent primal repression. Repression proper, therefore, is actually an after-expulsion. Moreover, it is a mistake to emphasize only the rejection which operates from the side of consciousness upon what is to be repressed. We have to consider just as much the attraction exercised by what was originally repressed upon everything with which it can establish a connection. Probably the tendency to repression would fail of its purpose if these forces did not co-operate, if there were not something previously repressed ready to assimilate that which is rejected from consciousness.

Under the influence of study of the psychoneuroses, which brings before us the important effects of repression, we are inclined to over-estimate their psychological content and to forget too readily that repression does not hinder the instinct-presentation from continuing to exist in the unconscious and from organizing itself further, putting forth derivatives and instituting connections. Really, repression interferes only with the relation of the instinct-presentation to one system of the mind, namely, to consciousness.

Psycho-analysis is able to show us something else which is important for understanding the effects of repression in the psychoneuroses. It shows us, for instance, that the instinct-presentation develops in a more unchecked and luxuriant fashion if it is withdrawn by repression from conscious influence. It ramifies like a fungus, so to speak, in the dark and takes on extreme forms of expression, which when translated and revealed to the neurotic are bound not merely to seem alien to him, but to terrify him by the way in which they reflect an extraordinary and dangerous strength of instinct. This illusory strength of instinct is the result of an uninhibited development of it in phantasy and of the damming-up consequent on lack of real satisfaction. The fact that this last result is bound up with repression points the direction in which we have to look for the true significance of the latter.

In reverting to the contrary aspect, however, let us state

definitely that it is not even correct to suppose that repression withholds from consciousness all the derivatives of what was primally repressed. If these derivatives are sufficiently far removed from the repressed instinct-presentation, whether owing to the process of distortion or by reason of the number of intermediate associations, they have free access to consciousness. It is as though the resistance of consciousness against them was in inverse proportion to their remoteness from what was originally repressed. During the practice of the psycho-analytic method, we continually require the patient to produce such derivatives of what has been repressed as, in consequence either of their remoteness or of distortion, can pass the censorship of consciousness. Indeed, the associations which we require him to give, while refraining from any consciously directed train of thought or any criticism, and from which we reconstruct a conscious interpretation of the repressed instinct-presentation, are precisely derivatives of this kind. We then observe that the patient can go on spinning a whole chain of such associations, till he is brought up in the midst of them against some thought-formation, the relation of which to what is repressed acts so intensely that he is compelled to repeat his attempt at repression. Neurotic symptoms, too, must have fulfilled the condition referred to, for they are derivatives of the repressed, which has finally by means of these formations wrested from consciousness the right of way previously denied it.

We can lay down no general rule concerning the degree of

distortion and remoteness necessary before the resistance of consciousness is abrogated. In this matter a delicate balancing takes place, the play of which is hidden from us; its mode of operation, however, leads us to infer that it is a question of a definite degree of intensity in the cathexis of the unconscious – beyond which it would break through for satisfaction. Repression acts, therefore, in a *highly specific* manner in each instance; every single derivative of the repressed may have its peculiar fate – a little more or a little less distortion alters the whole issue. In this connection it becomes comprehensible that those objects to which men give their preference, that is, their ideals, originate in the same perceptions and experiences as those objects of which they have most abhorrence, and that the two originally differed from one another only by slight modifications. Indeed, as we found in the origin of the fetish, it is possible for the original instinct-presentation to be split into two, one part undergoing repression, while the remainder, just an account of its intimate association with the other, undergoes idealization.

The same result as ensues from an increase or a decrease in the degree of distortion may also be achieved at the other end of the apparatus, so to speak, by a modification in the conditions producing pleasure and 'pain'. Special devices have been evolved, with the object of bringing about such changes in the play of mental forces that what usually gives rise to 'pain' may on this occasion result in pleasure, and whenever such a device comes into operation the repression of an instinct-presentation that is ordinarily repudiated is abrogated. The only one of these devices which has till now been studied in any detail is that of joking. Generally the lifting of the repression is only transitory; the repression is immediately re-established.

Observations of this sort, however, suffice to draw our attention to some further characteristics of repression. Not only is it, as we have just explained, *variable* and *specific*, but it is also exceedingly *mobile*. The process of repression is not to be regarded as something which takes place once for all, the results of which are permanent, as when some living thing has been killed and from that time onward is dead; on the contrary, repression demands a constant expenditure of energy, and if this were discontinued the success of the repression would be jeopardized, so that a fresh act of repression would be necessary. We may imagine that what is repressed exercises a continuous straining in the direction of consciousness, so that the balance has to be kept by means of a steady counter-pressure. A constant expenditure of energy, therefore, is entailed in maintaining a repression, and economically its abrogation denotes a saving. The mobility of the repression, incidentally, finds expression also in the mental characteristics of the condition of sleep which alone renders dream-formation possible. With a return to waking life the repressive cathexes which have been called in are once more put forth.

Finally, we must not forget that after all we have said very little about an instinctual impulse when we state it to be repressed.

Without prejudice to the repression such an impulse may find itself in widely different conditions; it may be inactive, i.e. cathected with only a low degree of mental energy, or its degree of cathexis (and consequently its capacity for activity) may vary. True, its activity will not result in a direct abrogation of the repression, but it will certainly set in motion all the processes which terminate in a breaking through into consciousness by circuitous routes. With unrepressed derivatives of the unconscious the fate of a particular idea is often decided by the degree of its activity or cathexis. It is an everyday occurrence that such a derivative can remain unrepressed so long as it represents only a small amount of energy, although its content is of such a nature as to give rise to a conflict with conscious control. But the quantitative factor is manifestly decisive for this conflict; as soon as an idea which is fundamentally offensive exceeds a certain degree of strength, the conflict takes on actuality, and it is precisely activation of the idea that leads to its repression. So that, where repression is concerned, an increase in energic cathexis operates in the same way as an approach to the unconscious, while a decrease in that energy operates like distance from the unconscious or like distortion. We understand that the repressing tendencies can find a substitute for repression in a weakening or lessening of whatever is distasteful to them.

In our discussion hitherto we have dealt with the repression of an instinct-presentation, and by that we understood an idea or group of ideas which is cathected with a definite amount of the mental energy (libido, interest) pertaining to an instinct. Now clinical observation forces us further to dissect something that hitherto we have conceived of as a single entity, for it shows us that beside the idea there is something else, another presentation of the instinct to be considered, and that this other element undergoes a repression which may be quite different from that of the idea. We have adopted the term *charge of affect* for this other element in the mental presentation; it represents that part of the instinct which has become detached from the idea, and finds proportionate expression, according to its quantity, in processes which become observable to perception as affects. From this point on, in describing a case of repression, we must follow up the fate of the idea which undergoes repression separately from that of the instinctual energy attached to the idea.

We should be glad enough to be able to give some general account of the outcome of both of these, and when we have taken our bearings a little we shall actually be able to do so. In general, repression of the ideational presentation of an instinct can surely only have the effect of causing it to vanish from consciousness if it had previously been in consciousness, or of holding it back if it is about to enter it. The difference, after all, is not important; it amounts to much the same thing as the difference between ordering an undesirable guest out of my drawing-room or out of my front hall, and refusing to let him cross my threshold once I have recognized him.[2] The fate of the quantitative factor in the instinct-presentation may be one of three, as we see by a cursory survey of the observations made through psycho-analysis: either the instinct is altogether suppressed, so that no trace of it is found, or it appears in the guise of an affect of a particular qualitative tone, or it is transformed into anxiety. With the two last possibilities we are obliged to focus our attention upon the *transformation* into *affects*, and especially into *anxiety*, of the mental energy belonging to the *instincts*, this being a new possible vicissitude undergone by an instinct.

We recall the fact that the motive and purpose of repression was simply the avoidance of 'pain'. It follows that the fate of the charge of affect belonging to the presentation is far more important than that of the ideational content of it and is decisive for the opinion we form of the process of repression. If a repression does not succeed in preventing feelings of 'pain' or anxiety from arising, we may say that it has failed, even though it may have achieved its aim as far as the ideational element is concerned. Naturally, the case of unsuccessful repression will have more claim on our interest than that of repression which is eventually successful; the latter will for the most part elude our study.

We now wish to gain some insight into the mechanism of the process of repression, and especially we want to know whether it has a single mechanism only, or more than one, and whether perhaps each of the psychoneuroses may be distinguished by a characteristic repression-mechanism peculiar to itself. At the outset of this inquiry, however, we encounter complications.

The mechanism of a repression becomes accessible to us only when we deduce it from its final results. If we confine our observations to the results of its effect on the ideational part of the instinct-presentation, we discover that as a rule repression creates a *substitute-formation*. What then is the mechanism of such a substitute-formation, or must we distinguish several mechanisms here also? Further, we know that repression leaves *symptoms* in its train. May we then regard substitute-formation and symptom-formation as coincident processes, and, if this is on the whole possible, does the mechanism of substitute-formation coincide with that of repression? So far as we know at present, it seems probable that the two are widely divergent, that it is not the repression itself which produces substitute-formations and symptoms, but that these latter constitute indications of a *return of the repressed* and owe their existence to quite other processes. It would also seem advisable to examine the mechanisms of substitute- and symptom-formation before those of repression.

Obviously there is no ground here for speculation to explore: on the contrary, the solution of the problem must be found by careful analysis of the results of repression observable in the individual neuroses. I must, however, suggest that we should postpone this task, too, until we have formed reliable conceptions of the relation of consciousness to the unconscious. Only, in order that the present discussion may not be quite unfruitful, I will anticipate by saying: (1) that the mechanism of repression does not in fact coincide with the mechanism or mechanisms of substitute-formation, (2) that there are many different mechanisms of substitute-formation, and (3) that the different mechanisms of repression have at least this one thing in common: *a withdrawal of energic cathexis* (or of *libido*, if it is a question of sexual instincts).

Further, confining myself to the three best-known forms of psychoneurosis, I will show by means of some examples how the conceptions here introduced find application to the study of repression. From *anxiety-hysteria* I will choose an instance which has been subjected to thorough analysis – that of an animal-phobia. The instinctual impulse subjected to repression here is a libidinal attitude towards the father, coupled with dread of him. After repression, this impulse vanishes out of consciousness: the father does not appear in consciousness as an object for the libido. As a substitute for him we find in a corresponding situation some animal which is more or less suited to be an object of dread. The substitute-formation of the ideational element has established itself by way of a displacement along the line of a series of associated ideas which is determined in some particular way. The quantitative element has not vanished, but has been transformed into anxiety. The result is a fear of a wolf, instead of a claim for love from the father. Of course the categories here employed are not enough to supply a complete explanation even of the simplest case of psychoneurosis: there are always other points of view to be taken into account.

Such a repression as that which takes place in an animal-phobia must be described as radically unsuccessful. All that it has done is to remove the idea and set another in its place; it has not succeeded at all in its aim of avoiding 'pain'. On this account, too, the work of the neurosis, far from ceasing, proceeds into a 'second movement', so to speak, which is designed to attain its immediate and more important aim. There follows an attempt at flight, the formation of the *phobia proper* – a number of things have to be *avoided* in order to prevent an outbreak of anxiety. A more particular investigation would enable us to understand the mechanism by which the phobia achieves its aim.

We are led to quite another view of the process of repression when we consider the picture of a true *conversion-hysteria*. Here the salient point is that it is possible to bring about a total disappearance of the charge of affect. The patient then displays towards his symptoms what Charcot called '*la belle indifférence des hystériques*'. At other times this suppression is not so completely successful: a part of the sensations of distress attaches to the symptoms themselves, or it has proved impossible entirely to prevent outbreaks of anxiety, and this in its turn sets the mechanism of phobia-formation working. The ideational content of the instinct-presentation is completely withdrawn from consciousness; as a substitute-formation – and concurrently, as a symptom – we have an excessive innervation (in typical cases, a somatic innervation), sometimes of a sensory, sometimes of a motor character, either as an excitation or as an inhibition. The area of over-innervation proves on closer observation to belong to the repressed instinct-presentation itself, and, as if by a process of *condensation*, to have absorbed the whole cathexis. Of course these remarks do not cover the whole mechanism of a conversion-hysteria; the element of *regression* especially, which will be appraised in another connection, has to be taken into account.

In so far as it is rendered possible only by means of extensive substitute-formations, the repression which takes place in hysteria may be pronounced entirely unsuccessful; with reference to mastering the charge of affect, however, which is the real task of repression, it generally betokens a complete success. Again, in conversion-hysteria the process of repression terminates with the formation of the symptom and does not, as in anxiety-hysteria, need to proceed to a 'second movement' – or, strictly speaking, an unlimited number of 'movements'.

A totally different aspect of repression is shown in the third affection to which we are referring for purposes of this comparison: in the *obsessional neurosis*. Here we are at first in doubt what it is that we have to regard as the repressed instinct-presentation – a libidinal or a hostile trend. This uncertainty arises because the obsessional neurosis rests on the premise of a regression by means of which a sadistic trend has been substituted for a tender one. It is this hostile impulse against a loved person which has undergone repression. The effect at an early phase of the work of repression is quite different from that produced later. At first the repression is completely successful, the idea-tional content is rejected and the affect made to disappear. As a substitute-formation there arises an alteration in the ego, an increased sensitiveness of conscience, which can hardly be called a symptom. Substitute- and symptom-formation do not coincide here. Here, too, we learn something about the mechanism of repression. Repression, as it invariably does, has brought about a withdrawal of libido, but for this purpose it has made use of a *reaction-formation*, by intensifying an antithesis. So here the substitute-formation has the same mechanism as the repression and at bottom coincides with it, while yet chronologically, as well as in its content, it is distinct from the symptom-formation. It is very probable that the whole process is made possible by the ambivalent relation into which the sadistic impulse destined for repression has been introduced.

But the repression, at first successful, does not hold; in the further course of things its failure becomes increasingly obvious. The ambivalence which has allowed repression to come into being by means of reaction-formation also constitutes the point at which the repressed succeeds in breaking through again. The vanished affect is transformed, without any diminution, into dread of the community, pangs of conscience, or self-reproaches; the rejected idea is replaced by a *displacement-substitute*, often by displacement on to something utterly trivial or indifferent. For the most part there is an unmistakable tendency to complete re-establishment of the repressed idea. Failure of repression of the quantitative factor brings into play, by means of various taboos and prohibitions, the same mechanism of flight as we have seen at work in the formation of hysterical phobias. The rejection of the idea from consciousness is, however, obstinately maintained, because it ensures abstention from action, preclusion of the motor expression of an impulse. So the final form of the work of repression in the obsessional neurosis is a sterile and never-ending struggle.

The short series of comparisons which have been presented here may easily convince us that more comprehensive investigations are necessary before we can hope to understand thoroughly the processes connected with repression and the formation of neurotic symptoms. The extraordinary intricacy of all the factors to be taken into consideration leaves us only one way open by which to present them. We must select first one and then another point of view, and follow it up through the material at our disposal as long as application of it seems to prove fruitful. Each separate point so treated will be incomplete in itself and there cannot fail to be obscurities where we touch upon material not previously dealt with; but we may hope that the final synthesis of them all will lead to a good understanding of the subject.

Mourning and Melancholia[1]

(1917)

NOW THAT DREAMS have proved of service to us as the normal prototypes of narcissistic mental disorders, we propose to try whether a comparison with the normal emotion of grief, and its expression in mourning, will not throw some light on the nature of melancholia. This time, however, we must make a certain prefatory warning against too great expectations of the result. Even in descriptive psychiatry the definition of melancholia is uncertain; it takes on various clinical forms (some of them suggesting somatic rather than psychogenic affections) that do not seem definitely to warrant reduction to a unity. Apart from those impressions which every observer may gather, our material here is limited to a small number of cases the psychogenic nature of which was indisputable. Any claim to general validity for our conclusions shall be forgone at the outset, therefore, and we will console ourselves by reflecting that, with the means of investigation at our disposal today, we could hardly discover anything that was not typical, at least of a small group if not of a whole class of disorders.

A correlation of melancholia and mourning seems justified by the general picture of the two conditions.[2] Moreover, wherever it is possible to discern the external influences in life which have brought each of them about, this exciting cause proves to be the same in both. Mourning is regularly the reaction to the loss of a loved person, or to the loss of some abstraction which has taken the place of one, such as fatherland, liberty, an ideal, and so on. As an effect of the same influences, melancholia instead of a state of grief develops in some people, whom we consequently suspect of a morbid pathological disposition. It is also well worth notice that, although grief involves grave departures from the normal attitude to life, it never occurs to us to regard it as a morbid condition and hand the mourner over to medical treatment. We rest assured that after a lapse of time it will be overcome, and we look upon any interference with it as inadvisable or even harmful.

The distinguishing mental features of melancholia are a profoundly painful dejection, abrogation of interest in the outside world, loss of the capacity to love, inhibition of all activity, and a lowering of the self-regarding feelings to a degree that finds utterance in self-reproaches and self-revilings, and culminates in a delusional expectation of punishment. This picture becomes a little more intelligible when we consider that, with one exception, the same traits are met with in grief. The fall in self-esteem is absent in grief; but otherwise the features are the same. Profound mourning, the reaction to the loss of a loved person, contains the same feeling of pain, loss of interest in the outside world – in so far as it does not recall the dead one – loss of capacity to adopt any new object of love, which would mean a replacing of the one mourned, the same turning from every active effort that is not connected with thoughts of the dead. It is easy to see that this inhibition and circumscription in the ego is the expression of an exclusive devotion to its mourning, which leaves nothing over for other purposes or other interests. It is really only because we know so well how to explain it that this attitude does not seem to us pathological.

We should regard it as a just comparison, too, to call the temper of grief 'painful'. The justification for this comparison will probably prove illuminating when we are in a position to define pain in terms of the economics of the mind.[3]

Now in what consists the work which mourning performs? I do not think there is anything far-fetched in the following representation of it. The testing of reality, having shown that the loved object no longer exists, requires forthwith that all the libido shall be withdrawn from its attachments to this object. Against this demand a struggle of course arises – it may be universally observed that man never willingly abandons a libido-position, not even when a substitute is already beckoning to him. This struggle can be so intense that a turning away from reality ensues, the object being clung to through the medium of an hallucinatory wish-psychosis.[4] The normal outcome is that deference for reality gains the day. Nevertheless its behest cannot be at once obeyed. The task is now carried through bit by bit, under great expense of time and cathectic energy, while all the time the existence of the lost object is continued in the mind. Each single one of the memories and hopes which bound the libido to the object is brought up and hyper-cathected, and the detachment of the libido from it accomplished. Why this process of carrying out the behest of reality bit by bit, which is in the nature of a compromise, should be so extraordinarily painful is not at all easy to explain in terms of mental economics. It is worth noting that this pain[5] seems natural to us. The fact is, however, that when the work of mourning is completed the ego becomes free and uninhibited again.

Now let us apply to melancholia what we have learnt about grief. In one class of cases it is evident that melancholia too may be the reaction to the loss of a loved object; where this is not the exciting cause one can perceive that there is a loss of a more ideal kind. The object has not perhaps actually died, but has become lost as an object of love (e.g. the case of a deserted bride). In yet other cases one feels justified in concluding that a loss of the kind has been experienced, but one cannot see clearly what has been lost, and may the more readily suppose that the patient too cannot consciously perceive what it is he has lost. This, indeed, might be so even when the patient was aware of the loss giving rise to the melancholia, that is, when he knows whom he has lost but not *what* it is he has lost in them. This would suggest that melancholia is in some way related to an unconscious loss of a love-object, in contradistinction to mourning, in which there is nothing unconscious about the loss.

In grief we found that the ego's inhibited condition and loss of interest was fully accounted for by the absorbing work of mourning. The unknown loss in melancholia would also result in an inner labour of the same kind and hence would be responsible for the melancholic inhibition. Only, the inhibition of the melancholiac seems puzzling to us because we cannot see what it is that absorbs him so entirely. Now the melancholiac displays something else which is lacking in grief – an extraordinary fall in his self-esteem, an impoverishment of his ego on a grand scale. In grief the world becomes poor and empty; in melancholia it is the ego itself. The patient represents his ego to us as worthless, incapable of any effort and morally despicable; he reproaches himself, vilifies himself and expects to be cast out and chastised. He abases himself before everyone and commiserates his own relatives for being connected with someone so unworthy. He does not realize that any change has taken place in him, but extends his self-criticism back over the past and declares that he was never any better. This picture of delusional belittling – which is predominantly moral – is completed by sleeplessness and refusal of nourishment, and by an overthrow, psychologically very remarkable, of that instinct which constrains every living thing to cling to life.

Both scientifically and therapeutically it would be fruitless to contradict the patient who brings these accusations against himself. He must surely be right in some way and be describing something that corresponds to what he thinks. Some of his statements, indeed, we are at once obliged to confirm without reservation. He really is as lacking in interest, as incapable of love and of any achievement as he says. But that, as we know, is secondary, the effect of the inner travail consuming his ego, of which we know nothing but which we compare with the work of mourning. In certain other self-accusations he also seems to us justified, only that he has a keener eye for the truth than others who are not melancholic. When in his exacerbation of self-criticism he describes himself as petty, egoistic, dishonest, lacking in independence, one whose sole aim has been to hide the weaknesses of his own nature, for all we know it may be that he has come very near to self-knowledge; we only wonder why a man must become ill before he can discover truth of this kind. For there can be no doubt that whoever holds and expresses to others such an opinion of himself – one that Hamlet harboured of himself and all men[6] – that man is ill, whether he speaks the truth or is more or less unfair to himself. Nor is it difficult to see that there is no correspondence, so far as we can judge, between the degree of self-abasement and its real justification. A good, capable, conscientious woman will speak no better of herself after she develops melancholia than one who is actually worthless; indeed, the first is more likely to fall ill of the disease than the other, of whom we too should have nothing good to say. Finally, it must strike us that after all the melancholiac's behaviour is not in every way the same as that of one who is normally devoured by remorse and self-reproach. Shame before others, which would characterize this condition above everything, is lacking in him, or at least there is little sign of it. One could almost say that the opposite trait of insistent talking about himself and pleasure in the consequent exposure of himself predominates in the melancholiac.

The essential thing, therefore, is not whether the melancholiac's distressing self-abasement is justified in the opinion of others. The point must be rather that he is correctly describing his psychological situation in his lamentations. He has lost his self-respect and must have some good reason for having done so. It is true that we are then faced with a contradiction which presents a very difficult problem. From the analogy with grief we should have to conclude that the loss suffered by the melancholiac is that of an object; according to what he says the loss is one in himself.

Before going into this contradiction, let us dwell for a moment on the view melancholia affords of the constitution of the ego. We see how in this condition one part of the ego sets itself over against the other, judges it critically, and, as it were, looks upon it as an object. Our suspicion that the critical institution in the mind which is here split off from the ego might also demonstrate its independence in other circumstances will be confirmed by all further observations. We shall really find justification for distinguishing this institution from the rest of the ego. It is the mental faculty commonly called conscience that we are thus recognizing; we shall count it, along with the censorship of consciousness and the testing of reality, among the great institutions of the ego and shall also find evidence elsewhere showing that it can become diseased independently. In the clinical picture of melancholia dissatisfaction with the self on moral grounds is far the most outstanding feature; the self-criticism much less frequently concerns itself with bodily infirmity, ugliness, weakness, social inferiority; among these latter ills that the patient dreads or asseverates the thought of, poverty alone has a favoured position.

There is one observation, not at all difficult to make, which supplies an explanation of the contradiction mentioned above. If one listens patiently to the many and various self-accusations of the melancholiac, one cannot in the end avoid the impression that often the most violent of them are hardly at all applicable to the patient himself, but that with insignificant modifications they do fit someone else, some person whom the patient loves, has loved or ought to love. This conjecture is confirmed every time one examines the facts. So we get the key to the clinical picture – by perceiving that the self-reproaches are reproaches against a loved object which have been shifted on to the patient's own ego.

The woman who loudly pities her husband for being bound to such a poor creature as herself is really accusing her husband of being a poor creature in some sense or other. There is no need to be greatly surprised that among those transferred from him some genuine self-reproaches are mingled: they are allowed to obtrude themselves since they help to mask the others and make recognition of the true state of affairs impossible; indeed, they derive from the 'for' and 'against' contained in the conflict that has led to the loss of the loved object. The behaviour of the patients too becomes now much more comprehensible. Their complaints are really 'plaints' in the legal sense of the word; it is because everything derogatory that they say of themselves at bottom relates to someone else that they are not ashamed and do not hide their heads. Moreover, they are far from evincing towards those around them the attitude of humility and sub-mission that alone would befit such worthless persons; on the contrary, they give a great deal of trouble, perpetually taking offence and behaving as if they had been treated with great in-justice. All this is possible only because the reactions expressed in their behaviour still proceed from an attitude of revolt, a mental constellation which by a certain process has become transformed into melancholic contrition.

Once this is recognized there is no difficulty in reconstructing this process. First there existed an object-choice, the libido had attached itself to a certain person; then, owing to a real injury or disappointment concerned with the loved person, this object-relationship was undermined. The result was not the normal one of withdrawal of the libido from this object and transference of it to a new one, but something different for which various conditions seem to be necessary. The object-cathexis proved to have little power of resistance, and was abandoned; but the free libido was withdrawn into the ego and not directed to another object. It did not find application there, however, in any one of several possible ways, but served simply to establish an *identification* of the ego with the abandoned object. Thus the shadow of the object fell upon the ego, so that the latter could henceforth be criticized by a special mental faculty like an object, like the forsaken object. In this way the loss of the object became transformed into a loss in the ego, and the conflict between the ego and the loved person transformed into a cleavage between the criticizing faculty of the ego and the ego as altered by the identification.

Certain things may be directly inferred with regard to the necessary conditions and effects of such a process. On the one hand, a strong fixation to the love-object must have been present; on the other hand, in contradiction to this, the object-cathexis can have had little power of resistance. As Otto Rank has aptly remarked, this contradiction seems to imply that the object-choice had been effected on a narcissistic basis, so that when obstacles arise in the way of the object-cathexis it can regress into narcissism. The narcissistic identification with the object then becomes a substitute for the erotic cathexis, the result of which is that in spite of the conflict with the loved person the love-relation need not be given up. This kind of substitution of identification for object-love is an important mechanism in the narcissistic affections; Karl Landauer has lately been able to point to it in the process of recovery in schizophrenia.[7] It of course represents a regression from one type of object-choice to the primal narcissism. We have elsewhere described how object-choice develops from a preliminary stage of identification, the way in which the ego first adopts an object and the ambivalence in which this is expressed. The ego wishes to incorporate this object into itself, and the method by which it would do so, in this oral or cannibalistic stage, is by devouring it. Abraham is undoubtedly right in referring to this connection the refusal of nourishment met with in severe forms of melancholia.

The conclusion which our theory would require, namely, that the disposition to succumb to melancholia – or some part of it – lies in the narcissistic type of object-choice, unfortunately still lacks confirmation by investigation. In the opening remarks of this paper I admitted that the empirical material upon which this study is founded does not supply all we could wish. On the assumption that the results of observation would accord with our inferences, we should not hesitate to include among the special characteristics of melancholia a regression from object-cathexis to the still narcissistic oral phase of the libido. Identifications with the object are by no means rare in the transference-neuroses too; indeed, they are a well-known mechanism in symptom-formation, especially in hysteria. The difference, however, between narcissistic and hysterical identification may be perceived in the object-cathexis, which in the first is relinquished, whereas in the latter it persists and exercises an influence, usually confined to certain isolated actions and innervations. Nevertheless, even in the transference-neuroses identification is the expression of a community which may signify love. The narcissistic identification is the older, and it paves the way to comprehension of the hysterical form, which has been less thoroughly studied.

Some of the features of melancholia, therefore, are borrowed from grief, and the others from the process of regression from narcissistic object-choice to narcissism. On the one hand, like mourning, melancholia is the reaction to a real loss of a loved object; but, over and above this, it is bound to a condition which is absent in normal grief or which, if it supervenes, transforms the latter into a pathological variety. The loss of a love-object constitutes an excellent opportunity for the ambivalence in love-relationships to make itself felt and come to the fore. Consequently where there is a disposition to obsessional neurosis the conflict of ambivalence casts a pathological shade on the grief, forcing it to express itself in the form of self-reproaches, to the effect that the mourner himself is to blame for the loss of the loved one, i.e. desired it. These obsessional states of depression following upon the death of loved persons show us what the conflict of ambivalence by itself can achieve, when there is no regressive withdrawal of libido as well. The occasions giving rise to melancholia for the most part extend beyond the clear case of a loss by death, and include all those situations of being wounded, hurt, neglected, out of favour, or disappointed, which can import opposite feelings of love and hate into the relationship or reinforce an already existing ambivalence. This conflict of ambivalence, the origin of which lies now more in actual experience, now more in constitution, must not be neglected among the conditioning factors in melancholia. If the object-love, which cannot be given up, takes refuge in narcissistic identification, while the object itself is abandoned, then hate is expended upon this new substitute-object, railing at it, depreciating it, making it suffer and deriving sadistic gratification from its suffering. The self-torments of melancholiacs, which are without doubt pleasurable, signify, just like the corresponding phenomenon in the obsessional neurosis, a gratification of sadistic tendencies and of hate,[8] both of which relate to an object and in this way have both been turned round upon the self. In both disorders the sufferers usually succeed in the end in taking revenge, by the circuitous path of self-punishment, on the original objects and in tormenting them by means of the illness, having developed the latter so as to avoid the necessity of openly expressing their hostility against the loved ones. After all, the person who has occasioned the injury to the patient's feelings, and against whom his illness is aimed, is usually to be found among those in his near neighbourhood. The melancholiac's erotic cathexis of his object thus undergoes a twofold fate: part of it regresses to identification, but the other part, under the influence of the conflict of ambivalence, is reduced to the stage of sadism, which is nearer to this conflict.

It is this sadism, and only this, that solves the riddle of the tendency to suicide which makes melancholia so interesting – and so dangerous. As the primal condition from which instinct-life proceeds we have come to recognize a self-love of the ego which is so immense, in the fear that rises up at the menace of death we see liberated a volume of narcissistic libido which is so vast, that we cannot conceive how this ego can connive at its own destruction. It is true we have long known that no neurotic harbours thoughts of suicide which are not murderous impulses against others re-directed upon himself, but we have never been able to explain what interplay of forces could carry such a purpose through to execution. Now the analysis of melancholia shows that the ego can kill itself only when, the object-cathexis having been withdrawn upon it, it can treat itself as an object, when it is able to launch against itself the animosity relating to an object – that primordial reaction on the part of the ego to all objects in the outer world.[9] Thus in the regression from narcissistic object-choice the object is indeed abolished, but in spite of all it proves itself stronger than the ego's self. In the two contrasting situations of intense love and of suicide the ego is overwhelmed by the object, though in totally different ways.

We may expect to find the derivation of that one striking feature of melancholia, the manifestations of dread of poverty, in anal erotism, torn out of its context and altered by regression.

Melancholia confronts us with yet other problems, the answer to which in part eludes us. The way in which it passes off after a certain time has elapsed without leaving traces of any gross change is a feature it shares with grief. It appeared that in grief this period of time is necessary for detailed carrying out of the behest imposed by the testing of reality, and that by accomplishing this labour the ego succeeds in freeing its libido from the lost object. We may imagine that the ego is occupied with some analogous task during the course of a melancholia; in neither case have we any insight into the economic processes going forward. The sleeplessness characteristic of melancholia evidently testifies to the inflexibility of the condition, the impossibility of effecting the general withdrawal of cathexes necessary for sleep. The complex of melancholia behaves like an open wound, drawing to itself cathectic energy from all sides (which we have called in the transference-neuroses 'anti-cathexes') and draining the ego until it is utterly depleted; it proves easily able to withstand the ego's wish to sleep. The amelioration in the condition that is regularly noticeable towards evening is probably due to a somatic factor and not explicable psychologically. These questions link up with the further one, whether a loss in the ego apart from any object (a purely narcissistic wound to the ego) would suffice to produce the clinical picture of melancholia and whether an impoverishment of ego-libido directly due to toxins would not result in certain forms of the disease.

The most remarkable peculiarity of melancholia, and one most in need of explanation, is the tendency it displays to turn into mania accompanied by a completely opposite symptomatology.

Not every melancholia has this fate, as we know. Many cases run their course in intermittent periods, in the intervals of which signs of mania may be entirely absent or only very slight. Others show that regular alternation of melancholic and manic phases which has been classified as circular insanity. One would be tempted to exclude these cases from among those of psychogenic origin, if the psycho-analytic method had not succeeded in effecting an explanation and therapeutic improvement of several cases of the kind. It is not merely permissible, therefore, but incumbent upon us to extend the analytic explanation of melancholia to mania.

I cannot promise that this attempt will prove entirely satisfying; it is much more in the nature of a first sounding and hardly goes beyond that. There are two points from which one may start: the first is a psycho-analytic point of view, and the second one may probably call a matter of general observation in mental economics. The psycho-analytic point is one which several analytic investigators have already formulated in so many words, namely, that the content of mania is no different from that of melancholia, that both the disorders are wrestling with the same 'complex', and that in melancholia the ego has succumbed to it, whereas in mania it has mastered the complex or thrust it aside. The other point of view is founded on the observation that all states such as joy, triumph, exultation, which form the normal counterparts of mania, are economically conditioned in the same way. First, there is always a long-sustained condition of great mental expenditure, or one established by long force of habit, upon which at last some influence supervenes making it super-fluous, so that a volume of energy becomes available for manifold possible applications and ways of discharge – for instance, when some poor devil, by winning a large sum of money, is suddenly relieved from perpetual anxiety about his daily bread, when any long and arduous struggle is finally crowned with success, when a man finds himself in a position to throw off at one blow some heavy burden, some false position he has long endured, and so on. All such situations are characterized by high spirits, by the signs of discharge of joyful emotion, and by increased readiness to all kinds of action, just like mania, and in complete contrast to the dejection and inhibition of melancholia. One may ven-ture to assert that mania is nothing other than a triumph of this sort, only that here again what the ego has surmounted and is triumphing over remains hidden from it. Alcoholic intoxication, which belongs to the same group of conditions, may be explained in the same way – in so far as it consists in a state of elation; here there is probably a relaxation produced by toxins of the expend-iture of energy in repression. The popular view readily takes for granted that a person in a maniacal state finds such delight in movement and action because he is so 'cheery'. This piece of false logic must of course be exploded. What has happened is that the economic condition described above has been fulfilled, and this is the reason why the maniac is in such high spirits on the one hand and is so uninhibited in action on the other.

If we put together the two suggestions reached, we have the following result. When mania supervenes, the ego must have surmounted the loss of the object (or the mourning over the loss, or perhaps the object itself), whereupon the whole amount of anti-cathexis which the painful suffering of melancholia drew from the ego and 'bound' has become available. Besides this, the maniac plainly shows us that he has become free from the object by whom his suffering was caused, for he runs after new object-cathexes like a starving man after bread.

This explanation certainly sounds plausible, but in the first place it is too indefinite, and, secondly, it gives rise to more new problems and doubts than we can answer. We will not evade a discussion of them, even though we cannot expect it to lead us to clear understanding.

First, then: in normal grief too the loss of the object is undoubtedly surmounted, and this process too absorbs all the energies of the ego while it lasts. Why then does it not set up the economic condition for a phase of triumph after it has run its course or at least produce some slight indication of such a state? I find it impossible to answer this objection off-hand. It reminds us again that we do not even know by what economic measures the work of mourning is carried through; possibly, however, a conjecture may help us here. Reality passes its verdict – that the object no longer exists – upon each single one of the memories and hopes through which the libido was attached to the lost object, and the ego, confronted as it were with the decision whether it will share this fate, is persuaded by the sum of its narcissistic satisfactions in being alive to sever its attachment to the non-existent object. We may imagine that, because of the slowness and the gradual way in which this severance is achieved, the expenditure of energy necessary for it becomes somehow dissipated by the time the task is carried through.[10]

It is tempting to essay a formulation of the work performed during melancholia on the lines of this conjecture concerning the work of mourning. Here we are met at the outset by an uncertainty. So far we have hardly considered the topographical situation in melancholia, nor put the question in what systems or between what systems in the mind the work of melancholia goes on. How much of the mental processes of the disease is still occupied with the unconscious object-cathexes that have been given up and how much with their substitute, by identification, in the ego?

Now, it is easy to say and to write that 'the unconscious (thing-)presentation of the object has been abandoned by the libido'. In reality, however, this presentation is made up of innumerable single impressions (unconscious traces of them), so that this withdrawal of libido is not a process that can be accomplished in a moment, but must certainly be, like grief, one in which progress is slow and gradual. Whether it begins simultaneously at several points or follows some sort of definite sequence is not at all easy to decide; in analyses it often becomes evident that first one, then another memory is activated and that the laments which are perpetually the same and wearisome in their monotony nevertheless each time take their rise in some different unconscious source. If the object had not this great significance, strengthened by a thousand links, to the ego, the loss of it would be no meet cause for either mourning or melancholia. This character of withdrawing the libido bit by bit is therefore to be ascribed alike to mourning and to melancholia; it is probably sustained by the same economic arrangements and serves the same purposes in both.

As we have seen, however, there is more in the content of melancholia than in that of normal grief. In melancholia the relation to the object is no simple one; it is complicated by the conflict of ambivalence. This latter is either constitutional, i.e. it is an element of every love-relation formed by this particular ego, or else it proceeds from precisely those experiences that involved a threat of losing the object. For this reason the exciting causes of melancholia are of a much wider range than those of grief, which is for the most part occasioned only by a real loss of the object, by its death. In melancholia, that is, countless single conflicts in which love and hate wrestle together are fought for the object; the one seeks to detach the libido from the object, the other to uphold this libido-position against assault. These single conflicts cannot be located in any system but the Ucs [unconscious system], the region of memory-traces of things (as contrasted with word-cathexes). The efforts to detach the libido are made in this system also during mourning; but in the latter nothing hinders these processes from proceeding in the normal way through the Pcs [preconscious system] to consciousness. For the work of melancholia this way is blocked, owing perhaps to a number of causes or to their combined operation. Constitutional ambivalence belongs by nature to what is repressed, while traumatic experiences with the object may have stirred to activity something else that has been repressed. Thus everything to do with these conflicts of ambivalence remains excluded from consciousness, until the outcome characteristic of melancholia sets in. This, as we know, consists in the libidinal cathexis that is being menaced at last abandoning the object, only, however, to resume its occupation of that place in the ego whence it came. So by taking flight into the ego love escapes annihilation. After this regression of the libido the process can become conscious; it appears in consciousness as a conflict between one part of the ego and its self-criticizing faculty.

That which consciousness is aware of in the work of melancholia is thus not the essential part of it, nor is it even the part which we may credit with an influence in bringing the suffering to an end. We see that the ego debases itself and rages against itself, and as little as the patient do we understand what this can lead to and how it can change. We can more readily credit such an achievement to the unconscious part of the work, because it is not difficult to perceive an essential analogy between the work performed in melancholia and in mourning. Just as the work of grief, by declaring the object to be dead and offering the ego the benefit of continuing to live, impels the ego to give up the object, so each single conflict of ambivalence, by disparaging the object, denigrating it, even as it were by slaying it, loosens the fixation of the libido to it. It is possible, therefore, for the process in the Ucs to come to an end, whether it be that the fury has spent itself or that the object is abandoned as no longer of value. We cannot tell which of these two possibilities is the regular or more usual one in bringing melancholia to an end, nor what influence this termination has on the future condition of the case. The ego may enjoy here the satisfaction of acknowledging itself as the better of the two, as superior to the object.

Even if we accept this view of the work of melancholia, it still does not supply an explanation of the one point upon which we hoped for light. By analogy with various other situations we expected to discover in the ambivalence prevailing in melancholia the economic condition for the appearance of mania when the melancholia has run its course. But there is one fact to which our expectations must bow. Of the three conditioning factors in melancholia – loss of the object, ambivalence, and regression of libido into the ego – the first two are found also in the obsessional reproaches arising after the death of loved persons. In these it is indubitably the ambivalence that motivates the conflict, and observation shows that after it has run its course nothing in the nature of a triumph or a manic state of mind is left. We are thus directed to the third factor as the only one that can have this effect. That accumulation of cathexis which is first of all 'bound' and then, after termination of the work of melancholia, becomes free and makes mania possible must be connected with the regression of the libido into narcissism. The conflict in the ego, which in melancholia is substituted for the struggle surging round the object, must act like a painful wound which calls out unusually strong anti-cathexes. Here again, however, it will be well to call a halt and postpone further investigations into mania until we have gained some insight into the economic conditions, first, of bodily pain, and then of the mental pain[11] which is its analogue. For we know already that, owing to the interdependence of the complicated problems of the mind, we are forced to break off every investigation at some point until such time as the results of another attempt elsewhere can come to its aid.[12]

*Papers on Applied
Psycho-Analysis*

The Most Prevalent Form of Degradation in Erotic Life[1]

(1912)

I

IF A PRACTISING psycho-analyst asks himself what disorder he is most often called upon to remedy, he is obliged to reply – apart from anxiety in all its many forms – psychical impotence. This strange disorder affects men of a strongly libidinous nature, and is manifested by a refusal on the part of the sexual organs to execute the sexual act, although both before and after the attempt they can show themselves intact and competent to do so, and although a strong mental inclination to carry out the act is present. The man gets his first inkling in the direction of understanding his condition by discovering that he fails in this way only with certain women, whereas it never happens with others. He knows then that the inhibition of his masculine potency is due to some quality in the sexual object, and sometimes he describes having had a sensation of holding back, of having perceived some check within him which interfered successfully with his conscious intention. What this inner opposition is, however, he cannot guess, or what quality in the sexual object makes it active. If the failure has been repeated several times he probably concludes, by the familiar erroneous line of argument, that a recollection of the first occasion acted as a disturbance by causing anxiety and brought about the subsequent failures; the first occasion itself he refers to some 'accidental' occurrence.

Psycho-analytic studies of psychical impotence have already been carried out and published by various writers.[2] Every analyst can, from his own experience, confirm the explanations adduced in them. The disorder is in fact due to the inhibiting influence of certain complexes in the mind that are withdrawn from the knowledge of the person in question. As the most universal feature of this pathogenic material an incestuous fixation on mother and sister which has not been surmounted stands out. In addition to this, the influence of accidental impressions of a painful kind connected with infantile sexuality comes into consideration, together with those factors which in general reduce the amount of libido available for the female sexual object.[3]

When cases of severe psychical impotence are subjected to exhaustive study by means of psycho-analysis, the following psycho-sexual processes are found to be operative. Here again – as very probably in all neurotic disorders – the root of the trouble lies in an arrest occurring during the course of development of the libido to that ultimate form which may be called normal. To ensure a fully normal attitude in love, two currents of feeling have to unite – we may describe them as the tender, affectionate feelings and the sensual feelings – and this confluence of the two currents has in these cases not been achieved.

Of these two currents affection is the older. It springs from the very earliest years of childhood, and was formed on the foundation provided by the interests of the self-preservative instinct; it is directed towards the members of the family and those who have care of the child. From the very beginning elements from the sexual instincts are taken up into it – component-parts of the erotic interest – which are more or less clearly visible in childhood and are invariably discovered in the neurotic by psycho-analysis in later years. This tender feeling represents the earliest childish choice of object. From this we see that the sexual instincts find their first *objects* along the path laid down by the ego-instincts and in accordance with the value set by the latter on their objects, in just the same way that the first sexual *satisfactions* are experienced, i.e. in connection with the bodily functions necessary for self-preservation. The 'affection' shown to the child by its parents and attendants which seldom fails to betray its erotic character ('a child is an erotic plaything') does a great deal to increase the erotic contributions to the cathexes that are put forth by the ego-instincts in the child, and to raise them to a level which is bound to leave its mark on future development, especially when certain other circumstances leading to the same result are present.

These fixations of the child's feelings of affection are maintained through childhood, continually absorbing erotic elements, which are thus deflected from their sexual aims. Then, when the age of puberty is reached, there supervenes upon this state of things a powerful current of 'sensual' feeling the aims of which can no longer be disguised. It never fails, apparently, to pursue the earlier paths and to invest the objects of the primary infantile choice with currents of libido that are now far stronger. But in relation to these objects it is confronted by the obstacle of the incest-barrier that has in the meanwhile been erected; consequently it seeks as soon as possible to pass on from these objects unsuited for real satisfaction to others in the world outside, with whom a real sexual life may be carried on. These new objects are still chosen after the pattern (imago) of the infantile ones; in time, however, they attract to themselves the tender feeling that had been anchored to those others. A man shall leave father and mother – according to the Biblical precept – and cleave to his wife; then are tenderness and sensuality united. The greatest intensity of sensual passion will bring with it the highest mental estimation of the object (the normal over-estimation of the sexual object characteristic of men).

Two factors will determine whether this advance in the development of the libido is accomplished successfully or otherwise. First, there is the degree of frustration in reality which is opposed to the new object-choice and reduces its value for the person concerned. For there is no sense in entering upon a choice of object if one is not to be allowed to choose at all or has no prospect of being able to choose one fit for the part. The second factor is the degree of attraction that may be exercised by the infantile objects which should be relinquished, and this is proportionate to the erotic cathexis already attaching to them in childhood. If these two factors are sufficiently powerful, the general mechanism leading to the formation of neurosis will come into operation. The libido turns away from reality, and is absorbed into the creation of phantasy (introversion), strengthens the images of the first sexual objects, and becomes fixated to them. The incest-barrier, however, necessarily has the effect that the libido attaching to these objects should remain in the unconscious. The sensual current of feeling is now attached to unconscious ideas of objects, and discharge of it in onanistic acts contributes to a strengthening of this fixation. It constitutes no change in this state of affairs if the step forward to extraneous objects which miscarried in reality is now made in phantasy, if in the phantasied situations leading up to onanistic gratification the extraneous objects are but replacements of the original ones. The phantasies become capable of entering consciousness by this replacement, but in the direction of applying the libido externally in the real world no advance has been made.

In this way it may happen that the whole current of sensual feeling in a young man may remain attached in the unconscious to incestuous objects, or, to put it in another way, may be fixated to incestuous phantasies. The result of this is then total impotence, which is perhaps even reinforced by an actual weakening, developing concurrently, of the organs destined to execute the sexual act.

Less severe conditions will suffice to bring about what is usually called psychical impotence. It is not necessary that the whole amount of sensual feeling should be fated to conceal itself behind the tender feelings; it may remain sufficiently strong and unchecked to secure some outlet for itself in reality. The sexual activity of such people shows unmistakable signs, however, that it has not behind it the whole mental energy belonging to the instinct. It is capricious, easily upset, often clumsily carried out, and not very pleasurable. Above all, however, it avoids all association with feelings of tenderness. A restriction has thus been laid upon the object-choice. The sensual feeling that has remained active seeks only objects evoking no reminder of the incestuous persons forbidden to it; the impression made by someone who seems deserving of high estimation leads, not to a sensual excitation, but to feelings of tenderness which remain erotically ineffectual. The erotic life of such people remains dissociated, divided between two channels, the same two that are personified in art as heavenly and earthly (or animal) love. Where such men love they have no desire and where they desire they cannot love. In order to keep their sensuality out of contact with the objects they love, they seek out objects whom they need not love; and, in accordance with the laws of the 'sensitivity of complexes' and the 'return of the repressed', the strange refusal implied in psychical impotence is made whenever the objects selected in order to avoid incest possess some trait, often quite inconspicuous, reminiscent of the objects that must be avoided.

The principal means of protection used by men against this complaint consists in *lowering* the sexual object in their own estimation, while reserving for the incestuous object and for those who represent it the over-estimation normally felt for the sexual object. As soon as the sexual object fulfils the condition of being degraded, sensual feeling can have free play, considerable sexual capacity and a high degree of pleasure can be developed. Another factor also contributes to this result. There is usually little refinement in the ways of obtaining erotic pleasure habitual to people in whom the tender and the sensual currents of feeling are not properly merged; they have remained addicted to perverse sexual aims which they feel it a considerable deprivation not to gratify, yet to such men this seems possible only with a sexual object who in their estimate is degraded and worth little.

The motives behind the phantasies mentioned in the preceding paper,[4] by which boys degrade the mother to the level of a prostitute, now become intelligible. They represent efforts to bridge the gulf between the two currents of erotic feeling, at least in phantasy: by degrading her, to win the mother as an object for sensual desires.

II

So far we have pursued our inquiry into psychical impotence from a medico-psychological angle which is not justified by the title of this paper. It will prove, however, that this introduction was necessary in order to provide an approach to our actual theme.

We have reduced psychical impotence to a disunion between the tender and sensual currents of erotic feeling, and have explained this inhibition in development itself as an effect of strong fixations in childhood and of frustration in reality later, after the incest-barrier has intervened. There is one principal objection to raise against this doctrine: it does too much, it explains why certain persons suffer from psychical impotence, but it makes it seem puzzling that others can escape the affliction. Since all the factors that appear to be involved, the strong fixation in childhood, the incest-barrier, and the frustration in the years of development after puberty, are demonstrably present in practically all civilized persons, one would be justified in expecting that psychical impotence was universally prevalent in civilized countries and not a disease of particular individuals.

It would not be difficult to escape from this conclusion by pointing to the quantitative element in the causation of disease, that greater or lesser amount of each single factor which determines whether or not recognizable disease results. But although this argument is in my opinion sound, I do not myself intend to employ it in refuting the objection advanced above. I shall, on the contrary, put forward the proposition that psychical impotence is far more widespread than is generally supposed, and that some degree of this condition does in fact characterize the erotic life of civilized peoples.

If one enlarges the meaning of the term psychical impotence, and ceases to limit it to failure to perform the act of coitus, although an intention to derive pleasure from it is present and the genital apparatus is intact, it would comprise, to begin with, all those men who are described as psycho-anaesthetic, i.e. who never fail in the act but who perform it without special pleasure – a state of things which is commoner than one might think. Psycho-analytic study of such cases has discovered the same aetiological factors in them as those found in psychical impotence, when employed in the narrower sense, without at first discovering any explanation of the symptomatic difference between the two. By an analogy which is easy to justify, one is led on from these anaesthetic men to consider the enormous number of frigid women, whose attitude to love can in fact not be described or understood better than by equating it with psychical impotence in men, although the latter is more conspicuous.[5]

If, however, instead of attributing a wide significance to the term psychical impotence, we look about for instances of its peculiar symptomatology in less marked forms, we shall not be able to deny that the behaviour in love of the men of present-day civilization bears in general the character of the psychically impotent type. In only very few people of culture are the two strains of tenderness and sensuality duly fused into one; the man almost always feels his sexual activity hampered by his respect for the woman and only develops full sexual potency when he finds himself in the presence of a lower type of sexual object; and this again is partly conditioned by the circumstance that his sexual aims include those of perverse sexual components, which he does not like to gratify with a woman he respects. Full sexual satisfaction only comes when he can give himself up wholeheartedly to enjoyment, which with his well-brought-up wife, for instance, he does not venture to do. Hence comes his need for a less exalted sexual object, a woman ethically inferior, to whom he need ascribe no aesthetic misgivings, and who does not know the rest of his life and cannot criticize him. It is to such a woman that he prefers to devote his sexual potency, even when all the tenderness in him belongs to one of a higher type. It is possible, too, that the tendency so often observed in men of the highest rank in society to take a woman of a low class as a permanent mistress, or even as a wife, is nothing but a consequence of the need for a lower type of sexual object on which, psychologically, the possibility of complete gratification depends.

I do not hesitate to lay the responsibility also for this very common condition in the erotic life of civilized men on the two factors operative in absolute psychical impotence, namely, the very strong incestuous fixation of childhood and the frustration by reality suffered during adolescence. It has an ugly sound and a paradoxical as well, but nevertheless it must be said that whoever is to be really free and happy in love must have overcome his deference for women and come to terms with the idea of incest with mother or sister. Anyone who in the face of this test subjects himself to serious self-examination will indubitably find that at the bottom of his heart he too regards the sexual act as something degrading, which soils and contaminates not only the body. And he will only be able to look for the origin of this attitude, which he will certainly not willingly acknowledge, in that period of his youth in which his sexual passions were already strongly developed but in which gratification of them with an object outside the family was almost as completely prohibited as with an incestuous one.

The women of our civilized world are similarly affected by their up-bringing and further, too, by the reaction upon them of this attitude in men. Naturally the effect upon a woman is just as unfavourable if the man comes to her without his full potency as if, after over-estimating her in the early stages of falling in love, he then, having successfully possessed himself of her, sets her at naught. Women show little need to degrade the sexual object; no doubt this has some connection with the circumstance that as a rule they develop little of the sexual over-estimation natural to men. The long abstinence from sexuality to which they are forced and the lingering of their sensuality in phantasy have in them, however, another important consequence. It is often not possible for them later on to undo the connection thus formed in their minds between sensual activities and something forbidden, and they turn out to be psychically impotent, i.e. frigid, when at last such activities do become permissible. This is the source of the desire in so many women to keep even legitimate relations secret for a time; and of the appearance of the capacity for normal sensation in others as soon as the condition of prohibition is restored by a secret intrigue – untrue to the husband, they can keep a second order of faith with the lover.

In my opinion the necessary condition of forbiddenness in the erotic life of women holds the same place as the man's need to lower his sexual object. Both are the consequence of the long period of delay between sexual maturity and sexual activity which is demanded by education for social reasons. The aim of both is to overcome the psychical impotence resulting from the lack of union between tenderness and sensuality. That the effect of the same causes differs so greatly in men and in women is perhaps due to another difference in the behaviour of the two sexes. Women belonging to the higher levels of civilization do not usually transgress the prohibition against sexual activities during the period of waiting, and thus they acquire this close association between the forbidden and the sexual. Men usually overstep the prohibition under the condition of lowering the standard of object they require, and so carry this condition on into their subsequent erotic life.

In view of the strenuous efforts being made in the civilized world at the present day to reform sexual life, it is not superfluous to remind the reader that psycho-analytic investigations have no more bias in any direction than has any other scientific research. In tracing back to its concealed sources what is manifest, psycho-analysis has no aim but that of disclosing connections. It can but be satisfied if what it has brought to light is of use in effecting reforms by substituting more advantageous for injurious conditions. It cannot, however, predict whether other, perhaps even greater, sacrifices may not result from other institutions.

III

The fact that the restrictions imposed by cultural education upon erotic life involve a general lowering of the sexual object may prompt us to turn our eyes from the object to the instincts themselves. The injurious results of the deprivation of sexual enjoyment at the beginning manifest themselves in lack of full satisfaction when sexual desire is later given free rein in marriage. But, on the other hand, unrestrained sexual liberty from the beginning leads to no better result. It is easy to show that the value the mind sets on erotic needs instantly sinks as soon as satisfaction becomes readily obtainable. Some obstacle is necessary to swell the tide of the libido to its height; and at all periods of history, wherever natural barriers in the way of satisfaction have not sufficed, mankind has erected conventional ones in order to be able to enjoy love. This is true both of individuals and of nations. In times during which no obstacles to sexual satisfaction existed, such as, maybe, during the decline of the civilizations of antiquity, love became worthless, life became empty, and strong reaction-formations were necessary before the indispensable emotional value of love could be recovered. In this context it may be stated that the ascetic tendency of Christianity had the effect of raising the psychical value of love in a way that heathen antiquity could never achieve; it developed greatest significance in the lives of the ascetic monks, which were almost entirely occupied with struggles against libidinous temptation.

One's first inclination undoubtedly is to see in this difficulty a universal characteristic of our organic instincts. It is certainly true in a general way that the importance of an instinctual desire is mentally increased by frustration of it. Suppose one made the experiment of exposing a number of utterly different human beings to hunger under the same conditions. As the imperative need for food rose in them all their individual differences would be effaced, and instead the uniform manifestations of one unsatisfied instinct would appear. But is it also true, conversely, that the mental value of an instinct invariably sinks with gratification of it? One thinks, for instance, of the relation of the wine-drinker to wine. Is it not a fact that wine always affords the drinker the same toxic satisfaction – one that in poetry has so often been likened to the erotic and that science as well may regard as comparable? Has one ever heard of a drinker being forced constantly to change his wine because he soon gets tired of always drinking the same? On the contrary, habit binds a man more and more to the particular kind of wine he drinks. Do we ever find a drinker impelled to go to another country where the wine is dearer or where alcohol is prohibited, in order to stimulate his dwindling pleasure in it by these obstacles? Nothing of the sort. If we listen to what our great lovers of alcohol say about their attitude to wine, for instance, B. Böcklin,[6] it sounds like the most perfect harmony, a model of a happy marriage. Why is the relation of the lover to his sexual object so very different?

However strange it may sound, I think the possibility must be considered that something in the nature of the sexual instinct itself is unfavourable to the achievement of absolute gratification. When we think of the long and difficult evolution the instinct goes through, two factors to which this difficulty might be ascribed at once emerge. First, in consequence of the two 'thrusts' of sexual development impelling towards choice of an object, together with the intervention of the incest-barrier between the two, the ultimate object selected is never the original one but only a surrogate for it. Psycho-analysis has shown us, however, that when the original object of an instinctual desire becomes lost in consequence of repression, it is often replaced by an endless series of substitute-objects, none of which ever give full satisfaction. This may explain the lack of stability in object-choice, the 'craving for stimulus', which is so often a feature of the love of adults.

Secondly, we know that at its beginning the sexual instinct is divided into a large number of components – or, rather, it develops from them – not all of which can be carried on into its final form; some have to be suppressed or turned to other uses before the final form results. Above all, the coprophilic elements in the instinct have proved incompatible with our aesthetic ideas, probably since the time when man developed an upright posture and so removed his organ of smell from the ground; further, a considerable proportion of the sadistic elements belonging to the erotic instinct have to be abandoned. All such developmental processes, however, relate only to the upper layers of the complicated structure. The fundamental processes which promote erotic excitation remain always the same. Excremental things are all too intimately and inseparably bound up with sexual things; the position of the genital organs – *inter urinas et faeces* – remains the decisive and unchangeable factor. One might say, modifying a well-known saying of the great Napoleon's, 'Anatomy is destiny.' The genitals themselves have not undergone the development of the rest of the human form in the direction of beauty; they have retained their animal cast; and so even today love, too, is in essence as animal as it ever was. The erotic instincts are hard to mould; training of them achieves now too much, now too little. What culture tries to make out of them seems attainable only at the cost of a sensible loss of pleasure; the persistence of the impulses that are not enrolled in adult sexual activity makes itself felt in an absence of satisfaction.

So perhaps we must make up our minds to the idea that altogether it is not possible for the claims of the sexual instinct to be reconciled with the demands of culture, that in consequence of his cultural development renunciation and suffering, as well as the danger of his extinction at some far future time, are not to be eluded by the race of man. This gloomy prognosis rests, it is true, on the single conjecture that the lack of satisfaction accompanying culture is the necessary consequence of certain peculiarities developed by the sexual instinct under the pressure of culture. This very incapacity in the sexual instinct to yield full satisfaction as soon as it submits to the first demands of culture becomes the source, however, of the grandest cultural achievements, which are brought to birth by ever greater sublimation of the components of the sexual instinct. For what motive would induce man to put his sexual energy to other uses if by any disposal of it he could obtain fully satisfying pleasure? He would never let go of this pleasure and would make no further progress. It seems, therefore, that the irreconcilable antagonism between the demands of the two instincts – the sexual and the egoistic – have made man capable of ever greater achievements, though, it is true, under the continual menace of danger, such as that of the neuroses to which at the present time the weaker are succumbing.

The purpose of science is neither to alarm nor to reassure. But I myself freely admit that such far-reaching conclusions as those drawn here should be built up on a broader foundation, and that perhaps developments in other directions will enable mankind to remedy the effects of these, which we have here been considering in isolation.

Some Character-Types Met with in Psycho-Analytic Work[1]

(1915)

WHEN THE PHYSICIAN is carrying out psycho-analytic treatment of a neurotic, his interest is by no means primarily directed to the patient's character. He is far more desirous to know what the symptoms signify, what instinctual impulses lurk behind them and are satisfied by them, and by what transitions the mysterious path has led from those impulses to these symptoms. But the technique which he is obliged to follow soon constrains him to direct his immediate curiosity towards other objectives. He observes that his investigation is threatened by resistances set up against him by the patient, and these resistances he may justly attribute to the latter's character, which now acquires the first claim on his interest.

What opposes itself to the physician's labours is not always those traits of character which the patient recognizes in himself and which are attributed to him by those around him. Peculiarities in the patient which he had seemed to possess only in a modest degree are often displayed in surprising intensity, or attitudes reveal themselves in him which in other relations of life would not have been betrayed. The following pages will be devoted to describing and tracing back to their origin some of these astonishing traits of character.

I

The 'Exceptions'

The psycho-analytic worker is continually confronted with the task of inducing the patient to renounce an immediate and directly attainable source of pleasure. He need not renounce all pleasure; that one could probably expect of no human being, and even religion is obliged to support its ordinance that earthly pleasure shall be set aside by the promise of an incomparably greater degree of more inestimable bliss in another world. No, the patient need merely renounce such gratifications as will inevitably be detrimental to him; he need only temporarily abjure, only learn to exchange an immediate source of pleasure for one better assured though longer delayed. Or, in other words, under the physician's guidance he must make that advance from the pleasure-principle to the reality-principle by which the mature human being is distinguished from the child. In this educative process, the clearer insight of the physician plays but an insignificant part; as a rule, he can say to his patient only what the latter's own reason can say to him. But it is not the same thing to know a thing in oneself and to hear it from someone outside oneself; the physician takes the part of this significant outsider; he makes use of the influence which one human being can exercise over another. Or – remembering that the practice of psycho-analysis is to replace etiolated derivatives by the original and fundamental – let us say that the physician in his educative work makes use of one of the components of love. In this work of after-education, he probably does no more than repeat the process which first of all made training of any kind possible. By the side of the necessities of existence, love is the great teacher; and it is by his love for those nearest him that the incomplete human being is induced to respect the decrees of necessity and to spare himself the punishment attendant on any infringement of it.

Thus, when one exacts from the patient a provisional renunciation of any source of pleasure, a sacrifice, a readiness to accept some temporary suffering in view of a better end, or even only the resolve to submit to a necessity which applies to all human beings, one will come upon individuals who resist such an appeal on special grounds. They say that they have renounced enough and suffered enough, and have a claim to be spared any further exactions; they will submit no longer to disagreeable necessity, for they are *exceptions* and intend to remain so too. In one patient of the kind this claim had grown into the conviction that a special providence watched over him, which would protect him from any painful sacrifices of the sort. Against an inner confidence expressing itself thus strongly the arguments of the physician will achieve nothing; even his influence, indeed, is powerless at first, and it becomes clear to him that he must find out the sources which are feeding the injurious prepossession.

Now it is surely indubitable that everyone would fain consider himself an 'exception' and claim privileges over others. But precisely because of this there must be a particular reason, and one not universally available, if any individual actually proclaims himself an exception and behaves as such. This reason may be of more than one kind; in the cases I investigated I succeeded in tracing it to a common peculiarity in the earlier experiences of these patients' lives. Their neuroses were connected with an event or painful experience from which they had suffered in their earliest childhood, one in respect of which they knew themselves to be guiltless, and which they could look upon as an unjust injury inflicted upon them. The privileges that they claimed as a result of this injustice, and the rebelliousness it engendered, had contributed not a little to intensifying the conflicts leading to the outbreak of neurosis. In one of these patients, a woman, the attitude in question developed when she learnt that a painful organic trouble, which had hindered her from attaining the aim of her life, was of congenital origin. So long as she looked upon this trouble as an accidental acquisition during later life, she bore it patiently; as soon as she knew it was part of her congenital inheritance, she became rebellious. The young man who believed himself watched over by a special providence had been in infancy the victim of an accidental infection from his wet-nurse, and had lived his whole later life on the 'insurance-dole', as it were, of his claims to compensation, without having any idea on what he based those claims. In his case the analysis, which reconstructed this event out of obscure glimmerings of memory and interpretations of the symptoms, was confirmed objectively by information from the family.

For reasons which will be easily understood I cannot communicate very much about these and other case-histories. Nor do I propose to go into the obvious analogy between deformities of character resulting from protracted sickliness in childhood and the behaviour of whole nations whose past history has been full of suffering. Instead, however, I will take the opportunity of pointing to that figure in the creative work of the greatest of poets in whose character the claim to be an exception is closely bound up with and motivated by the circumstance of congenital injury.

In the opening soliloquy to Shakespeare's *Richard III*, Gloucester, who subsequently becomes King, says:

> But I, that am not shap'd for sportive tricks,
> Nor made to court an amorous looking-glass;
> I, that am rudely stamp'd, and want love's majesty

To strut before a wanton ambling nymph;
I, that am curtail'd of this fair proportion,
Cheated of feature by dissembling Nature,
Deform'd, unfinish'd, sent before my time
Into this breathing world, scarce half made up,
And that so lamely and unfashionable,
That dogs bark at me as I halt by them . . .
And therefore, since I cannot prove a lover,
To entertain these fair well-spoken days,
I am determined to prove a villain,
And hate the idle pleasures of these days.

At a first glance this tirade will possibly seem unrelated to our present theme. Richard seems to say nothing more than 'I find this idle way of life tedious, and I want to enjoy myself. As I cannot play the lover on account of my deformity, I will play the villain; I will intrigue, murder, do anything I please.' So wanton a cause of action could not but stifle any stirring of sympathy in the audience, if it were not a screen for something much more serious. And besides, the play would be psychologically impossible, for the writer must know how to furnish us with a secret background of sympathy for his hero, if we are to admire his boldness and adroitness without some inward protest; and such sympathy can only be based on understanding or on a sense of a possible inner fellowship with him.

I think, therefore, that Richard's soliloquy does not say

everything; it merely gives a hint, and leaves us to fill up the indications. When we complete it, however, the appearance of wantonness vanishes, the bitterness and minuteness with which Richard has depicted his deformity make their full effect, and we clearly perceive the bond of fellowship which constrains us to sympathy with the miscreant. The soliloquy then signifies: 'Nature has done me a grievous wrong in denying me that beauty of form which wins human love. Life owes me reparation for this, and I will see that I get it. I have a right to be an exception, to overstep those bounds by which others let themselves be circumscribed. I may do wrong myself, since wrong has been done to me' – and now we feel that we ourselves could be like Richard, nay, that we are already a little like him. Richard is an enormously magnified representation of something we can all discover in ourselves. We all think we have reason to reproach nature and our destiny for congenital and infantile disadvantages; we all demand reparation for early wounds to our narcissism, our self-love. Why did not nature give us the golden curls of Balder or the strength of Siegfried or the lofty brow of genius or the noble profile of aristocracy? Why were we born in a middle-class dwelling instead of in a royal palace? We could as well carry off beauty and distinction as any of those whom now we cannot but envy.

It is, however, a subtle economy of art in the poet not to permit his hero to give complete expression to all his secret springs of action. By this means he obliges us to supplement, he engages our intellectual activity, diverts it from critical reflections, and keeps us closely identified with his hero. A bungler in his place would deliberately express all that he wishes to reveal to us, and would then find himself confronted by our cool, untrammelled intelligence, which would preclude any great degree of illusion.

We will not, however, dismiss the 'exceptions' without pointing out that the claim of women to privileges and to exemption from so many of the importunities of existence rests upon the same foundation. As we learn from psycho-analytic work, women regard themselves as wronged from infancy, as undeservedly cut short and set back; and the embitterment of so many daughters against their mothers derives, in the last analysis, from the reproach against her of having brought them into the world as women instead of as men.

II

Those Wrecked by Success

Psycho-analytic work has furnished us with the rule that people fall ill of a neurosis as a result of *frustration*. The frustration meant is that of satisfaction for their libidinal desires and a long circumlocution is necessary before the law becomes comprehensible. That is to say, for a neurosis to break out there must be a conflict between the libidinal desires of a person and that part of his being which we call his ego, the expression of his instinct of self-preservation which also contains his ideals of his own character. A pathogenic conflict of this kind takes place only when the libido is desirous of pursuing paths and aims which the ego has long overcome and despised, and has therefore henceforth proscribed; and this the libido never does until it is deprived of the possibility of an ideal satisfaction consistent with the ego. Hence privation, frustration of a real satisfaction, is the first condition for the outbreak of a neurosis, although, indeed, it is far from being the only one.

So much the more surprising, indeed bewildering, must it appear when as a physician one makes the discovery that people occasionally fall ill precisely because a deeply rooted and long-cherished wish has come to fulfilment. It seems then as though they could not endure their bliss, for of the causative connection between this fulfilment and the falling-ill there can be no question. I had an opportunity in this way of obtaining insight into a woman's story, which I propose to describe as typical of these tragic occurrences.

Well-born and well-brought-up, as a quite young girl she could not restrain her zest for life; she ran away from home and roved adventurously till she made the acquaintance of an artist who could appreciate her feminine charms but could also divine, despite her degradation, the finer qualities she possessed. He took her to live with him, and she proved a faithful and devoted companion, apparently needing only social rehabilitation for complete happiness. After many years of life together, he succeeded in getting his family to recognize her, and was then prepared to make her his legal wife. At this critical moment she began to go to pieces. She neglected the house whose rightful mistress she was now about to become, imagined herself persecuted by his relatives, who wanted to take her into the family, debarred her lover, through senseless jealousy, from all social intercourse, hindered him in his artistic work, and soon fell into incurable mental illness.

On another occasion I observed a most respectable man who, himself professor at a university, had for many years cherished the natural wish to succeed the master who had initiated him into the life of learning. When this elder man retired, and the other's colleagues intimated that it was he whom they desired as successor, he began to hesitate, depreciated his own merits, declared himself unworthy to fill the position designed for him, and fell into a state of melancholy which unfitted him for all activity for some years after.

Different as these two cases are, they yet coincide on this one point – that illness followed close upon the wish-fulfilment, and annihilated all enjoyment of it.

The contradiction between such experiences and the rule that frustration induces illness is not insoluble. The distinction between an *internal* and an *external* frustration dispels it. When in actuality the object in which the libido can find its satisfaction is withheld, this is an external frustration. In itself it is inoperative, not pathogenic, until an internal frustration has joined hands with it. This must proceed from the ego, and must dispute the right of the libido to the other objects that it then desires to possess. Only then does a conflict arise, and the possibility of neurotic illness, i.e. of a substitutive gratification proceeding circuitously by way of the repressed unconscious. The internal frustration is present, therefore, in every case, only it does not come into operation until the external, actual frustration has prepared the ground for it. In those exceptional cases where illness ensues on success, the internal frustration has operated alone – has indeed only made its appearance when an external frustration has been replaced by fulfilment of the wish. At first sight there remains something astonishing about this; but on closer consideration we shall reflect that it is not so very unusual for the ego to tolerate a wish as harmless so long as this exists in phantasy alone and seems remote from fulfilment, while it will defend itself hotly against such a wish as soon as it approaches fulfilment and threatens to become an actuality. The distinction between this and familiar situations in neurosis-formation is merely that usually it is internal intensifications of the libidinal cathexis which turn the phantasy, that has hitherto been thought little of and tolerated, into a dreaded opponent; while in these cases of ours the signal for the outbreak of conflict is given by an actual external alteration in circumstances.

Analytic work soon shows us that it is forces of conscience which forbid the person to gain the long-hoped-for enjoyment from the fortunate change in reality. It is a difficult task, however, to discover the essence and origin of these censuring and punishing tendencies, which so often surprise us by their presence where we do not expect to find them. What we know or conjecture on the point I shall discuss, for the usual reasons, in relation not to cases of clinical observation, but to figures which great writers have created from the wealth of their knowledge of the soul.

A person who collapses on attaining her aim, after striving for it with single-minded energy, is Shakespeare's Lady Macbeth. In the beginning there is no hesitation, no sign of any inner conflict in her, no endeavour but that of overcoming the scruples of her ambitious and yet gentle-hearted husband. She is ready to sacrifice even her womanliness to her murderous intention, without reflecting on the decisive part which this womanliness must play when the question arises of preserving the aim of her ambition, which has been attained through a crime.

> Come, you spirits
> That tend on mortal thoughts, unsex me here . . .
> Come to my woman's breasts,
> And take my milk for gall, you murdering ministers!
>   (Act I, Scene 5)

> I have given suck, and know
> How tender 'tis to love the babe that milks me:
> I would, while it was smiling in my face,
> Have pluck'd my nipple from his boneless gums,
> And dashed the brains out, had I so sworn
> As you have done to this.
>
> (Act I, Scene 7)

One solitary stirring of unwillingness comes over her before the deed:

> Had he not resembled
> My father as he slept, I had done it.

Then, when she has become Queen by the murder of Duncan, she betrays for a moment something like disillusion, like satiety. We know not why.

> Nought's had, all's spent,
> Where our desire is got without content:
> 'Tis safer to be that which we destroy,
> Than by destruction dwell in doubtful joy.
>
> (Act III, Scene 2)

Nevertheless, she holds out. In the banquet-scene which follows on these words, she alone keeps her head, cloaks her husband's distraction, and finds a pretext for dismissing the guests. And then we see her no more; until (in the first scene of the fifth act) we again behold her as a sleep-walker, with the impressions of that night of murder fixed on her mind. Again, as then, she seeks to put heart into her husband: 'Fie, my lord, fie! a soldier, and afeard? What need we fear who knows it, when none can call our power to account?' She hears the knocking at the door, which terrified her husband after the deed. Next, she strives to 'undo the deed which cannot be undone'. She washes her hands, which are blood-stained and smell of blood, and is conscious of the futility of the attempt. Remorse seems to have borne her down – she who had seemed so remorseless. When she dies, Macbeth, who meanwhile has become as inexorable as she had been in the beginning, can find only a brief epitaph for her:

> She should have died hereafter;
> There would have been a time for such a word.
>
> (Act V, Scene 5)

And now we ask ourselves what it was that broke this character which had seemed forged from the most perdurable metal? Is it only disillusion, the different aspect shown by the accomplished deed, and are we to infer that even in Lady Macbeth an originally gentle and womanly nature had been worked up to a concentration and high tension which could not long endure, or ought we to seek for such signs of a deeper motivation as will make this collapse more humanly intelligible to us?

It seems to me impossible to come to any decision. Shakespeare's *Macbeth* is a *pièce d'occasion*, written for the accession of James, who had hitherto been King of Scotland. The plot was ready-made, and had been handled by other contemporary writers, whose work Shakespeare probably made use of in his customary manner. It offered remarkable analogies to the actual situation. The 'virginal' Elizabeth, of whom it was rumoured that she had never been capable of childbearing and who had once described herself as 'a barren stock',[2] in an anguished outcry at the news of James's birth, was obliged by this very childlessness of hers to let the Scottish king become her successor. And he was the son of that Mary Stuart whose execution she, though reluctantly, had decreed, and who, despite the clouding of their relations by political concerns, was yet of her blood and might be called her guest.

The accession of James I was like a demonstration of the curse of unfruitfulness and the blessings reserved for those who carry on the race. And Shakespeare's *Macbeth* develops on the theme of this same contrast. The three Fates, the 'weird sisters', have assured him that he shall indeed be king, but to Banquo they promise that *his* children shall obtain possession of the crown. Macbeth is incensed by this decree of destiny; he is not content with the satisfaction of his own ambition, he desires to found a dynasty and not to have murdered for the benefit of strangers.

This point is overlooked when Shakespeare's play is regarded only as a tragedy of ambition. It is clear that Macbeth cannot live for ever, and thus there is but one way for him to disprove that part of the prophecy which opposes his wishes – namely, to have children himself, children who can succeed him. And he seems to expect them from his vigorous wife:

> Bring forth men-children only!
> For thy undaunted mettle should compose
> Nothing but males . . .
>
> (Act I, Scene 7)

And equally it is clear that if he is deceived in this expectation he must submit to destiny; otherwise his actions lose all purpose and are transformed into the blind fury of one doomed to destruction, who is resolved to destroy beforehand all that he can reach. We watch Macbeth undergo this development, and at the height of the tragedy we hear that shattering cry from Macduff, which has often ere now been recognized to have many meanings and possibly to contain the key to the change in Macbeth: 'He has no children!' (Act IV, Scene 3).

Undoubtedly that signifies 'Only because he is himself child-less could he murder my children'; but more may be implied in it, and above all it might be said to lay bare the essential motive which not only forces Macbeth to go far beyond his own true nature, but also assails the hard character of his wife at its only

366

weak place. If one looks back upon *Macbeth* from the culmination reached in these words of Macduff's, one sees that the whole play is sown with references to the father-and-children relation. The murder of the kindly Duncan is little else than parricide; in Banquo's case, Macbeth kills the father while the son escapes him; and he kills Macduff's children because the father has fled from him. A bloody child, and then a crowned one, are shown him by the witches in the conjuration-scene; the armed head seen previously is doubtless Macbeth's own. But in the background arises the sinister form of the avenger, Macduff, who is himself an exception to the laws of generation, since he was not born of his mother but ripp'd from her womb.

It would be a perfect example of poetic justice in the manner of the talion if the childlessness of Macbeth and the barrenness of his Lady were the punishment for their crimes against the sanctity of geniture – if Macbeth could not become a father because he had robbed children of their father and a father of his children, and if Lady Macbeth had suffered the unsexing she had demanded of the spirits of murder. I believe one could without more ado explain the illness of Lady Macbeth, the transformation of her callousness into penitence, as a reaction to her childlessness, by which she is convinced of her impotence against the decrees of nature, and at the same time admonished that she has only herself to blame if her crime has been barren of the better part of its desired results.

In the *Chronicle* of Holinshed (1577), whence Shakespeare

took the plot of *Macbeth*, Lady Macbeth is only once mentioned as the ambitious wife who instigates her husband to murder that she may herself be queen. Of her subsequent fate and of the development of her character there is no word at all. On the other hand, it would seem that there the change in Macbeth to a sanguinary tyrant is motivated just in the way we have suggested. For in Holinshed ten years pass between the murder of Duncan, whereby Macbeth becomes king, and his further misdeeds; and in these ten years he is shown as a stern but righteous ruler. It is not until after this period that the change begins in him, under the influence of the tormenting apprehension that the prophecy to Banquo will be fulfilled as was that of his own destiny. Then only does he contrive the murder of Banquo, and, as in Shakespeare, is driven from one crime to another. Holinshed does not expressly say that it was his childlessness which urged him to these courses, but there is warrant enough – both time and occasion – for this probable motivation. Not so in Shakespeare. Events crowd breathlessly on one another in the tragedy, so that to judge by the statements made by the persons in the play, about one week represents the duration of time assigned to it.[3] This acceleration takes the ground from under our attempts at reconstructing the motives for the change in the characters of Macbeth and his wife. There is no time for a long-drawn disappointment of their hopes of offspring to enervate the woman and drive the man to an insane defiance; and it remains impossible to resolve the contradiction that so many subtle inter-relations in the plot, and between it and its occasion, point to a common origin of them in the motive of childlessness, and that yet the period of time in the tragedy expressly precludes a development of character from any but a motive contained in the play.

What, however, these motives can have been which in so short a space of time could turn the hesitating, ambitious man into an unbridled tyrant, and his steely-hearted instigator into a sick woman gnawed by remorse, it is, in my view, impossible to divine. I think we must renounce the hope of penetrating the triple obscurity of the bad preservation of the text, the unknown intention of the dramatist, and the hidden purport of the legend. But I should not admit that such investigations are idle in view of the powerful effect which the tragedy has upon the spectator. The dramatist can indeed, during the representation, overwhelm us by his art and paralyse our powers of reflection; but he cannot prevent us from subsequently attempting to grasp the psychological mechanism of that effect. And the contention that the dramatist is at liberty to shorten at will the natural time and duration of the events he brings before us, if by the sacrifice of common probability he can enhance the dramatic effect, seems to me irrelevant in this instance. For such a sacrifice is justified only when it merely affronts probability,[4] and not when it breaks the causal connection; besides, the dramatic effect would hardly have suffered if the time-duration had been left in uncertainty, instead of being expressly limited to some few days.

One is so unwilling to dismiss a problem like that of *Macbeth* as insoluble that I will still make another attempt, by introducing another comment which points towards a new issue. Ludwig Jekels, in a recent Shakespearean study, thinks he has divined a technical trick of the poet, which might have to be reckoned with in *Macbeth*, too. He is of opinion that Shakespeare frequently splits up a character into two personages, each of whom then appears not altogether comprehensible until once more conjoined with the other. It might be thus with Macbeth and the Lady; and then it would of course be futile to regard her as an independent personage and seek to discover her motivation without considering the Macbeth who completes her. I shall not follow this hint any further, but I would add, nevertheless, a remark which strikingly confirms the idea – namely, that the stirrings of fear which arise in Macbeth on the night of the murder, do not develop further in him, but in the Lady.⁵ It is he who has the hallucination of the dagger before the deed, but it is she who later succumbs to mental disorder; he, after the murder, hears the cry from the house: 'Sleep no more! Macbeth does murder sleep . . .', and so 'Macbeth shall sleep no more', but we never hear that King Macbeth could not sleep, while we see that the Queen rises from her bed and betrays her guilt in somnambulistic wanderings. He stands helpless with bloody hands, lamenting that not great Neptune's ocean can wash them clean again, while she comforts him: 'A little water clears us of this deed'; but later it is she who washes her hands for a quarter of an hour and cannot get rid of the bloodstains. 'All the perfumes of Arabia will not sweeten this little hand.' Thus is fulfilled in her what his pangs of conscience had apprehended; she is incarnate remorse after the deed, he incarnate defiance – together they exhaust the possibilities of reaction to the crime, like two disunited parts of the mind of a single individuality, and perhaps they are the divided images of a single prototype.

If we have been unable to give any answer to the question why Lady Macbeth should collapse after her success, we may perhaps have a better chance with the creation of another great dramatist, who loves to pursue with unrelenting rigour the task of the psychological reckoning.

Rebecca Gamvik, the daughter of a midwife, has become, under the influence of her adoptive father, Dr West, a freethinker and a contemner of all those restrictions upon desires in life which are imposed by morality founded on religious belief. After the doctor's death she obtains a footing at Rosmersholm, the ancestral seat of an old family whose members are unacquainted with laughter and have sacrificed joy to stern fulfilment of duty. At Rosmersholm dwell Pastor Johannes Rosmer and his invalid wife, the childless Beata. Overcome by 'a wild, uncontrollable passion' for the love of the aristocratic Rosmer, Rebecca resolves to remove the wife who stands in her way, and to this end is served by her 'fearless, freeborn' will, which is restrained by no ethical considerations. She contrives that Beata shall read a medical book in which the begetting of offspring is represented as the sole aim of marriage, so that the poor woman begins to doubt whether her own union is an honourable one. Rebecca then hints that Rosmer, whose studies and ideas she shares, is about to abandon the old faith and join the party of enlightenment; and after she has thus shaken the wife's confidence in the moral uprightness of her husband, gives her finally to understand that she, Rebecca, must soon leave the house in order to conceal the consequences of illicit intercourse with Rosmer. The criminal scheme succeeds. The poor wife, who has passed for melancholic and crazy, throws herself from the path beside the mill into the mill-race, possessed by the sense of her own worthlessness and desirous of standing no longer between her beloved husband and his bliss.

For more than a year Rebecca and Rosmer have been living alone at Rosmersholm in a relationship which he wishes to regard as a purely intellectual and ideal friendship. But when from outside the first shadow of evil gossip falls upon this relationship, and at the same time there arise tormenting doubts in Rosmer in regard to the motives for which his wife had put an end to herself, he begs Rebecca to become his second wife, so that they may oppose to the unhappy past a new living reality (Act II). For one instant she cries out with joy at this proposal, but immediately afterwards declares that it can never be, and that if he urges her further she will 'go the way Beata went'. Rosmer cannot at all understand this rejection; and still less can we, who know more of Rebecca's actions and designs. All we can be certain of is that her 'No' is meant in good earnest.

How has it come about that the adventuress with the fearless, freeborn will, which forged its way relentlessly to its desired goal, should now refuse to pluck the fruit which is offered her? She herself gives us the explanation in the fourth Act: '*This* is the terrible part of it: that now when all life's happiness is within my grasp – my heart is changed, and my own past bars my way to happiness.' That is, she has become a different being, her conscience has awakened, she has a conviction of guilt which denies her happiness.

And how has her conscience been awakened? Let us listen to her, and consider whether we can accord her our full credence: 'It is the Rosmer view of life – or your view, at any rate – that has infected my will . . . And made it sick. Enslaved it to laws that had no power over me before. You – life with you – has ennobled my mind.'

This influence, we are further to understand, has only become effective since she has been living alone with Rosmer: 'In quiet – in solitude – when you showed me all your thoughts without reserve – every tender and delicate feeling, just as it came to you – then the great change came over me.'

Shortly before this she has lamented the other aspect of the change: 'Because Rosmersholm has sapped my strength, my old fearless will has had its wings clipped here. It is paralysed! The time is past when I had courage for anything in the world. I have lost the power of action, Rosmer.'

Rebecca makes this declaration after she has revealed herself

373

a wrong-doer in a voluntary confession to Rosmer and Rector Kroll, the brother of the dead wife. Ibsen has made it clear by many little touches, worked in with masterly subtlety, that this Rebecca does not actually lie, but is never entirely straightforward. Just as, in spite of all her freedom from prejudice, she understated her age by a year, so is her confession to the two men not entirely complete, and through the persistence of Kroll it is supplemented on some important points. Hence it is open to us, too, to conjecture that the explanation of her refusal only exposes one motive in order to conceal another.

Assuredly we have no reason to disbelieve her when she declares that the atmosphere of Rosmersholm and her intercourse with the high-souled Rosmer have ennobled and – paralysed her. She expresses there what she knows and has felt. But this is not necessarily all that has happened to her, nor is she necessarily competent to explain to herself that all. The influence of Rosmer might even only be a cloak which conceals another influence that was operative, and a notable indication points in this new direction.

Even after her confession, in their last interview which brings the play to an end, Rosmer again beseeches her to be his wife. He forgives her the crime committed for love of him. And now she does not answer, as she might, that no forgiveness can rid her of the consciousness of guilt incurred by her malignant deception of poor Beata; but charges herself with another reproach which affects us as coming strangely from this freethinking woman, and in no wise corresponds to the importance which Rebecca attaches to it: 'Dear – never speak of this again! It is impossible. – For you must know, Rosmer, I have – a past behind me.' She means, of course, that she has had sexual relations with another man; and we do not fail to observe that these relations, which occurred at a time when she was free and accountable to nobody, seem to her a greater hindrance to the union with Rosmer than her truly criminal action against his wife.

Rosmer refuses to hear anything about this past. We can divine what it was, though everything that refers to it in the play is, so to speak, subterranean and has to be pieced together from hints. But it is true they are hints inserted with such art that it is impossible to misunderstand them.

Between Rebecca's first refusal and her confession something occurs which has a decisive influence on her future destiny. Rector Kroll arrives one day at the house on purpose to humiliate Rebecca by telling her that he knows she is an illegitimate child, the daughter of that very Dr West who had adopted her after her mother's death. Hate has sharpened his perceptions, yet he does not suppose that this is any news to her. 'I really did not suppose you were ignorant of this, otherwise it would have been very odd that you should have let Dr West adopt you—'; 'And then he takes you into his house – as soon as your mother dies. He treats you harshly. And yet you stay with him. You know that he won't leave you a halfpenny – as a matter of fact you got only a case of books – and yet you stay on; you bear with him; you nurse him to the last'; 'I attribute your care for him to the natural filial instinct of a daughter. Indeed, I believe your whole conduct is a natural result of your origin.'

But Kroll was mistaken. Rebecca had no idea at all that she could be West's daughter. When Kroll began with dark hints at her past, she could not but think he was referring to something else. After she knew what he did mean, she could still retain her composure awhile, for she was able to suppose that her enemy was basing his calculations on her age, which she had given falsely on an earlier visit of his. But when Kroll demolished this objection by saying: 'Well, so be it, but my calculation may be right, none the less; for Dr West was up there on a short visit the year before he got the appointment . . .' After this new information, she loses all control. 'It is not true!' She walks about wringing her hands. 'It is impossible. You want to cheat me into believing it. This can never, never be true. It cannot be true. Never in this world!—' Her agitation is so extreme that Kroll cannot attribute it to his information alone.

> KROLL But, my dear Miss West – why in Heaven's name are you so terribly excited? You quite frighten me. What am I to think – to believe—?
>
> REBECCA Nothing! You are not to think anything or believe anything.
>
> KROLL Then you must really tell me how you can take this affair – this possibility – so terribly to heart.

REBECCA (*controlling herself*) It is perfectly simple, Rector Kroll. I have no wish to be taken for an illegitimate child.

The enigma of Rebecca's behaviour is susceptible of only one solution. The news that Dr West was her father is the heaviest blow that can befall her, for she was not only the adopted daughter, but she had been the mistress of this man. When Kroll began to speak, she thought that he was hinting at these relations, the truth about which she would probably have admitted and justified by her emancipated ideas. But this was far from the Rector's intention; he knew nothing of the love-affair with Dr West, as she knew nothing of West being her father. She *cannot* have had anything else in her mind when she accounted for her final rejection of Rosmer on the ground that she had a past which made her unworthy to be his wife. Probably, if Rosmer had consented to hear of this past, she would have made only a half-confession and have kept silence on the more serious part of it.

But now we do indeed understand that this past must seem to her the more serious obstacle to their union – the more serious . . . crime.

After she has learnt that she has been the mistress of her own father, she surrenders herself wholly to her now overmastering sense of guilt. She confesses to Rosmer and Kroll that she was a murderess; she rejects for ever the happiness to which she has paved the way by crime; and prepares for departure. But the true origin of her sense of guilt, which wrecks her at the moment of attainment, remains a secret. We have seen that it is something quite other than the atmosphere of Rosmersholm and the refining influence of Rosmer.

No one who has followed us so far will neglect to bring forward an objection which may justify some doubts. The first refusal of Rosmer by Rebecca occurs before the second visit of Kroll, and therefore before his exposure of her illicit origin and at a time when she as yet knows nothing of her incest — if we have rightly understood the dramatist. Yet her first refusal is given in very serious earnest. The sense of guilt which bids her renounce the fruit of her actions is thus effective before she knows anything of her cardinal crime; and if we grant so much it is perhaps incumbent on us to ignore the incest as the source of that sense of guilt.

Hitherto, we have treated Rebecca West as if she were a living person and not a creation of Ibsen's phantasy, one which is always subject to the most critical tests of reason. We shall attempt to meet the objection aforesaid on this same ground. It is a just objection that, before the knowledge of her incest, conscience was in some sort awakened in Rebecca. There is nothing to prevent our making the influence which is acknowledged and accused by Rebecca herself responsible for this change. But we shall not thus escape recognition of the second motive. The behaviour of Rebecca on hearing what Kroll has to tell her, the confession which is her immediate reaction, leave no doubt that now only does the stronger and more decisive motive for renunciation begin to take effect. It is in fact a case of manifold motivation, in which a deeper motive comes to the surface from beneath the superficial one. Laws of poetical economy necessitate this way of presenting the situation, for this deeper motive could not be explicitly set forth, it had to be dissimulated, kept from the direct perception of the spectator or the reader; otherwise such serious resistances, based on most painful emotions, would have arisen that the effect of the tragedy might have been imperilled.

We have, however, a right to demand that the ostensible motive shall not be without an inherent relation to the dissimulated one, but shall appear as a mitigation of, and a derivation from, the latter. And relying on the dramatist to have arranged his conscious dramatic combination in logical accordance with unconscious possibilities, we can now try to show that he has fulfilled this demand. Rebecca's feeling of guilt finds its source in the shame of incest, even before Kroll with his analytic insight has made her aware of it. When we fully reconstruct and supplement the past indicated by the author, we shall feel sure that she cannot have been without an inkling of the intimate relation between her mother and Dr West. It must have made a strong impression on her when she became her mother's successor with this man; and she thus stood under the domination of the Oedipus-complex, even though she did not know that this universal phantasy had been a reality in her case. When she came to Rosmersholm, the inward force of this first experience drove her to bring about, by definite action, the same situation which had been realized in the original instance, though not by her doing – to get rid of the wife and mother, that she might take her place with the husband and father. She describes with a convincing insistence how against her will she was obliged to proceed, step by step, to the removal of Beata.

> You think then that I was cool and calculating and self-possessed all the time! I was not the same woman then that I am now, as I stand here telling it all. Besides, there are two sorts of will in us, I believe. I wanted Beata away by one means or another, but I never really believed that it would come to pass. As I felt my way forward, at each step I ventured, I seemed to hear something within me cry out: No further! Not a step further! – And yet I could not stop. I *had* to venture the least little bit further. And only one hair's-breadth more. And then one more – and always one more . . . And so it happened. That is the way such things come about.

That is no plea for extenuation, but an authentic description. Everything that befell her at Rosmersholm, the passion for Rosmer and the enmity towards his wife, was from the first a consequence of the Oedipus-complex – a compulsive replica of her relations with her mother and Dr West.

And so the sense of guilt which first causes her to reject

Rosmer's proposal is at bottom indistinguishable from the deeper one which drives her to confession after Kroll has opened her eyes. But just as under the influence of Dr West she had become a freethinker and contemner of religious morality, so she is transformed by her love for Rosmer into a being with a conscience and an ideal. This much of the mental processes within her she does herself understand, and so she is justified in describing Rosmer's influence as the motive of the change in her – the only one of which she could be aware.

The practising psycho-analytic physician knows how frequently, or how invariably, the girl who enters a household as servant, companion or governess, will consciously or unconsciously weave a day-dream, which derives from the Oedipus-complex, about the disappearance of the mistress of the house and the master taking the newcomer to wife in her stead. *Rosmersholm* is the greatest work of art among those which treat of this common girlish phantasy. What makes it a tragedy is the circumstance that the early history of the heroine in actual fact had completely anticipated her day-dream.[6]

After long lingering in the sphere of literature, we now return to clinical experience. But only to establish in a few words the complete agreement between them. Psycho-analytic work teaches that the forces of conscience which induce illness on attainment of success, as in other cases on a frustration, are closely connected with the Oedipus-complex, the relation to father and mother, as perhaps, indeed, is all our sense of guilt in general.

One of the Difficulties of Psycho-Analysis[1]

(1917)

I WILL SAY AT once that it is not an intellectual difficulty I am thinking of, not anything that makes psycho-analysis hard for the hearer or reader to understand, but an affective one – something that alienates the feelings of those who come into contact with it, so that they become less inclined to believe in it or take an interest in it. As may be observed, the two kinds of difficulty amount to the same thing in the end. Where sympathy is lacking, understanding will not come very easily.

My present readers are, I take it, as yet unconcerned with the subject and I shall be obliged, therefore, to go back some distance. Out of a great number of individual observations and impressions something like a theory has at last shaped itself in psycho-analysis, and this is known by the name of the 'libido-theory'. As is known, psycho-analysis is concerned with the explanation and cure of what are called nervous disorders. A starting-point had to be found from which to approach this problem, and it was decided to look for it in the life of the instincts in the mind. Hypotheses relating to the instincts in man came to form the basis, therefore, of our conception of nervous disease.

The psychology that is taught in the schools gives us but very inadequate replies to questions concerning our mental life, but in no direction is its information so meagre as in this matter of the instincts.

We are left to take the first sounding in our own way. The popular view distinguishes between hunger and love, seeing them as the two representatives of those instincts which aim at self-preservation and at reproduction of the species respectively. We acknowledge this very evident distinction, so that in psycho-analysis also we postulate a similar one between the self-preservative or ego-instincts, on the one hand, and the sexual instincts on the other; that force by which the sexual instinct is represented in the mind we call 'libido' – sexual hunger – regarding it as analogous to the force of hunger, or the will to power, and other such trends among the ego-tendencies.

With this as a starting-point we then make our first important discovery. We learn that, when we come to try to comprehend neurotic disorders, by far the most significance attaches to the sexual instincts; in fact neuroses are the specific disorders, so to speak, of the sexual function; that in general whether or not a person develops a neurosis depends upon the strength of his libido, and upon the possibility of gratifying it and of discharging it through gratification; that the form taken by the disease is determined by the path which the sexual function of the person in question takes in its development, or, as we put it, by the fixations his libido has undergone in the course of its development; and, further, that by a special, not very simple technique for influencing the mind we are able to throw light on the nature of many groups of neuroses and at the same time to resolve them. The greatest success of our therapeutic efforts has been with a certain class of neuroses proceeding from a conflict between ego-instincts and sexual instincts. For in human beings it may happen that the demands of the sexual instincts, which of course extend far beyond the individual, seem to the ego to constitute a danger menacing his self-preservation or his self-respect. The ego then takes up the defensive, denies the sexual instincts the satisfaction they claim and forces them into those by-paths of substitutive gratification which become manifest as symptoms of a neurosis.

The psycho-analytic method of treatment is then able to subject this process of repression to revision and to bring about a better solution of the conflict, one compatible with health. Opponents who do not understand the matter accuse us of one-sidedness and of over-estimating the sexual instincts: 'Human beings have other interests besides sexual things.' We have not forgotten or denied this for a moment. Our one-sidedness is like that of the chemist who traces all compounds back to the force of chemical attraction. In doing so, he does not deny the force of gravity; he leaves that to the physicist to reckon with.

During the work of treatment we have to consider the distribution of the patient's libido; we look for the objects (ideas of them) to which it is attached and free it from them, so as to place it at the disposal of the ego. In the course of this, we have come to form a very curious picture of the direction taken at the outset by the libido in man. We have had to infer that at the beginning of its development the libido (all the erotic tendencies, all capacity for love) in each individual is directed towards the self — as we say, it cathects the self. It is only later that, in association with the satisfaction of the chief natural functions, the libido flows over beyond the ego towards objects outside the self, and not till then are we able to recognize the libidinal trends as such and distinguish them from the ego-instincts. It is possible for the libido to become detached from these objects and withdrawn again into the self.

The condition in which the libido is contained within the ego is called by us 'narcissism', in reference to the Greek myth of the youth Narcissus who remained faithful to his love for his own reflection.

Thus we look upon the development of the individual as a progress from narcissism to object-love; but we do not believe that the whole of the libido is ever transferred from the ego to objects outside itself. A certain amount of libido is always retained in the ego; even when object-love is highly developed, a certain degree of narcissism continues. The ego is a great reservoir from which the libido that is destined for objects flows outward and into which it can flow back from those objects. Object-libido was at first ego-libido and can be again transformed into ego-libido. For complete health it is essential that the libido should not lose this full mobility. As an illustration of this state of things we may think of an amoeba, the protoplasm of which puts out pseudopodia, elongations into which the substance of the body extends but which can be retracted at any time so that the form of the protoplasmic mass is reinstated.

What I have been trying to describe in this outline is the *libido-theory* of the neuroses, upon which are founded all our conceptions of the nature of these morbid states, together with our therapeutic measures for relieving them. We naturally regard the premises of the libido-theory as valid for normal behaviour as well. We employ the term 'narcissism' in relation to little children, and it is to the excessive 'narcissism' of primitive man that we ascribe his belief in the omnipotence of his thoughts and his consequent attempts to influence the course of events in the outer world by magical practices.

After this introduction I shall describe how the general narcissism of man, the self-love of humanity, has up to the present been three times severely wounded by the researches of science.

(*a*) When the first promptings of curiosity about his dwelling-place, the earth, began to arise in him, man believed that it was the stationary centre of the universe, with the sun, moon and planets circling round it. With this he was naively following the dictates of his sense-perceptions, for he felt no movement of the earth, and wherever he had an unimpeded view he found himself in the centre of a circle that enclosed the whole world outside him. The central position of the earth was to him a token of its sovereignty in the universe and it appeared to accord very well with his proclivity to regard himself as lord of the world.

The destruction of this narcissistic illusion is associated with the name and work of Copernicus in the sixteenth century. Long before his day the Pythagoreans had already cast doubts upon the privileged position of the earth, and in the third century BC Aristarchus of Samos had declared that the earth was much smaller than the sun and moved round that celestial body. Even the great discovery of Copernicus, therefore, had already been made before. But when it achieved general recognition, the self-love of humanity suffered its first blow, the *cosmological* one.

(*b*) In the course of his development towards culture, man acquired a dominating position over his fellow-creatures in the animal kingdom. Not content with this supremacy, however, he began to place a gulf between his nature and theirs. He denied the possession of reason to them, and to himself he attributed an immortal soul, and made claims to a divine descent which permitted him to annihilate the bond of community between him and the animal kingdom. It is noteworthy that this piece of arrogance is still as foreign to the child as it is to the savage or to primitive man. It is the result of a later, more pretentious stage of development. At the level of totemism primitive man has no repugnance to tracing his descent from an animal ancestor. In myths, which contain the deposit of this ancient attitude of mind, the gods take animal shapes, and in the art of prehistoric times they are portrayed with animals' heads. A child can see no difference between his own nature and that of animals; he is not astonished at animals thinking and talking in fairy-tales; he will transfer to a dog or a horse an emotion of fear which refers to his human father, without thereby intending any derogation of his father. Not until he is grown-up does he become so far estranged from the animals as to use their names in vilification of others.

We all know that, little more than half a century ago, the researches of Charles Darwin, his collaborators and predecessors put an end to this presumption on the part of man. Man is not a being different from animals or superior to them; he himself originates in the animal race and is related more closely to some of its members and more distantly to others. The accretions he has subsequently developed have not served to efface the evidences, both in his physical structure and in his mental dispositions, of his parity with them. This was the second, the *biological* blow to human narcissism.

(*c*) The third blow, which is psychological in nature, is probably the most wounding.

Although thus humbled in his external relations, man feels himself to be supreme in his own soul. Somewhere in the core of his ego he has developed an organ of observation to keep a watch on his impulses and actions and see that they accord with its demands. If they do not, they are inexorably prohibited and retracted. His inner perception, consciousness, gives the ego news of all the important occurrences in the mind's working, and the will, set in motion by these reports, carries out what the ego directs, and modifies all that tends to accomplish itself independently. For this soul is not a simple thing; on the contrary, it is a hierarchy of superordinated and subordinated agents, a labyrinth of impulses striving independently of one another towards action, corresponding with the multiplicity of instincts and of relations with the outer world, many of which are antagonistic to one another and incompatible. For proper functioning it is necessary that the highest among these agents should have knowledge of all that is going forward and that its will should penetrate throughout to exert its influence. But the ego feels itself secure of the completeness and trustworthiness both of the reports it receives and of the channels by which it can enforce its commands.

In certain diseases, including indeed the very neuroses of which we have made special study, things are different. The ego feels uneasy; it finds a limit to its power in its own house, the mind. Thoughts suddenly break in without the conscious mind knowing where they come from, nor can it do anything to drive them away. These unwelcome guests seem to be more powerful even than those which are at the ego's command; they resist all the well-proven measures instituted by the will, remain unmoved by logical rebuttal, and unaffected though reality refutes them. Or else impulses make themselves felt which seem like those of a stranger, so that the ego disowns them; yet it has to fear them and take precautions against them. The ego says to itself: 'This is an illness, a foreign invasion'; it increases its vigilance, but cannot understand why it feels so strangely paralysed.

Psychiatry, it is true, denies that such things mean the intrusion into the mind of evil spirits from without; beyond this, however, it can only say with a shrug: 'Degeneracy, hereditary disposition, constitutional inferiority!' Psycho-analysis sets out to explain these eerie disorders; it engages in scrupulous and laborious investigations, devises hypotheses and scientific expedients, until at length it can say to the ego: 'Nothing has entered into you from without; a part of the activity of your own mind has been withdrawn from your knowledge and from the command of your will. That, too, is why you are so weak in your defences; with one part of your forces you are fighting the other part and you cannot concentrate the whole of your energy as you would against an outer enemy. And it is not even the worst or least effective part of your mental powers that has thus become antagonistic to you and independent of you. The blame, I must tell you, lies with yourself. You over-estimated your strength when you thought you could do as you liked with your sexual instincts and could utterly ignore their aims. The result is that they have rebelled and have gone their own way in the dark to rid themselves of this oppression; they have extorted their rights in a manner you cannot sanction. How they have achieved this and the paths by which they have reached their purpose, you have not learnt; only the result of their work, the symptom which you experience as suffering, has come to your knowledge. Then you do not recognize it as a product of your own rejected impulses and do not know that it is a substitutive gratification of them.

'The whole process, however, only becomes possible through the single circumstance that you are mistaken in another important point as well. You believe that you are informed of all that goes on in your mind if it is of any importance at all, because your consciousness then gives you news of it. And if you have heard nothing of any particular thing in your mind you confidently assume that it does not exist there. Indeed, you go so far as to regard "the mind" as co-extensive with "consciousness", that is, with what is known to you, in spite of the most obvious evidence that a great deal more is perpetually going on in your mind than can be known to your consciousness. Come, let yourself be taught something on this one point. What is in your mind is not identical with what you are conscious of; whether something is going on in your mind and whether you hear of it, are two different things. In the ordinary way, I will admit, the intelligence which reaches your consciousness is enough for your needs; and you may cherish the illusion that you learn of all the more important things. But in some cases, as in that of a conflict between instincts such as I have described, the intelligence department breaks down and your will then extends no further than your knowledge. In all cases, however, the news that reaches your consciousness is incomplete and often not to be relied on; often enough, too, it happens that you get news of what has taken place only when it is all over and when you can no longer do anything to change it. Even if you are not ill, who can tell all that is stirring in your mind of which you know nothing or are falsely informed? You conduct yourself like an absolute sovereign who is content with the information supplied him by his highest officials and never goes among the people to hear their voice. Look into the depths of your own soul and learn first to know yourself, then you will understand why this illness was bound to come upon you and perhaps you will thenceforth avoid falling ill.'

It is thus that psycho-analysis wishes to educate the ego. But these two discoveries – that the life of the sexual instincts cannot be totally restrained, and that mental processes are in themselves unconscious and only reach the ego and come under its control through incomplete and untrustworthy perceptions – amount to a statement that *the ego is not master in its own house*. Together they represent the third wound inflicted on man's self-love, that which I call the *psychological* one. No wonder, therefore, that the ego shows no favour to psycho-analysis and persistently refuses to believe in it.

Probably but very few people have realized the momentous

significance for science and life of the recognition of unconscious mental processes. It was not psycho-analysis, however, let us hasten to add, which took this first step. There are renowned names among the philosophers who may be cited as its predecessors, above all the great thinker Schopenhauer, whose unconscious 'Will' is equivalent to the instincts in the mind as seen by psycho-analysis. It was this same thinker, moreover, who in words of unforgettable impressiveness admonished mankind of the importance of their sexual craving, still so depreciated. Psycho-analysis has only this to its credit, that it has not affirmed these two propositions that are so wounding to narcissism on an abstract basis – the importance of sexuality in the mind and the unconsciousness of mental activity – but has demonstrated them in matters that touch every individual personally and force him to take up some attitude towards these problems. It is just for this reason, however, that it brings on itself the aversion and antagonism which still keep at a respectful distance from the name of the great philosopher.

The 'Uncanny'[1]

(1919)

IT IS ONLY RARELY that a psycho-analyst feels impelled to investigate the subject of aesthetics even when aesthetics is understood to mean not merely the theory of beauty, but the theory of feeling. He works in other planes of mental life and has little to do with those subdued emotional activities which, inhibited in their aims and dependent upon a multitude of concurrent factors, usually furnish the material for the study of aesthetics. But it does occasionally happen that he has to interest himself in some particular province of that subject; and then it usually proves to be a rather remote region of it and one that has been neglected in standard works.

The subject of the 'uncanny' is a province of this kind. It undoubtedly belongs to all that is terrible – to all that arouses dread and creeping horror; it is equally certain, too, that the word is not always used in a clearly definable sense, so that it tends to coincide with whatever excites dread. Yet we may expect that it implies some intrinsic quality which justifies the use of a special name. One is curious to know what this peculiar quality is which allows us to distinguish as 'uncanny' certain things within the boundaries of what is 'fearful'.

As good as nothing is to be found upon this subject in elaborate treatises on aesthetics, which in general prefer to concern themselves with what is beautiful, attractive and sublime, that is with feelings of a positive nature, with the circumstances and the objects that call them forth, rather than with the opposite feelings of unpleasantness and repulsion. I know of only one attempt in medico-psychological literature, a fertile but not exhaustive paper by E. Jentsch.[2] But I must confess that I have not made a very thorough examination of the bibliography, especially the foreign literature, relating to this present modest contribution of mine, for reasons which must be obvious at this time;[3] so that my paper is presented to the reader without any claim to priority.

In his study of the 'uncanny', Jentsch quite rightly lays stress on the obstacle presented by the fact that people vary so very greatly in their sensitivity to this quality of feeling. The writer of the present contribution, indeed, must himself plead guilty to a special obtuseness in the matter, where extreme delicacy of perception would be more in place. It is long since he has experienced or heard of anything which has given him an uncanny impression, and he will be obliged to translate himself into that state of feeling, and to awaken in himself the possibility of it before he begins. Still, difficulties of this kind make themselves felt powerfully in many other branches of aesthetics; we need not on this account despair of finding instances in which the quality in question will be recognized without hesitation by most people.

Two courses are open to us at the start. Either we can find out what meaning has come to be attached to the word 'uncanny' in the course of its history; or we can collect all those properties of persons, things, sensations, experiences and situations which arouse in us the feeling of uncanniness, and then infer the unknown nature of the uncanny from what they all have in common. I will say at once that both courses lead to the same result: the 'uncanny' is that class of the terrifying which leads back to something long known to us, once very familiar. How this is possible, in what circumstances the familiar can become uncanny and frightening, I shall show in what follows. Let me also add that my investigation was actually begun by collecting a number of individual cases, and only later received confirmation after I had examined what language could tell us. In this discussion, however, I shall follow the opposite course.

The German word *unheimlich*[4] is obviously the opposite of *heimlich*, *heimisch*, meaning 'familiar'; 'native', 'belonging to the home'; and we are tempted to conclude that what is 'uncanny' is frightening precisely because it is *not* known and familiar. Naturally not everything which is new and unfamiliar is frightening, however; the relation cannot be inverted. We can only say that what is novel can easily become frightening and uncanny; some new things are frightening but not by any means all. Something has to be added to what is novel and unfamiliar to make it uncanny.

On the whole, Jentsch did not get beyond this relation of the uncanny to the novel and unfamiliar. He ascribes the essential factor in the production of the feeling of uncanniness to intellectual uncertainty; so that the uncanny would always be that in which one does not know where one is, as it were. The better orientated in his environment a person is, the less readily will he get the impression of something uncanny in regard to the objects and events in it.

It is not difficult to see that this definition is incomplete, and we will therefore try to proceed beyond the equation of *unheimlich* with unfamiliar. We will first turn to other languages. But foreign dictionaries tell us nothing new, perhaps only because we speak a different language. Indeed, we get the impression that many languages are without a word for this particular variety of what is fearful.

I wish to express my indebtedness to Dr Th. Reik for the following excerpts:

LATIN (K. E. Georges, *Deutschlateinisches Wörterbuch*, 1898): Ein *unheimlicher* Ort [an uncanny place] – locus suspectus; in *unheimlicher* Nachtzeit [in the dismal night hours] – intempesta nocte.

GREEK (Rost's and Schenkl's Lexikons): ξένος – strange, foreign.

ENGLISH (from dictionaries by Lucas, Bellow, Flügel, Muret–Sanders): Uncomfortable, uneasy, gloomy, dismal, uncanny, ghastly; (of a house) haunted; (of a man) a repulsive fellow.

FRENCH (Sachs–Villatte): Inquiétant, sinistre, lugubre, mal à son aise.

SPANISH (Tollhausen, 1889): Sospechoso, de mal agüero, lugubre, siniestro.

The Italian and the Portuguese seem to content themselves with words which we should describe as circumlocutions. In Arabic and Hebrew 'uncanny' means the same as 'daemonic', 'gruesome'.

Let us therefore return to the German language. In Daniel Sanders' *Wörterbuch der deutschen Sprache* (1860), the following remarks [abstracted in translation] are found upon the word *heimlich*; I have laid stress on certain passages by italicizing them.

Heimlich, adj.: I. Also *heimelich*, *heimelig*, belonging to the house, not strange, familiar, tame, intimate, comfortable, homely, etc.

(*a*) (Obsolete) belonging to the house or the family, or regarded as so belonging (cf. Latin *familiaris*): *Die Heimlichen*, the members of the household; *Der heimliche Rat* [him to whom

398

secrets are revealed], Genesis 41, 45; 2 Samuel 23, 23; now more usually *Geheimer Rat* [Privy Councillor], cf. *Heimlicher*.

(*b*) Of animals: tame, companionable to man. As opposed to wild, e.g. 'Wild animals . . . that are trained to be *heimlich* and accustomed to men.' 'If these young creatures are brought up from early days among men they become quite *heimlich*, friendly', etc.

(*c*) Friendly, intimate, homelike; the enjoyment of quiet content, etc., arousing a sense of peaceful pleasure and security as in one within the four walls of his house. 'Is it still *heimlich* to you in your country where strangers are felling your woods?' 'She did not feel all too *heimlich* with him.' 'To destroy the *Heimlichkeit* of the home.' I could not readily find another spot so intimate and *heimlich* as this.' 'In quiet *Heimlichkeit*, surrounded by close walls.' 'A careful housewife, who knows how to make a pleasing *Heimlichkeit* (*Häuslichkeit*)' out of the smallest means.' 'The protestant rulers do not feel . . . *heimlich* among their catholic subjects.' 'When it grows *heimlich* and still, and the evening quiet alone watches over your cell.' 'Quiet, lovely and *heimlich*, no place more fitted for her rest.' 'The in- and outflowing waves of the current, dreamy and *heimlich* as a cradle-song.' Cf. in especial *Unheimlich*. Among Swabian and Swiss authors in especial, often as a trisyllable: 'How *heimelich* it seemed again of an evening, back at home.' 'The warm room and the *heimelig* afternoon.' 'Little by little they grew at ease and *heimelig* among themselves.' 'That which comes from afar . . . assuredly does not live quite *heimelig* (*heimatlich* [at home], *freundnachbarlich* [in a neighbourly way]) among the people.' 'The sentinel's horn sounds so *heimelig* from the tower, and his voice invites so hospitably.' *This form of the word ought to become general in order to protect the word from becoming obsolete in its good sense through an easy confusion with II.* [see below]. '"*The Zecks* [a family name] *are all 'heimlich'.*" "'*Heimlich'? What do you understand by 'heimlich'?" "Well . . . they are like a buried spring or a dried-up pond. One cannot walk over it without always having the feeling that water might come up there again." "Oh, we call it 'unheimlich'; you call it 'heimlich'. Well, what makes you think that there is something secret and untrustworthy about this family?"'* – Gutzkow.

II. Concealed, kept from sight, so that others do not get to know about it, withheld from others, cf. *geheim* [secret]; so also *Heimlichkeit* for *Geheimnis* [secret]. To do something *heimlich*, i.e. behind someone's back; to steal away *heimlich*; *heimlich* meetings and appointments; to look on with *heimlich* pleasure at someone's discomfiture; to sigh or weep *heimlich*; to behave *heimlich*, as though there was something to conceal; *heimlich* love, love-affair, sin; *heimlich* places (which good manners oblige us to conceal). 1 Samuel 5, 6; 'The *heimlich* chamber' [privy]. 2 Kings 10, 27 etc.; 'To throw into pits or *Heimlichkeit*.' 'Led the steeds *heimlich* before Laomedon.' 'As secretive, *heimlich*, deceitful and malicious towards cruel masters . . . as frank, open, sympathetic and helpful towards a friend in misfortune.' 'The *heimlich* art' (magic). 'Where public ventilation has to stop, there *heimlich* machinations begin.' 'Freedom is the whispered watchword of *heimlich* conspirators and the loud battle-cry of professed revolutionaries.' 'A holy, *heimlich* effect.' 'I have roots that are most *heimlich*, I am grown in the deep earth.' 'My *heimlich* pranks' (Cf. *Heimtücke* [mischief]). To discover, disclose, betray someone's *Heimlichkeiten*; 'to concoct *Heimlichkeiten* behind my back.' Cf. *Geheimnis*.

Compounds and especially also the opposite follow meaning I (above): *Unheimlich*, uneasy, eerie, blood-curdling; 'Seeming almost *unheimlich* and ghostly to him.' 'I had already long since felt an *unheimlich*, even gruesome feeling.' 'Feels an *unheimlich* horror.' '*Unheimlich* and motionless like a stone-image.' 'The *unheimlich* mist called hill-fog.' 'These pale youths are *unheimlich* and are brewing heaven knows what mischief.' '"*Unheimlich*" is the name for everything that ought to have remained ... hidden and secret and has become visible' – Schelling. 'To veil the divine, to surround it with a certain *Unheimlichkeit*.' – *Unheimlich* is not often used as opposite to meaning II (above).

What interests us most in this long extract is to find that among its different shades of meaning the word *heimlich* exhibits one which is identical with its opposite, *unheimlich*. What is *heimlich* thus comes to be *unheimlich*. (Cf. the quotation from Gutzkow: 'We call it *unheimlich*; you call it *heimlich*.') In general we are reminded that the word *heimlich* is not unambiguous, but belongs to two sets of ideas, which without being contradictory are yet very different: on the one hand, it means that which is familiar and congenial, and on the other, that which is concealed and kept out of sight. The word *unheimlich* is only used customarily, we are told, as the contrary of the first signification, and not of the second. Sanders tells us nothing concerning a possible genetic connection between these two sets of meanings. On the other hand, we notice that Schelling says something which throws quite a new light on the concept of the 'uncanny', one which we had certainly not awaited. According to him everything is uncanny that ought to have remained hidden and secret, and yet comes to light.

Some of the doubts that have thus arisen are removed if we consult Grimm's dictionary.

We read:

Heimlich; adj. and adv. *vernaculus, occultus*; MHG. heimelîch, heimlîch.

P. 874. In a slightly different sense: 'I feel *heimlich*, well, free from fear. . . .'

(*b*) *Heimlich*, also in the sense of a place free from ghostly influences . . . familiar, friendly, intimate.

4. *From the idea of 'homelike', 'belonging to the house', the further idea is developed of something withdrawn from the eyes of others, something concealed, secret, and this idea is expanded in many ways . . .*

P. 876. ' On the left bank of the lake there lies a meadow *heimlich* in the wood.' Schiller, *Tell* . . . Poetic licence, rarely so used in modern speech . . . In conjunction with a verb expressing the act of concealing: 'In the secret of his tabernacle he shall hide me (*heimlich*)', Psalms 27, 5 . . . *Heimlich* places in the human body, pudenda . . . 'the men that died not were smitten' (on their *heimlich* parts), 1 Samuel 5, 12 . . .

(*c*) Officials who give important advice which has to be kept secret in matters of state are called *heimlich* councillors; the adjective, according to modern usage, having been replaced by *geheim* [secret] . . . 'Pharaoh called Joseph's name "him to whom secrets are revealed"' [*heimlich* councillor), Genesis 41, 45.

P. 878. 6. *Heimlich*, as used of knowledge, mystic, allegorical: a *heimlich* meaning, *mysticus, divinus, occultus, figuratus*.

P. 878. *Heimlich* in a different sense, as withdrawn from knowledge, unconscious . . . *Heimlich* also has the meaning of that which is obscure, inaccessible to knowledge . . . 'Do you not see? They do not trust me; they fear the *heimlich* face of the Duke of Friedland', *Wallensteins Lager*, Act II.

9. *The notion of something hidden and dangerous, which is expressed in the last paragraph, is still further developed, so that 'heimlich' comes to have the meaning usually ascribed to 'unheimlich'.* Thus: 'At times I feel like a man who walks in the night and believes in ghosts; every corner is *heimlich* and full of terrors for him' – Klinger.

Thus *heimlich* is a word the meaning of which develops towards an ambivalence, until it finally coincides with its opposite, *unheimlich*. *Unheimlich* is in some way or other a sub-species of *heimlich*. Let us retain this discovery, which we do not yet properly understand, alongside of Schelling's definition of the 'uncanny'. Then if we examine individual instances of uncanniness, these indications will become comprehensible to us.

II

In proceeding to review those things, persons, impressions, events and situations which are able to arouse in us a feeling of the uncanny in a very forcible and definite form, the first requirement is obviously to select a suitable example to start upon. Jentsch has taken as a very good instance 'doubts whether an apparently animate being is really alive; or conversely, whether a lifeless object might not be in fact animate'; and he refers in this connection to the impression made by wax-work figures, artificial dolls and automatons. He adds to this class the uncanny effect of epileptic seizures and the manifestations of insanity, because these excite in the spectator the feeling that automatic, mechanical processes are at work, concealed beneath the ordinary appearance of animation. Without entirely accepting the author's view, we will take it as a starting-point for our investigation because it leads us on to consider a writer who has succeeded better than anyone else in producing uncanny effects.

Jentsch says: 'In telling a story, one of the most successful devices for easily creating uncanny effects is to leave the reader in uncertainty whether a particular figure in the story is a human being or an automaton; and to do it in such a way that his attention is not directly focused upon his uncertainty, so that he may not be urged to go into the matter and clear it up immediately, since that, as we have said, would quickly dissipate the peculiar emotional effect of the thing. Hoffmann has repeatedly employed this psychological artifice with success in his fantastic narratives.'

This observation, undoubtedly a correct one, refers primarily to the story of 'The Sand-Man' in Hoffmann's *Nachtstücken*,[6] which contains the original of Olympia, the doll in the first act of Offenbach's opera, *Tales of Hoffmann*. But I cannot think – and I hope that most readers of the story will agree with me – that the theme of the doll, Olympia, who is to all appearances a living being, is by any means the only element to be held responsible for the quite unparalleled atmosphere of uncanniness which the story evokes; or, indeed, that it is the most important among them. Nor is this effect of the story heightened by the fact that the author himself treats the episode of Olympia with a faint touch of satire and uses it to make fun of the young man's idealization of his mistress. The main theme of the story is, on the contrary, something different, something which gives its name to the story, and which is always re-introduced at the critical moment: it is the theme of the 'Sand-Man' who tears out children's eyes.

This fantastic tale begins with the childhood-recollections of the student Nathaniel: in spite of his present happiness, he cannot banish the memories associated with the mysterious and terrifying death of the father he loved. On certain evenings his mother used to send the children to bed early, warning them that 'the Sand-Man was coming'; and sure enough Nathaniel would not fail to hear the heavy tread of a visitor with whom his father would then be occupied that evening. When questioned about the Sand-Man, his mother, it is true, denied that such a person existed except as a form of speech; but his nurse could give him more definite information: 'He is a wicked man who comes when children won't go to bed, and throws handfuls of sand in their eyes so that they jump out of their heads all bleeding. Then he puts the eyes in a sack and carries them off to the moon to feed his children. They sit up there in their nest, and their beaks are hooked like owls' beaks, and they use them to peck up naughty boys' and girls' eyes with.'

Although little Nathaniel was sensible and old enough not to believe in such gruesome attributes to the figure of the Sand-Man, yet the dread of him became fixed in his breast. He determined to find out what the Sand-Man looked like; and one evening, when the Sand-Man was again expected, he hid himself in his father's study. He recognized the visitor as the lawyer Coppelius, a repulsive person of whom the children were frightened when he occasionally came to a meal; and he now identified this Coppelius with the dreaded Sand-Man. Concerning the rest of the scene, Hoffmann already leaves us in doubt whether we are witnessing the first delirium of the panic-stricken boy, or a succession of events which are to be regarded in the story as being real. His father and the guest begin to busy themselves at a hearth with glowing flames. The little eavesdropper hears Coppelius call out, 'Here with your eyes!' and betrays himself by screaming aloud; Coppelius seizes him and is about to drop grains of red-hot coal out of the fire into his eyes, so as to cast them out on to the hearth. His father begs him off and saves his eyes. After this the boy falls into a deep swoon; and a long illness followed upon his experience. Those who lean towards a rationalistic interpretation of the Sand-Man will not fail to recognize in the child's phantasy the continued influence of his nurse's story. The grains of sand that are to be thrown into the child's eyes turn into red-hot grains of coal out of the flames; and in both cases they are meant to make his eyes jump out. In the course of another visit of the Sand-Man's, a year later, his father was killed in his study by an explosion. The lawyer Coppelius vanished from the place without leaving a trace behind.

Nathaniel, now a student, believes that he has recognized this childhood's phantom of horror in an itinerant optician, an Italian called Giuseppe Coppola. This man had offered him barometers for sale in his university town, and when Nathaniel refused had added: 'Eh, not barometers, not barometers – also got fine eyes, beautiful eyes.' The student's terror was allayed on finding that the proffered eyes were only harmless spectacles, and he bought a pocket-telescope from Coppola. With its aid he looks across into Professor Spalanzani's house opposite and there spies Spalanzani's beautiful, but strangely silent and motionless daughter, Olympia. He soon falls in love with her so violently that he quite forgets his clever and sensible betrothed on her account. But Olympia was an automaton whose works Spalanzani had made, and whose eyes Coppola, the Sand-Man, had put in. The student surprises the two men quarrelling over their handiwork. The optician carries off the wooden, eyeless doll; and the mechanician, Spalanzani, takes up Olympia's bleeding eye-balls from the ground and throws them at Nathaniel's breast, saying that Coppola had stolen them from him (Nathaniel). Nathaniel succumbs to a fresh attack of madness, and in his delirium his recollection of his father's death is mingled with this new experience. He cries, 'Faster – faster – faster – rings of fire – rings of fire! Whirl about, rings of fire – round and round! Wooden doll, ho! lovely wooden doll, whirl about—', then falls upon the professor, Olympia's so-called father, and tries to strangle him.

Rallying from a long and serious illness, Nathaniel seemed at last to have recovered. He was going to marry his betrothed with whom he was reconciled. One day he was walking through the town and market-place, where the high tower of the Town Hall threw its huge shadow. On the girl's suggestion they mounted the tower, leaving her brother, who was walking with them, down below. Up there, Clara's attention is drawn to a curious object coming along the street. Nathaniel looks at this thing through Coppola's spyglass, which he finds in his pocket, and falls into a new fit of madness. Shouting out, 'Whirl about, my wooden doll!' he tries to fling the girl into the depths below. Her brother, brought to her side by her cries, rescues her and hastens down to safety with her. Up above, the raving man rushes round, shrieking 'Rings of fire, whirl about!' – words whose origin we know. Among the people who begin to gather below there comes forward the figure of the lawyer Coppelius, suddenly returned. We may suppose it was his approach, seen through the telescope, that threw Nathaniel into his madness. People want to go up and overpower the madman, but Coppelius[7] laughs and says, 'Wait a bit; he'll come down of himself.' Nathaniel suddenly stands still, catches sight of Coppelius, and with a wild shriek – 'Yes! "Fine eyes – beautiful eyes"' – flings himself down over the parapet. No sooner does he lie on the paving-stones with a shattered skull than the Sand-Man vanishes in the throng.

This short summary leaves, I think, no doubt that the feeling of something uncanny is directly attached to the figure of the Sand-Man, that is, to the idea of being robbed of one's eyes; and that Jentsch's point of an intellectual uncertainty has nothing to do with this effect. Uncertainty whether an object is living or inanimate, which we must admit in regard to the doll Olympia, is quite irrelevant in connection with this other, more striking instance of uncanniness. It is true that the writer creates a kind of uncertainty in us in the beginning by not letting us know, no doubt purposely, whether he is taking us into the real world or into a purely fantastic one of his own creation. He has admittedly the right to do either; and if he chooses to stage his action in a world peopled with spirits, demons and ghosts, as Shakespeare does in *Hamlet*, in *Macbeth* and, in a different sense, in *The Tempest* and *A Midsummer Night's Dream*, we must bow to his decision and treat his setting as though it were real for as long as we put ourselves into his hands. But this uncertainty disappears in the course of Hoffmann's story, and we perceive that he means to make us, too, look through the fell Coppola's glasses – perhaps, indeed, that he himself once gazed through such an instrument. For the conclusion of the story makes it quite clear that Coppola the optician really is the lawyer Coppelius and thus also the Sand-Man.

There is no question, therefore, of any 'intellectual uncertainty'; we know now that we are not supposed to be looking on at the products of a madman's imagination behind which we, with the superiority of rational minds, are able to detect the sober truth; and yet this knowledge does not lessen the impression of uncanniness in the least degree. The theory of 'intellectual uncertainty' is thus incapable of explaining that impression.

We know from psycho-analytic experience, however, that this fear of damaging or losing one's eyes is a terrible fear of childhood. Many adults still retain their apprehensiveness in this respect, and no bodily injury is so much dreaded by them as an injury to the eye. We are accustomed to say, too, that we will treasure a thing as the apple of our eye. A study of dreams, phantasies and myths has taught us that a morbid anxiety connected with the eyes and with going blind is often enough a substitute for the dread of castration. In blinding himself, Oedipus, that mythical law-breaker, was simply carrying out a mitigated form of the punishment of castration — the only punishment that according to the *lex talionis* was fitted for him. We may try to reject the derivation of fears about the eye from the fear of castration on rationalistic grounds, and say that it is very natural that so precious an organ as the eye should be guarded by a proportionate dread; indeed, we might go further and say that the fear of castration itself contains no other significance and no deeper secret than a justifiable dread of this kind. But this view does not account adequately for the substitutive relation between the eye and the male member which is seen to exist in dreams and myths and phantasies; nor can it dispel the impression one gains that it is the threat of being castrated in especial which excites a peculiarly violent and obscure emotion, and that this emotion is what first gives the idea of losing other organs its intense colouring. All further doubts are removed when we get the details of their 'castration-complex' from the analyses of neurotic patients, and realize its immense importance in their mental life.

Moreover, I would not recommend any opponent of the psycho-analytic view to select precisely the story of the Sand-Man upon which to build his case that morbid anxiety about the eyes has nothing to do with the castration-complex. For why does Hoffmann bring the anxiety about eyes into such intimate connection with the father's death? And why does the Sand-Man appear each time in order to interfere with love? He divides the unfortunate Nathaniel from his betrothed and from her brother, his best friend; he destroys his second object of love, Olympia, the lovely doll; and he drives him into suicide at the moment when he has won back his Clara and is about to be happily united to her. Things like these and many more seem arbitrary and meaningless in the story so long as we deny all connection between fears about the eye and castration; but they become intelligible as soon as we replace the Sand-Man by the dreaded father at whose hands castration is awaited.[8]

We shall venture, therefore, to refer the uncanny effect of the Sand-Man to the child's dread in relation to its castration-complex. But having gained the idea that we can take this infantile factor to account for feelings of uncanniness, we are drawn to examine whether we can apply it to other instances of uncanny things. We find in the story of the Sand-Man the other theme upon which Jentsch lays stress, of a doll that appears to be alive. Jentsch believes that a particularly favourable condition for awakening uncanny sensations is created when there is intellectual uncertainty whether an object is alive or not, and when an inanimate object becomes too much like an animate one. Now, dolls happen to be rather closely connected with infantile life.

We remember that in their early games children do not distinguish at all sharply between living and lifeless objects, and that they are especially fond of treating their dolls like live people. In fact I have occasionally heard a woman patient declare that even at the age of eight she had still been convinced that her dolls would be certain to come to life if she were to look at them in a particular way, with as concentrated a gaze as possible. So that here, too, it is not difficult to discover a factor from childhood; but curiously enough, while the Sand-Man story deals with the excitation of an early childhood fear, the idea of a 'living doll' excites no fear at all; the child had no fear of its doll coming to life, it may even have desired it. The source of the feeling of an uncanny thing would not, therefore, be an infantile fear in this case, but rather an infantile wish or even only an infantile belief. There seems to be a contradiction here; but perhaps it is only a complication, which may be helpful to us later on.

Hoffmann is in literature the unrivalled master of conjuring up the uncanny. His *Elixire des Teufels* ['The Devil's Elixir'] contains a mass of themes to which one is tempted to ascribe the uncanny effect of the narrative; but it is too obscure and intricate a story to venture to summarize. Towards the end of the book the reader is told the facts, hitherto concealed from him, from which the action springs; with the result, not that he is at last enlightened, but that he falls into a state of complete bewilderment. The author has piled up too much of a kind; one's comprehension of the whole suffers as a result, though not the impression it makes. We must content ourselves with selecting those themes of uncanniness which are most prominent, and seeing whether we can fairly trace them also back to infantile sources. These themes are all concerned with the idea of a 'double' in every shape and degree, with persons, therefore, who are to be considered identical by reason of looking alike; Hoffmann accentuates this relation by transferring mental processes from the one person to the other – what we should call telepathy – so that the one possesses knowledge, feeling and experience in common with the other, identifies himself with another person, so that his self becomes confounded, or the foreign self is substituted for his own – in other words, by doubling, dividing and interchanging the self. And finally there is the constant recurrence of similar situations, a same face, or character-trait, or twist of fortune, or a same crime, or even a same name recurring throughout several consecutive generations.

The theme of the 'double' has been very thoroughly treated by Otto Rank.[9] He has gone into the connections the 'double' has with reflections in mirrors, with shadows, guardian spirits, with the belief in the soul and the fear of death; but he also lets in a flood of light on the astonishing evolution of this idea. For the 'double' was originally an insurance against destruction to the ego, an 'energetic denial of the power of death', as Rank says; and probably the 'immortal' soul was the first 'double' of the body. This invention of doubling as a preservation against extinction has its counterpart in the language of dreams, which is fond of representing castration by a doubling or multiplication of the genital symbol; the same desire spurred on the ancient Egyptians to the art of making images of the dead in some lasting material. Such ideas, however, have sprung from the soil of unbounded self-love, from the primary narcissism which holds sway in the mind of the child as in that of primitive man; and when this stage has been left behind the double takes on a different aspect. From having been an assurance of immortality, he becomes the ghastly harbinger of death.

The idea of the 'double' does not necessarily disappear with the passing of the primary narcissism, for it can receive fresh meaning from the later stages of development of the ego. A special faculty is slowly formed there, able to oppose the rest of the ego, with the function of observing and criticizing the self and exercising a censorship within the mind, and this we become aware of as our 'conscience'. In the pathological case of delusions of being watched, this mental institution becomes isolated, dissociated from the ego, and discernible to a physician's eye. The fact that a faculty of this kind exists, which is able to treat the rest of the ego like an object – the fact, that is, that man is capable of self-observation – renders it possible to invest the old idea of a 'double' with a new meaning and to ascribe many things to it, above all, those things which seem to the new faculty of self-criticism to belong to the old surmounted narcissism of the earliest period of all.[10]

But it is not only this narcissism, offensive to the ego-criticizing faculty, which may be incorporated in the idea of a double. There are also all those unfulfilled but possible futures to which we still like to cling in phantasy, all those strivings of the ego which adverse external circumstances have crushed, and all our suppressed acts of volition which nourish in us the illusion of Free Will.[11]

But, after having thus considered the manifest motivation of the figure of a 'double', we have to admit that none of it helps us to understand the extraordinarily strong feeling of something uncanny that pervades the conception; and our knowledge of pathological mental processes enables us to add that nothing in the content arrived at could account for that impulse towards self-protection which has caused the ego to project such a content outward as something foreign to itself. The quality of uncanniness can only come from the circumstance of the 'double' being a creation dating back to a very early mental stage, long since left behind, and one, no doubt, in which it wore a more friendly aspect. The 'double' has become a vision of terror, just as after the fall of their religion the gods took on daemonic shapes.[12]

It is not difficult to judge, on the same lines as his theme of the 'double', the other forms of disturbance in the ego made use of by Hoffmann. They are a harking-back to particular phases in the evolution of the self-regarding feeling, a regression to a time when the ego was not yet sharply differentiated from the external world and from other persons. I believe that these factors are partly responsible for the impression of the uncanny, although it is not easy to isolate and determine exactly their share of it.

That factor which consists in a recurrence of the same situations, things and events, will perhaps not appeal to everyone as a source of uncanny feeling. From what I have observed, this phenomenon does undoubtedly, subject to certain conditions and combined with certain circumstances, awaken an uncanny feeling, which recalls that sense of helplessness sometimes experienced in dreams. Once, as I was walking through the deserted streets of a provincial town in Italy which was strange to me, on a hot summer afternoon, I found myself in a quarter the character of which could not long remain in doubt. Nothing but painted women were to be seen at the windows of the small houses, and I hastened to leave the narrow street at the next turning. But after having wandered about for a while without being directed, I suddenly found myself back in the same street, where my presence was now beginning to excite attention. I hurried away once more, but only to arrive yet a third time by devious paths in the same place. Now, however, a feeling overcame me which I can only describe as uncanny, and I was glad enough to abandon my exploratory walk and get straight back to the piazza I had left a short while before. Other situations having in common with my adventure an involuntary return to the same situation, but which differ radically from it in other respects, also result in the same feeling of helplessness and of something uncanny. As, for instance, when one is lost in a forest in high altitudes, caught, we will suppose, by the mountain mist, and when every endeavour to find the marked or familiar path ends again and again in a return to one and the same spot, recognizable by some particular landmark. Or when one wanders about in a dark, strange room, looking for the door or the electric switch, and collides for the hundredth time with the same piece of furniture – a situation which, indeed, has been made irresistibly comic by Mark Twain, through the wild extravagance of his narration.

Taking another class of things, it is easy to see that here, too, it is only this factor of involuntary repetition which surrounds with an uncanny atmosphere what would otherwise be innocent enough, and forces upon us the idea of something fateful and unescapable where otherwise we should have spoken of 'chance' only. For instance, we of course attach no importance to the event when we give up a coat and get a cloakroom ticket with the number, say, 62; or when we find that our cabin on board ship is numbered 62. But the impression is altered if two such events, each in itself indifferent, happen close together, if we come across the number 62 several times in a single day, or if we begin to notice that everything which has a number – addresses, hotel-rooms, compartments in railway trains – always has the same one, or one which at least contains the same figures. We do feel this to be 'uncanny', and unless a man is utterly hardened and proof against the lure of superstition he will be tempted to ascribe a secret meaning to this obstinate recurrence of a number, taking it, perhaps, as an indication of the span of life allotted to him. Or take the case that one is engaged at the time in reading the works of Hering, the famous physiologist, and then receives within the space of a few days two letters from two different countries, each from a person called Hering; whereas one has never before had any dealings with anyone of that name. Not long ago an ingenious scientist attempted to reduce coincidences of this kind to certain laws, and so deprive them of their uncanny effect.[13] I will not venture to decide whether he has succeeded or not.

How exactly we can trace back the uncanny effect of such recurrent similarities to infantile psychology is a question I can only lightly touch upon in these pages; and I must refer the reader instead to another pamphlet,[14] now ready for publication, in which this has been gone into in detail, but in a different connection. It must be explained that we are able to postulate the principle of a *repetition-compulsion* in the unconscious mind, based upon instinctual activity and probably inherent in the very nature of the instincts – a principle powerful enough to overrule the pleasure-principle, lending to certain aspects of the mind their daemonic character, and still very clearly expressed in the tendencies of small children; a principle, too, which is responsible for a part of the course taken by the analyses of neurotic patients. Taken in all, the foregoing prepares us for the discovery that whatever reminds us of this inner *repetition-compulsion* is perceived as uncanny.

Now, however, it is time to turn from these aspects of the matter, which are in any case difficult to decide upon, and look for undeniable instances of the uncanny, in the hope that analysis of them will settle whether our hypothesis is a valid one.

In the story of 'The Ring of Polycrates', the guest turns away from his friend with horror because he sees that his every wish is at once fulfilled, his every care immediately removed by kindly fate. His host has become 'uncanny' to him. His own explanation, that the too fortunate man has to fear the envy of the gods, seems still rather obscure to us; its meaning is veiled in mythological language. We will therefore turn to another example in a less grandiose setting. In the case history of an obsessional neurotic,[15] I have described how the patient once stayed in a hydropathic establishment and benefited greatly by it. He had the good sense, however, to attribute his improvement not to the therapeutic properties of the water, but to the situation of his room, which immediately adjoined that of a very amiable nurse. So on his second visit to the establishment he asked for the same room but was told that it was already occupied by an old gentleman, whereupon he gave vent to his annoyance in the words, 'Well, I hope he'll have a stroke and die.' A fortnight later the old gentleman really did have a stroke. My patient thought this an 'uncanny' experience. And that impression of uncanniness would have been stronger still if less time had elapsed between his exclamation and the untoward event, or if he had been able to produce innumerable similar coincidences. As a matter of fact, he had no difficulty in producing coincidences of this sort, but then not only he but all obsessional neurotics I have observed are able to relate analogous experiences. They are never surprised when they invariably run up against the person they have just been thinking of, perhaps for the first time for many months. If they say one day, 'I haven't had news of so-and-so for a long time,' they will be sure to get a letter from him the next morning. And an accident or a death will rarely take place without having cast its shadow before on their minds. They are in the habit of mentioning this state of affairs in the most modest manner, saying that they have 'presentiments' which 'usually' come true.

One of the most uncanny and widespread forms of super-stition is the dread of the evil eye.[16] There never seems to have been any doubt about the source of this dread. Whoever possesses something at once valuable and fragile is afraid of the envy of others, in that he projects on to them the envy he would have felt in their place. A feeling like this betrays itself in a look even though it is not put into words; and when a man attracts the attention of others by noticeable, and particularly by unattractive, attributes, they are ready to believe that his envy is rising to more than usual heights and that this intensity in it will convert it into effective action. What is feared is thus a secret intention of harming someone, and certain signs are taken to mean that such an intention is capable of becoming an act.

These last examples of the uncanny are to be referred to that principle in the mind which I have called 'omnipotence of thoughts', taking the name from an expression used by one of my patients. And now we find ourselves on well-known ground. Our analysis of instances of the uncanny has led us back to the old, animistic conception of the universe, which was character-ized by the idea that the world was peopled with the spirits of human beings, and by the narcissistic over-estimation of sub-jective mental processes (such as the belief in the omnipotence of thoughts, the magical practices based upon this belief, the carefully proportioned distribution of magical powers or 'mana' among various outside persons and things), as well as by all those other figments of the imagination with which man, in the unrestricted narcissism of that stage of development, strove to withstand the inexorable laws of reality. It would seem as though each one of us has been through a phase of individual development corresponding to that animistic stage in primitive men, that none of us has traversed it without preserving certain traces of it which can be re-activated, and that everything which now strikes us as 'uncanny' fulfils the condition of stirring those vestiges of animistic mental activity within us and bringing them to expression.[17]

This is the place now to put forward two considerations which, I think, contain the gist of this short study. In the first place, if psycho-analytic theory is correct in maintaining that every emotional affect, whatever its quality, is transformed by repression into morbid anxiety, then among such cases of anx-iety there must be a class in which the anxiety can be shown to come from something repressed which *recurs*. This class of morbid anxiety would then be no other than what is uncanny, irrespective of whether it originally aroused dread or some other affect. In the second place, if this is indeed the secret nature of the uncanny, we can understand why the usage of speech has extended *das Heimliche* into its opposite *das Unheimliche*;[18] for this uncanny is in reality nothing new or foreign, but something familiar and old-established in the mind that has been estranged only by the process of repression. This reference to the factor of repression enables us, furthermore, to understand Schelling's definition of the uncanny as something which ought to have been kept concealed but which has nevertheless come to light.

It only remains for us to test our new hypothesis on one or two more examples of the uncanny.

Many people experience the feeling in the highest degree in relation to death and dead bodies, to the return of the dead, and to spirits and ghosts. As we have seen, many languages in use today can only render the German expression 'an *unheimliches* house' by 'a *haunted* house'. We might indeed have begun our investigation with this example, perhaps the most striking of all, of something uncanny, but we refrained from doing so because the uncanny in it is too much mingled with and in part covered by what is purely gruesome. There is scarcely any other matter, however, upon which our thoughts and feelings have changed so little since the very earliest times, and in which discarded forms have been so completely preserved under a thin disguise, as that of our relation to death. Two things account for our conservatism: the strength of our original emotional reaction to it, and the insufficiency of our scientific knowledge about it. Biology has not yet been able to decide whether death is the inevitable fate of every living being or whether it is only a regular but yet perhaps avoidable event in life. It is true that the proposition 'All men are mortal' is paraded in text-books of logic as an example of a generalization, but no human being really grasps it, and our unconscious has as little use now as ever for the idea of its own mortality. Religions continue to dispute the undeniable fact of the death of each one of us and to postulate a life after death; civil governments still believe that they cannot maintain moral order among the living if they do not uphold this prospect of a better life after death as a recompense for earthly existence. In our great cities, placards announce lectures which will tell us how to get into touch with the souls of the departed; and it cannot be denied that many of the most able and penetrating minds among our scientific men have come to the conclusion, especially towards the close of their lives, that a contact of this kind is not utterly impossible. Since practically all of us still think as savages do on this topic, it is no matter for surprise that the primitive fear of the dead is still so strong within us and always ready to come to the surface at any opportunity. Most likely our fear still contains the old belief that the deceased becomes the enemy of his survivor and wants to carry him off to share his new life with him. Considering our unchanged attitude towards death, we might rather inquire what has become of the repression, that necessary condition for enabling a primitive feeling to recur in the shape of an uncanny effect. But repression is there, too. All so-called educated people have ceased to believe, officially at any rate, that the dead can become visible as spirits, and have hedged round any such appearances with improbable and remote circumstances; their emotional attitude towards their dead, moreover, once a highly dubious and ambivalent one, has been toned down in the higher strata of the mind into a simple feeling of reverence.[19]

We have now only a few more remarks to add, for animism, magic and witchcraft, the omnipotence of thoughts, man's attitude to death, involuntary repetition and the castration-complex comprise practically all the factors which turn something fearful into an uncanny thing.

We also call a living person uncanny, usually when we ascribe evil motives to him. But that is not all; we must not only credit him with bad intentions but must attribute to these intentions capacity to achieve their aim in virtue of certain special powers. A good instance of this is the 'Gettatore', that uncanny figure of Roman superstition which Schaeffer, with intuitive poetic feeling and profound psycho-analytic knowledge, has transformed into a sympathetic figure in his *Josef Montfort*. But the question of these secret powers brings us back again to the realm of animism. It is her intuition that he possesses secret power of this kind that makes Mephistopheles so uncanny to the pious Gretchen. 'She divines that I am certainly a spirit, even the devil himself perchance.'[20]

The uncanny effect of epilepsy and of madness has the same origin. The ordinary person sees in them the workings of forces hitherto unsuspected in his fellow-man but which at the same time he is dimly aware of in a remote corner of his own being. The Middle Ages quite consistently ascribed all such maladies to daemonic influences, and in this their psychology was not so far out. Indeed, I should not be surprised to hear that psycho-analysis, which is concerned with laying bare these hidden forces, has itself become uncanny to many people for that very reason. In one case, after I had succeeded – though none too rapidly – in effecting a cure which had lasted many years in a girl who had been an invalid, the patient's own mother confessed to this attitude long after the girl's recovery.

Dismembered limbs, a severed head, a hand cut off at the wrist,[21] feet which dance by themselves[22] – all these have some-thing peculiarly uncanny about them, especially when, as in the last instance, they prove able to move of themselves in addition. As we already know, this kind of uncanniness springs from its association with the castration-complex. To many people the idea of being buried alive while appearing to be dead is the most uncanny thing of all. And yet psycho-analysis has taught us that this terrifying phantasy is only a transformation of another phantasy which had originally nothing terrifying about it at all, but was filled with a certain lustful pleasure – the phantasy, I mean, of intra-uterine existence.

*

There is one more point of general application I should like to add, though, strictly speaking, it has been included in our statements about animism and mechanisms in the mind that have been surmounted: for I think it deserves special mention. This is that an uncanny effect is often and easily produced by effacing the distinction between imagination and reality, such as when something that we have hitherto regarded as imaginary appears before us in reality, or when a symbol takes over the full functions and significance of the thing it symbolizes, and so on. It is this element which contributes not a little to the uncanny effect attaching to magical practices. The infantile element in this, which also holds sway in the minds of neurotics, is the over-accentuation of psychical reality in comparison with physical reality – a feature closely allied to the belief in the omnipotence of thoughts. In the midst of the isolation of war-time a number of the English *Strand Magazine* fell into my hands; and, amongst other not very interesting matter, I read a story about a young married couple, who move into a furnished flat in which there is a curiously shaped table with carvings of crocodiles on it. Towards evening they begin to smell an intolerable and very typical odour that pervades the whole flat; things begin to get in their way and trip them up in the darkness; they seem to see a vague form gliding up the stairs – in short, we are given to understand that the presence of the table causes ghostly crocodiles to haunt the place, or that the wooden monsters come to life in the dark, or something of that sort. It was a thoroughly silly story, but the uncanny feeling it produced was quite remarkable.

To conclude this collection of examples, which is certainly not complete, I will relate an instance taken from psycho-analytical experience; if it does not rest upon mere coincidence, it furnishes a beautiful confirmation of our theory of the uncanny. It often happens that male patients declare that they feel there is something uncanny about the female genital organs. This *unheimlich* place, however, is the entrance to the former *heim* [home] of all human beings, to the place where everyone dwelt once upon a time and in the beginning. There is a humorous saying: 'Love is home-sickness'; and whenever a man dreams of a place or a country and says to himself, still in the dream, 'This place is familiar to me, I have been there before,' we may interpret the place as being his mother's genitals or her body. In this case, too, the *unheimlich* is what was once *heimisch*, home-like, familiar; the prefix 'un' is the token of repression.

III

Having followed the discussion as far as this the reader will have felt certain doubts arising in his mind about much that has been said; and he must now have an opportunity of collecting them and bringing them forward.

It may be true that the uncanny is nothing else than a hidden, familiar thing that has undergone repression and then emerged from it, and that everything that is uncanny fulfils this condition. But these factors do not solve the problem of the uncanny. For our proposition is clearly not convertible. Not everything that fulfils this condition — not everything that is connected with repressed desires and archaic forms of thought belonging to the past of the individual and of the race — is therefore uncanny.

Nor would we, moreover, conceal the fact that for almost every example adduced in support of our hypothesis some other analogous one may be found which rebuts it. The story of the severed hand in Hauff's fairy-tale certainly has an uncanny effect, and we have derived that effect from the castration-complex. But in the story in Herodotus of the treasure of Rhampsenitus, where the master-thief leaves his brother's severed hand behind him in that of the princess who wants to hold him fast, most readers will agree with me that the episode has no trace of uncanniness. Again, the instant fulfilment of the king's wishes in 'The Ring of Polycrates' undoubtedly does affect us in the same uncanny way as it did the king of Egypt. Yet our own fairy-tales are crammed with instantaneous wish-fulfilments which produce no uncanny effect whatever. In the story of 'The Three Wishes', the woman is tempted by the savoury smell of a sausage to wish that she might have one too, and immediately it lies on a plate before her. In his annoyance at her forwardness her husband wishes it may hang on her nose. And there it is, dangling from her nose. All this is very vivid but not in the least uncanny. Fairy-tales quite frankly adopt the animistic standpoint of the omnipotence of thoughts and wishes, and yet I cannot think of any genuine fairy-story which has anything uncanny about it. We have heard that it is in the highest degree uncanny when inanimate objects – a picture or a doll – come to life; nevertheless in Hans Andersen's stories the household utensils, furniture and tin soldiers are alive, and nothing could perhaps be more remote from the uncanny. And we should hardly call it uncanny when Pygmalion's beautiful statue comes to life.

Catalepsy and the re-animation of the dead have been represented as most uncanny themes. But things of this sort again are very common in fairy-stories. Who would be so bold as to call it an uncanny moment, for instance, when Snow White opens her eyes once more? And the resuscitation of the dead in miracles, as in the New Testament, elicits feelings quite unrelated to the uncanny. Then the theme that achieves such an indubitably uncanny effect, the involuntary recurrence of the like, serves, too, other and quite different purposes in another class of cases. One case we have already heard about in which it is employed to call forth a feeling of the comic; and we could multiply instances of this kind. Or again, it works as a means of emphasis, and so on. Another consideration is this: whence come the uncanny influences of silence, darkness and solitude? Do not these factors point to the part played by danger in the aetiology of what is uncanny, notwithstanding that they are also the most frequent accompaniment of the expression of fear in infancy? And are we in truth justified in entirely ignoring intellectual uncertainty as a factor, seeing that we have admitted its importance in relation to death?

It is evident that we must be prepared to admit that there are other elements besides those set down here determining the production of uncanny feelings. We might say that these preliminary results have satisfied psycho-analytic interest in the problem of the uncanny, and that what remains probably calls for an aesthetic valuation. But that would be to open the door to doubts about the exact value of our general contention that the uncanny proceeds from something familiar which has been repressed.

One thing we may observe which may help us to resolve these uncertainties: nearly all the instances which contradict our hypothesis are taken from the realm of fiction and literary productions. This may suggest a possible differentiation between the uncanny that is actually experienced, and the uncanny as we merely picture it or read about it.

Something uncanny in *real experience* is conditioned much more simply, but is limited to much fewer occasions. We shall find, I think, that it fits in perfectly with our attempt at solution, and can be traced back without exception to something familiar that has been repressed. But here, too, we must make a certain important and psychologically significant differentiation in our material, best illustrated by turning to suitable examples.

Let us take the uncanny in connection with the omnipotence

of thoughts, instantaneous wish-fulfilments, secret power to do harm and the return of the dead. The condition under which the feeling of uncanniness arises here is unmistakable. We – or our primitive forefathers – once believed in the possibility of these things and were convinced that they really happened. Nowadays we no longer believe in them, we have *surmounted* such ways of thought; but we do not feel quite sure of our new set of beliefs, and the old ones still exist within us ready to seize upon any confirmation. As soon as something actually happens in our lives which seems to support the old, discarded beliefs, we get a feeling of the uncanny; and it is as though we were making a judgement something like this: 'So, after all, it is true that one can kill a person by merely desiring his death!' or, 'Then the dead do continue to live and appear before our eyes on the scene of their former activities!', and so on. And conversely, he who has completely and finally dispelled animistic beliefs in himself, will be insensible to this type of the uncanny. The most remarkable coincidences of desire and fulfilment, the most mysterious recurrence of similar experiences in a particular place or on a particular date, the most deceptive sights and suspicious noises – none of these things will take him in or raise that kind of fear which can be described as 'a fear of something uncanny'. For the whole matter is one of 'testing reality', pure and simple, a question of the material reality of the phenomena.[23]

The state of affairs is somewhat different when the uncanny proceeds from repressed infantile complexes, from the castration-complex, womb-phantasies, etc.; but experiences which arouse this kind of uncanny feeling are not of very frequent occurrence in real life. Actual occurrences of the uncanny belong for the most part to the first group; nevertheless the distinction between the two is theoretically very important. Where the uncanny comes from infantile complexes, the question of external reality is quite irrelevant; its place is taken by psychical reality. What is concerned is an actual repression of some definite material and a return of this repressed material, not a removal of the *belief* in its objective reality. We might say that in the one case what had been repressed was a particular ideational content, and in the other the belief in its physical existence. But this last way of putting it no doubt strains the term 'repression' beyond its legitimate meaning. It would be more correct to respect a perceptible psychological difference here, and to say that the animistic beliefs of civilized people have been *surmounted* – more or less. Our conclusion could then be stated thus: An uncanny experience occurs either when repressed infantile complexes have been revived by some impression, or when the primitive beliefs we have surmounted seem once more to be confirmed. Finally, we must not let our predilection for smooth solution and lucid exposition blind us to the fact that these two classes of uncanny experience are not always sharply distinguishable. When we consider that primitive beliefs are most intimately connected with infantile complexes, and are, in fact, based upon them, we shall not be greatly astonished to find the distinction often rather a hazy one.

The uncanny as it is depicted in *literature*, in stories and imaginative productions, merits in truth a separate discussion. To begin with, it is a much more fertile province than the uncanny in real life, for it contains the whole of the latter and something more besides, something that cannot be found in real life. The distinction between what has been repressed and what has been surmounted cannot be transposed on to the uncanny in fiction without profound modification; for the realm of phantasy depends for its very existence on the fact that its content is not submitted to the reality-testing faculty. The somewhat paradoxical result is that *in the first place a great deal that is not uncanny in fiction would be so if it happened in real life; and in the second place that there are many more means of creating uncanny effects in fiction than there are in real life.*

The story-teller has this licence among many others, that he can select his world of representation so that it either coincides with the realities we are familiar with or departs from them in what particulars he pleases. We accept his ruling in every case. In fairy-tales, for instance, the world of reality is left behind from the very start, and the animistic system of beliefs is frankly adopted. Wish-fulfilments, secret powers, omnipotence of thoughts, animation of lifeless objects, all the elements so common in fairy-stories, can exert no uncanny influence here; for, as we have learnt, that feeling cannot arise unless there is a conflict of judgement whether things which have been 'surmounted' and are regarded as incredible are not, after all, possible; and this problem is excluded from the beginning by the setting of the story. And thus we see that such stories as have furnished us with most of the contradictions to our hypothesis of the uncanny confirm the first part of our proposition – that in the realm of fiction many things are not uncanny which would be so if they happened in real life. In the case of the fairy-story there are other contributory factors, which we shall briefly touch upon later.

The story-teller can also choose a setting which, though less imaginary than the world of fairy-tales, does yet differ from the real world by admitting superior spiritual entities such as daemonic influences or departed spirits. So long as they remain within their setting of poetic reality, their usual attribute of uncanniness fails to attach to such beings. The souls in Dante's *Inferno*, or the ghostly apparitions in *Hamlet*, *Macbeth* or *Julius Caesar*, may be gloomy and terrible enough, but they are no more really uncanny than is Homer's jovial world of gods. We order our judgement to the imaginary reality imposed on us by the writer, and regard souls, spirits and spectres as though their existence had the same validity in their world as our own has in the external world. And then in this case too we are spared all trace of the uncanny.

The situation is altered as soon as the writer pretends to move in the world of common reality. In this case he accepts all the conditions operating to produce uncanny feelings in real life; and everything that would have an uncanny effect in reality has it in his story. But in this case, too, he can increase his effect and multiply it far beyond what could happen in reality, by bringing about events which never or very rarely happen in fact. He takes advantage, as it were, of our supposedly surmounted superstitiousness; he deceives us into thinking that he is giving us the sober truth, and then after all oversteps the bounds of possibility. We react to his inventions as we should have reacted to real experiences; by the time we have seen through his trick it is already too late and the author has achieved his object; but it must be added that his success is not unalloyed. We retain a feeling of dissatisfaction, a kind of grudge against the attempted deceit; I have noticed this particularly after reading Schnitzler's *Die Weissagung* and similar stories which flirt with the supernatural. The writer has then one more means he can use to escape our rising vexation and at the same time to improve his chances of success. It is this: that he should keep us in the dark for a long time about the precise nature of the conditions he has selected for the world he writes about, or that he should cunningly and ingeniously avoid any definite information on the point at all throughout the book. Speaking generally, however, we find a confirmation of the second part of our proposition – that fiction presents more opportunities for creating uncanny sensations than are possible in real life.

Strictly speaking, all these complications relate only to that class of the uncanny which proceeds from forms of thought that have been surmounted. The class which proceeds from repressed complexes is more irrefragable and remains as powerful in fiction as in real experience, except in one point. The uncanny belonging to the first class – that proceeding from forms of thought that have been surmounted – retains this quality in fiction as in experience so long as the setting is one of physical reality; but as soon as it is given an arbitrary and unrealistic setting in fiction, it is apt to lose its quality of the uncanny.

It is clear that we have not exhausted the possibilities of poetic licence and the privileges enjoyed by story-writers in evoking or in excluding an uncanny feeling. In the main we adopt an unvarying passive attitude towards experience and are acted upon by our physical environment. But the story-teller has a peculiarly directive influence over us; by means of the states of mind into which he can put us and the expectations he can rouse in us, he is able to guide the current of our emotions, dam it up in one direction and make it flow in another, and he often obtains a great variety of effects from the same material. All this is nothing new, and has doubtless long since been fully taken into account by professors of aesthetics. We have drifted into this field of research half involuntarily, through the temptation to explain certain instances which contradicted our theory of the causes of the uncanny. And accordingly we will now return to the examination of a few instances.

We have already asked why it is that the severed hand in the story of the treasure of Rhampsenitus has no uncanny effect in the way that Hauff's story of the severed hand has. The question seems to us to have gained in importance now that we have recognized that class of the uncanny which proceeds from repressed complexes to be the more durable of the two. The answer is easy.

In the Herodotus story our thoughts are concentrated much more on the superior cunning of the master-thief than on the feelings of the princess. The princess may well have had an uncanny feeling, indeed she very probably fell into a swoon; but we have no such sensations, for we put ourselves in the thief's place, not in hers. In Nestroy's farce, *Der Zerrissene*, another means is used to avoid any impression of the uncanny in the scene in which the fleeing man, convinced that he is a murderer, lifts up one trap-door after another and each time sees what he takes to be the ghost of his victim rising up out of it. He calls out in despair, 'But I've only killed *one* man. Why this horrid multiplication?' We know the truth and do not share the error of the *Zerrissener*, so what must be uncanny to him has an irresistibly comic effect on us. Even a 'real' ghost, as in Oscar Wilde's *Canterville Ghost*, loses all power of arousing at any rate an uncanny horror in us as soon as the author begins to amuse himself at its expense and allows liberties to be taken with it. Thus we see how independent emotional effects can be of the actual subject-matter in the world of fiction. In fairy-stories feelings of fear – including uncanny sensations – are ruled out altogether. We understand this, and that is why we ignore the opportunities we find there for any development of a feeling of this kind.

Concerning the factors of silence, solitude and darkness, we can only say that they are actually elements in the production of that infantile morbid anxiety from which the majority of human beings have never become quite free. This problem has been discussed from a psycho-analytical point of view in another place.

Endnotes

Preface

1. James Strachey, 'Joan Riviere', *International Journal of Psychoanalysis* 44 (1963), 263–5 (p. 263).
2. Ibid.
3. Freud to Jones, *The Complete Correspondence of Sigmund Freud and Ernest Jones, 1908–1939*, ed. R. Andrew Paskauskas (Cambridge, Mass., and London: Harvard University Press, 1993), 21 January 1922.
4. Freud to Jones, ibid., 1 April 1922.
5. Freud to Jones, ibid., 4 June 1922.
6. Joan Riviere, *The Inner World and Joan Riviere: Collected Papers 1920–1958*, ed. Athol Hughes, quoted in Lisa Appignanesi and John Forrester, *Freud's Women* (Phoenix, 2005), pp. 383–4.
7. 'A Last Word about Freud', in *Collected Papers*, p. 351.

The following abbreviations are used in the notes:

Collected Papers: Sigmund Freud, *Collected Papers*, 5 vols (The Hogarth Press and the Institute of Psycho-Analysis, 1925–50)

Jahrbuch: *Jahrbuch für psychoanalytische und psychopathologische Forschungen* (Vienna)

Sammlung: Sigmund Frued, *Sammlung kleiner Schriften zur Nueurosenlehre* (Vienna)

Zeitschrift: *Internationale Zeitschrift für ärztliche Psychoanalyse* (later *Internationale Zeitschrift für Psychoanalyse*) (Vienna)

Zentralblatt: *Zentralblatt für Psychoanalyse* (Vienna)

The Aetiology of Hysteria

1. First published in the *Wiener klinische Rundschau* (1896), Nos. 22–26. Amplification of a lecture delivered at the Society of Psychiatry and Neurology in Vienna, 2 May 1896. [Translated by Cecil M. Baines.]

2. We purposely refrain from discussing what type of association unites the two memories (whether their relation is temporal, causal or that of similarity of content, etc.) and from asking what psychological character (conscious or unconscious) is to be attributed to these 'memories'.

3. *Wiener Medizinische Blätter* (18 April 1896).

The Sexual Enlightenment of Children

1. First published in *Soziale Medizin und Hygiene*, vol. 2 (1907); reprinted in *Sammlung*, second series. [Translated by E. B. M. Herford.]

2. Multatuli, *Briefe* (1906), vol. 1, p. 26.

3. Emma Eckstein, *Die Sexualfrage in der Erziehung des Kindes* (1904).

4. [The original has also: *am Schlusse des Volksschulunterrichtes und vor Eintritt in die Mittelschule.* –Trans.]

A Case of Paranoia Running Counter to the Psycho-Analytical Theory of Disease

1. First published in *Zeitschrift*, vol. 3 (1915); reprinted in *Sammlung*, fourth series. [Translated by Edward Glover.]

The Psychogenesis of a Case of Homosexuality in a Woman

1. First published in *Zeitschrift*, vol. 6 (1920); reprinted in *Sammlung*, fifth series. [Translated by Barbara Low and R. Gabler.]
2. I do not see any progress or advantage in the introduction of the term 'Electra-complex', and do not advocate its use.
3. Cf. J. Sadger, 'Jahresbericht über sexuelle Perversionen', *Jahrbuch*, vol. 6 (1914).
4. It is by no means rare for a love-relation to be broken off by means of a process of identification on the part of the lover with the loved object, a process equivalent to a kind of regression to narcissism. After this has been accomplished, it is easy in making a fresh choice of object to direct the libido to a member of the sex opposite to that of the earlier choice.
5. The displacements of the libido here described are doubtless familiar to every analyst from investigation of the anamneses of neurotics. With the latter, however, they occur in early childhood, at the beginning of the love-life; with our patient, who was in no way neurotic, they took place in the first years following puberty, though, by the way, they were just as completely unconscious. Perhaps one day this temporal factor may turn out to be of great importance.
6. As 'retiring in favour of someone else' has not previously been mentioned among the causes of homosexuality, or in the mechanism of libido-fixation in general, I will adduce here another analytical

observation of the same kind which has a special feature of interest. I once knew two twin brothers, both of whom were endowed with strong libidinal impulses. One of them was very successful with women, and had innumerable affairs with women and girls. The other went the same way at first, but it became unpleasant for him to be trespassing on his brother's beat, and, owing to the likeness between them, to be mistaken for him on intimate occasions, so he got out of the difficulty by becoming homosexual. He left the women to his brother, and thus 'retired' in his favour. Another time I treated a young man, an artist, unmistakably bisexual in disposition, in whom the homosexual trend had come to the fore simultaneously with a disturbance in his work. He fled from both women and work together. The analysis, which was able to bring him back to both, showed that the fear of the father was the most powerful psychic motive for both the disturbances, which were really renunciations. In his imagination all women belonged to the father, and he sought refuge in men out of submission, so as to 'retire from' the conflict in favour of the father. Such a motivation of the homosexual object-choice must be by no means uncommon; in the primeval ages of the human race all women presumably belonged to the father and head of the primal horde.

Among brothers and sisters who are not twins this 'retirement' plays a great part in other spheres as well as in that of the love-choice. For example, an elder brother studies music and is admired for it; the younger, far more gifted musically, soon gives up his own musical studies, in spite of his longing, and cannot be persuaded to touch an instrument again. This is one example of a very frequent occurrence, and investigation of the motives leading to this 'retirement' rather than to open rivalry discloses very complicated conditions in the mind.

7. Collected Papers, vol. 4.
8. [In the text there is a play on the word *niederkommen*, which means both 'to fall' and 'to be delivered of a child'. There is also in English

442

a colloquial use of the verb 'to fall', meaning pregnancy or childbirth. – Trans.]

9. That the various means of suicide can represent sexual wish-fulfilments has long been known to all analysts. (To poison oneself = to become pregnant; to drown = to bear a child; to throw oneself from a height = to be delivered of a child.)

10. Cf. 'Reflections upon War and Death', Collected Papers, vol. 4.

11. [A reference to the European War, 1914–18. – Trans.]

12. [I.e. believed on condition that it is regarded as not certain. – Trans.]

13. Cf. Kriemhilde's confession in the *Nibelungenlied*.

14. Cf. A. Lipschütz, *Die Pubertätsdrüse und ihre Wirkungen* (Berne, 1919).

The Economic Problem in Masochism

1. First published in *Zeitschrift*, vol. 10 (1924). [Translated by Joan Riviere.]

2. [*Unlust*, usually translated by 'pain'. – Trans.]

3. Freud, *Beyond the Pleasure-Principle* (London, 1922).

4. {See 'The Infantile Genital Organization of the Libido' (1923), in Collected Papers, vol. 2.}

5. *Das Ich und das Es* (Vienna, 1923).

6. Ibid.

7. Freud, *Totem und Tabu* (Vienna, 1913), Part Four.

8. Ed. Douwes Dekker (1820–1887).

Observations on 'Wild' Psycho-Analysis

1. First published in *Zentralblatt*, vol. 1 (1910); reprinted in *Sammlung*, fourth series. [Translated by Joan Riviere.]

The Dynamics of the Transference

1. First published in *Zentralblatt*, vol. 2 (1912); reprinted in *Sammlung*, fourth series. [Translated by Joan Riviere.]

2. *Zentralblatt*, vol. 2, No. 2, p. 26.

3. We will here provide against misconceptions and reproaches to the effect that we have denied the importance of the inborn (constitutional) factor because we have emphasized the importance of infantile impressions. Such an accusation arises out of the narrowness with which mankind looks for causes, inasmuch as one single causal factor satisfies him, in spite of the many commonly underlying the face of reality. Psycho-Analysis has said much about the 'accidental' component in aetiology and little about the constitutional, but only because it could throw new light upon the former, whereas of the latter it knows no more so far than is already known. We deprecate the assumption of an essential opposition between the two series of aetiological factors; we presume rather a perpetual interchange of both in producing the results observed, δαίμων καί τύχη determine the fate of man; seldom, perhaps never, one of these powers alone. The relative aetiological effectiveness of each is only to be measured individually and in single instances. In a series comprising varying degrees of both factors extreme cases will certainly also be found. According to the knowledge we possess we shall estimate the parts played by the forces of heredity and of environment differently in each case, and retain the right to modify our opinion in consequence of new knowledge. Further, we may venture to regard the constitution itself as a residue from the effects of accidental influences upon the endless procession of our forefathers.

4. 'Symbole und Wandlungen der Libido', *Jahrbuch*, vol. 3 (1911).

5. I mean here, when really nothing comes to his mind, and not when he keeps silence on account of some slight disagreeable feeling.

6. *Aus guter Familie* (1895).

7. Although many of Jung's utterances give the impression that he sees introversion as something characteristic of dementia praecox and not observable to the same extent in the other neuroses.

8. It would be easy to say: the libido has re-invested the infantile 'complexes'. But this would be erroneous; it would be correct only if expressed thus: 'the unconscious part of these complexes'. The exceptional intricacy of the theme dealt with in this essay tempts one to discuss further a number of adjunct problems, which require elucidation before one can speak definitely enough about the psychical processes here described. Such problems are: the definition of the boundary between introversion and regression; the incorporation of the complex-doctrine into the libido-theory; the relationship of phantasy-creation to the conscious, the unconscious, and to reality; etc. I need not apologize for having resisted these temptations here.

9. From which, however, one need not infer in general any very particular pathogenic importance in the point selected for resistance by transference. In warfare, when a bitter fight is raging over the possession of some little chapel or a single farmhouse, we do not necessarily assume that the church is a national monument, or that the barns contain the military funds. Their value may be merely tactical; in the next onslaught they will very likely be of no importance.

10. Ferenczi, 'Introjection and Transference', (1909). First published in German, *Zeitschrift*, vol. 1 (1913).

11. E. Bleuler, 'Dementia Praecox oder Gruppe der Schizophrenien', in Aschaffenburg's *Handbuch der Psychiatrie* (1911); also 'A Lecture on Ambivalence in Berne' (1910), abstracted in *Zentralblatt*, vol. 1., p. 266. W. Stekel had previously suggested the term *bipolarity* for the same phenomenon.

On Beginning the Treatment

1. First published in *Zeitschrift*, vol. 1 (1913); reprinted in *Sammlung*, fourth series. [Translated by Joan Riviere.]

2. 'On Psychotherapy', Collected Papers, vol. 1.

3. There is much to be said on the subject of this uncertainty in diagnosis, on the prospects of analysis in the milder forms of paraphrenia, and on the explanation of the similarity between the two diseases, which I cannot bring forward in this connection. I should be willing to contrast hysteria and the obsessional neurosis, under the name of 'transference neuroses', with the paraphrenic group, under the name of 'introversion neuroses', in accordance with Jung's formula, if the term 'introversion' (of the libido) were not alienated by such usage from its only legitimate meaning.

4. Much might be said about our experience with the fundamental rule of psycho-analysis. One meets occasionally with people who behave as if they had instituted this rule for themselves; others offend against it from the beginning. It is indispensable, and also advantageous, to mention it at the first stage of the treatment; later, under the influence of resistances, obedience to it weakens and there comes a time in every analysis when the patient disregards it. One must remember how irresistible was the temptation in one's self-analysis to yield to those cavilling pretexts for rejecting certain thoughts. The feeble effect of the patient's agreement to the bargain made with him about the 'fundamental rule' is regularly demonstrated when something of an intimate nature about a third person rises to his mind for the first time; the patient knows that he must say everything, but he makes a new obstacle out of the discretion required on behalf of others. 'Must I really say everything? I thought that only applied to what concerns myself.' It is naturally impossible to carry out an analysis if the patient's relations with other people and his thoughts about them are

excluded. *Pour faire une omelette il faut casser des œufs.* An honourable man readily forgets such of the private affairs of strangers as do not seem important for him to know. Names, too, cannot be excepted from communication; otherwise the patient's narratives become rather shadowy, like the scenes of Goethe's *Natural Daughter*, and do not remain in the physician's memory; moreover, the names withheld cover the approach to all kinds of important connections. One may perhaps leave names until the patient has become more familiar with the physician and the process of analysis. It is a most remarkable thing that the whole undertaking becomes lost labour if a single concession is made to secrecy. If at any one spot in a town the right of sanctuary existed, one can well imagine that it would not be long before all the riff-raff of the town would gather there. I once treated a high official who was bound by oath not to communicate certain State secrets, and the analysis came to grief as a consequence of this restriction. The psycho-analytic treatment must override everything which comes in its way, because the neurosis and the resistances are equally relentless.

5. Exceptions may be made only of such data as the family relationships, visits, operations, and so on.

Recollection, Repetition, and Working Through

1. First published in *Zeitschrift*, vol. 2 (1914); reprinted in *Sammlung*, fourth series. [Translated by Joan Riviere.]
2. [Cf. Freud, 'From the History of an Infantile Neurosis', Collected Papers, vol. 3. – Trans.]

Observations on Transference-Love

1. First published in *Zeitschrift*, vol. 3 (1915); reprinted in *Sammlung*, fourth series. [Translated by Joan Riviere.]
2. 'On the History of the Psycho-Analytic Movement' (1914), Collected Papers, vol. 1.
3. We know that the transference can express itself by other less tender feelings, but I do not propose to go into that side of the matter here.
4. Cf. pp. 149 and 185 *et seq.*

Formulations regarding the Two Principles in Mental Functioning

1. First published in *Jahrbuch*, vol. 3 (1911); reprinted in *Sammlung*, third series. [Translated by M. N. Searl.]
2. Pierre Janet, *Les Névroses* (1909).
3. A remarkably clear presentiment of this causation has recently been pointed out by Otto Rank in Schopenhauer's *The World as Will and Idea* (*Zentralblatt*, 1910).
4. The General Section of *Die Traumdeutung*.
5. The state of sleep can recover the likeness of mental life as it was before the recognition of reality, because a prerequisite of sleep is a deliberate rejection of reality (the wish to sleep).
6. I will attempt to amplify the above schematic presentation with some further details. It will rightly be objected that an organization which is a slave to the pleasure-principle and neglects the reality of the outer world could not maintain itself alive for the shortest time, so that it could not have come into being at all. The use of a fiction of this kind is, however, vindicated by the consideration that the infant,

if one only includes the maternal care, does almost realize such a state of mental life. Probably it hallucinates the fulfilment of its inner needs; it betrays its 'pain' due to increase of stimulation and delay of satisfaction by the motor discharge of crying and struggling and then experiences the hallucinated satisfaction. Later, as a child, it learns to employ intentionally these modes of discharge as means of expression. Since the care of the infant is the prototype of the later care of the child, the supremacy of the pleasure-principle can end in actuality only with complete mental detachment from the parents. A beautiful example of a state of mental life shut off from the stimuli of the outer world, and able to satisfy even its nutritional requirements autistically (to use Bleuler's word), is given by the bird inside the egg together with its food supply; for it, maternal care is limited to the provision of warmth. I shall not look upon it as a correction, but as an amplification of the scheme in question, if anyone demands by what devices the system living according to the pleasure-principle can withdraw itself from the stimuli of reality. These contrivances are only the correlate of 'repression', which treats inner 'painful' stimuli as if they were outer, i.e. reckons them as belonging to the outer world.

7. Just as a nation whose wealth rests on the exploitation of its land yet reserves certain territory to be preserved in its original state and protected from cultural alterations, e.g. Yellowstone Park.

8. The superiority of the reality-ego over the pleasure-ego is aptly expressed by Bernard Shaw in these words: 'To be able to choose the line of greatest advantage instead of yielding in the direction of least resistance' (*Man and Superman: A Comedy and a Philosophy*).

9. Cf. the similar position taken by Otto Rank in *Der Künstler* (Vienna, 1907).

449

On Narcissism: An Introduction

1. First published in *Jahrbuch*, vol. 6 (1914); reprinted in *Sammlung*, fourth series. [Translated by Cecil M. Baines.]

2. [In a later paper Professor Freud has corrected this slip and added the name of Havelock Ellis. – Ed.]

3. Otto Rank, 'Ein Beitrag zum Narzissmus', *Jahrbuch*, vol. 3 (1911).

4. Compare with these propositions my discussion of the 'end of the world' in the analysis of Senatspräsident Schreber, Collected Papers, vol. 3, No. 4. Also Karl Abraham, 'Die psychosexuellen Differenzen der Hysterie und der Dementia Praecox', *Zentralblatt für Nervenheilkunde und Psychiatrie* (1908).

5. Cf. the corresponding sections on this subject in my *Totem und Tabu* (1913).

6. Cf. Ferenczi, 'Stages in the Development of the Sense of Reality' (1913), *Contributions to Psycho-Analysis*, trans. Ernest Jones (Boston, 1916).

7. There are two mechanisms in this 'end of the world' idea: in one case, the whole libidinal cathexis is drained off to the loved object, while, in the other, it all flows back to the ego.

8. 'Wandlungen und Symbole der Libido', *Jahrbuch*, vol. 4 (1912).

9. *Zeitschrift*, vol. 1 (1913).

10. 'Versuch einer Darstellung der psychoanalytischen Theorie', *Jahrbuch*, vol. 5 (1913).

11. Cf. 'Types of Neurotic Nosogenesis', Collected Papers, vol. 2.

12. 'Disease at bottom brought about / Creative urgence – for, creating, / I soon could feel the pain abating, / Creating, I could work it out.'

13. [*Anlehnungstypus*. Literally, 'leaning-up-against'-type. In the first phase of their development the sexual instincts find their satisfaction through propping themselves upon or 'leaning up against' the self-preservative instincts. – Ed.]

14. I should like to add, merely by way of suggestion, that the process of development and strengthening of this watching institution might contain within it the genesis later on of (subjective) memory and of the time-factor, the latter of which has no application to unconscious processes.

15. I cannot here determine whether the differentiation of the censorial function from the rest of the ego is capable of forming the basis of the philosophic distinction between consciousness and self-consciousness.

Instincts and their Vicissitudes

1. First published in *Zeitschrift*, vol. 3 (1915); reprinted in *Sammlung*, fourth series. [Translated by Cecil M. Baines.]

2. Assuming, of course, that these internal processes constitute the organic basis of the needs described as thirst and hunger.

3. *Additional Note*, 1924. In later works (cf. 'The Economic Problem in Masochism', 1924) relating to problems of instinctual life, I have expressed the opposite view. {See above, p. 109.}

4. See the previous note.

5. *Zeitschrift*, vol. 1 (1913).

6. Some of the sexual instincts are, as we know, capable of this auto-erotic satisfaction and so are adapted to be the channel for that development under the sway of the pleasure-principle which we shall describe later. The sexual instincts which from the outset require an object and the needs of the ego-instincts, which are never capable of auto-erotic satisfaction, interfere, of course, with this condition and prepare the way for progress. More, the primal narcissistic condition would not have been able to attain such a development were it not that every individual goes through a period of helplessness and dependence on fostering care, during which his urgent needs are satisfied by agencies outside himself and thereby withheld from developing along their own line.

Repression

1. First published in *Zeitschrift*, vol. 3 (1915); reprinted in *Sammlung*, fourth series. [Translated by Cecil M. Baines.]
2. This metaphor, applicable to the process of repression, may also be extended to include one of the characteristics of repression mentioned earlier. I need only add that I have to place a sentinel to keep constant guard over the door which I have forbidden this guest to pass, lest he should burst it open (see above).

Mourning and Melancholia

1. First published in *Zeitschrift*, vol. 4 (1916–18); reprinted in *Sammlung*, fourth series. [Translated by Joan Riviere.]
2. Abraham, to whom we owe the most important of the few analytic studies on this subject, also took this comparison as his starting-point. (*Zentralblatt*, vol. 2, 1912.)
3. [The words 'painful' and 'pain' in this paragraph represent the German *Schmerz* (i.e. the ordinary connotation of *pain* in English) and not *Unlust*, the mental antithesis of pleasure, also technically translated 'pain'. – Trans.]
4. {Cf. 'Metaphychological Supplement to the Theory of Dreams', in Collected Papers, vol. 4.}
5. [Cf. note 3 above. The German here is *Schmerzunlust*, a combination of the two words for *pain*. –Trans.]
6. 'Use every man after his desert, and who should 'scape whipping?' (Act II, Scene 2).
7. *Zeitschrift*, vol. 2 (1914).
8. For the distinction between the two, see the paper entitled 'Instincts and their Vicissitudes', p. 289 above.

9. Cf. 'Instincts and their Vicissitudes', p. 284 above.

10. The economic point of view has up till now received little attention in psycho-analytic researches. I would mention as an exception a paper by Viktor Tausk, 'Compensation as a Means of Discounting the Motive of Repression', *International Journal of Psycho-Analysis*, vol. 5 (*Zeitschrift*, vol. 1, 1913).

11. [*Schmerz*.]

12. *Additional Note*, 1924. Cf. the continued discussion of this problem in *Group Psychology and the Analysis of the Ego* (London, 1922).

The Most Prevalent Form of Degradation in Erotic Life

1. First published in *Jahrbuch*, vol. 4 (1912); reprinted in *Sammlung*, fourth series. [Translated by Joan Riviere.]

2. M. Steiner, *Die funktionelle Impotenz des Mannes und ihre Behandlung* (1907); W. Stekel, in *Nervöse Angstzustände und ihre Behandlung* (1908); Ferenczi, 'The Analytic Interpretation and Treatment of Psychosexual Impotence' (1908), *Contributions to Psycho-Analysis*, trans. Ernest Jones (Boston, 1916).

3. W. Stekel, *loc. cit.*, p. 191 *et seq.*

4. {'A Special Type of Choice of Object Made by Men' (1910), in Collected Papers, vol. 4, p. 199.}

5. At the same time I willingly admit that the frigidity of women is a complicated subject which can also be approached from another angle.

6. G. Floerke, *Zehn Jahre mit Böcklin* (2nd ed., 1902), p. 16.

Some Character-Types Met with in Psycho-Analytic Work

1. First published in *Imago*, vol. 4 (1915–16); reprinted in *Sammlung*, fourth series. [Translated by E. Colburn Mayne.]

2. Cf. *Macbeth*, Act III, Scene I: 'Upon my head they plac'd a fruitless crown, / And put a barren sceptre in my gripe, / Thence to be wrench'd with an unlineal hand, / No son of mine succeeding . . .'

3. J. Darmstetter, *Macbeth* (Édition classique: Paris, 1887), p. lxxv.

4. As in Richard III's wooing of Anne beside the bier of the King whom he has murdered.

5. Cf. Darmstetter, *loc. cit.*

6. An exposition of the incest-theme in *Rosmersholm* has already been made, by similar methods to my own, in the extremely comprehensive work by Otto Rank, *Das Inzest-Motiv in Dichtung und Sage* (Vienna, 1912).

One of the Difficulties of Psycho-Analysis

1. First published (in Hungarian) in the *Nyugat* (1917), and subsequently in *Imago*, vol. 5 (1917); reprinted in *Sammlung*, fourth series. [Translated by Joan Riviere.]

The 'Uncanny'

1. First published in *Imago*, vol. 5 (1919); reprinted in *Sammlung*, fifth series. [Translated by Alix Strachey.]

2. 'Zur Psychologie des Unheimlichen', *Psychiatrisch-neurologische Wochenschrift*, Nos. 22 and 23 (1906).

3. [An allusion to the European War only just concluded.—Trans.]

4. [Throughout this paper 'uncanny' is used as the English translation of '*unheimlich*', literally 'unhomely'. – Trans.]

5. From *Haus* = house; *Häuslichkeit* = domestic life. –Trans.]

6. Hoffmann's *Sämtliche Werke*, Grisebach edition, vol. 3.

7. Frau Dr Rank has pointed out the association of the name with 'Coppella' = crucible, connecting it with the chemical operations that caused the father's death; and also with 'coppo' = eye-socket.

8. In fact, Hoffmann's imaginative treatment of his material has not played such havoc with its elements that we cannot reconstruct their original arrangement. In the story from Nathaniel's childhood, the figures of his father and Coppelius represent the two opposites into which the father-imago is split by the ambivalence of the child's feeling; whereas the one threatens to blind him, that is, to castrate him, the other, the loving father, intercedes for his sight. That part of the complex which is most strongly repressed, the death-wish against the father, finds expression in the death of the good father, and Coppelius is made answerable for it. Later, in his student days, Professor Spalanzani and Coppola the optician reproduce this double representation of the father-imago: the Professor is a member of the father-series, Coppola openly identified with the lawyer Coppelius. Just as before they used to work together over the fire, so now they have jointly created the doll Olympia: the Professor is even called the father of Olympia. This second occurrence of work in common shows that the optician and the mechanician are also components of the father-imago, that is, both are Nathaniel's father as well as Olympia's. I ought to have added that in the terrifying scene in childhood, Coppelius, after sparing Nathaniel's eyes, had screwed off his arms and legs as an experiment; that is, he had experimented on him as a mechanician would on a doll. This singular feature, which seems quite out of perspective in the picture of the Sand-Man, introduces a new castration-equivalent; but it also emphasizes the identity of Coppelius and his later counterpart, Spalanzani the mechanician, and

helps us to understand who Olympia is. She, the automatic doll, can be nothing else than a personification of Nathaniel's feminine attitude towards his father in his infancy. The father of both, Spalanzani and Coppola, are, as we know, new editions, reincarnations of Nathaniel's 'two' fathers. Now Spalanzani's otherwise incomprehensible statement that the optician has stolen Nathaniel's eyes so as to set them in the doll becomes significant and supplies fresh evidence for the identity of Olympia and Nathaniel. Olympia is, as it were, a dissociated complex of Nathaniel's which confronts him as a person, and Nathaniel's enslavement to this complex is expressed in his senseless obsessive love for Olympia. We may with justice call such love narcissistic, and can understand why he who has fallen victim to it should relinquish his real, external object of love. The psychological truth of the situation in which the young man, fixated upon his father by his castration-complex, is incapable of loving a woman, is amply proved by numerous analyses of patients whose story, though less fantastic, is hardly less tragic than that of the student Nathaniel.

Hoffmann was the child of an unhappy marriage. When he was three years old, his father left his small family, never to be united to them again. According to Grisebach, in his biographical introduction to Hoffmann's works, the writer's relation to his father was always a most sensitive subject with him.

9. 'Der Doppelgänger', *Imago*, vol. 3 (1914).
10. I cannot help thinking that when poets complain that two souls dwell within the human breast, and when popular psychologists talk of the splitting of the ego in an individual, they have some notion of this division (which relates to the sphere of ego-psychology) between the critical faculty and the rest of the ego, and not of the antithesis discovered by psycho-analysis between the ego and what is unconscious and repressed. It is true that the distinction is to some extent effaced by the circumstance that derivatives of what is repressed are foremost among the things reprehended by the ego-criticizing faculty.

11. In Ewers's *Der Student von Prag*, which furnishes the starting-point of Rank's study on the 'double', the hero has promised his beloved not to kill his antagonist in a duel. But on his way to the duelling-ground he meets his 'double', who has already killed his rival.

12. Heine, *Die Götter im Exil*.

13. P. Kammerer, *Das Gesetz der Serie*.

14. [*Beyond the Pleasure-Principle*. – Trans.]

15. Freud, 'Notes upon a Case of Obsessional Neurosis', Collected Papers, vol. 3.

16. Seligmann, the Hamburg ophthalmologist, has made a thorough study of this superstition in his *Der böse Blick und Verwandtes*, 2 vols (Berlin, 1910–1911).

17. Cf. my book *Totem und Tabu*, Part Four, 'Animismus, Magie und Allmacht der Gedanken'; also the footnote on p. 7 of the same book: 'It would appear that we invest with a feeling of uncanniness those impressions which lend support to a belief in the omnipotence of thoughts, and to the animistic attitude of mind, at a time when our judgement has already rejected these same beliefs.'

18. Cf. the abstract on p. ooo<p. 242 of t/s>.

19. Cf. *Totem und Tabu*: 'Das Tabu und die Ambivalenz'.

20. 'Sie ahnt, dass ich ganz sicker ein Genie, / Vielleicht sogar der Teufel bin.'

21. Cf. a fairy-tale of Hauff's.

22. As in Schaeffer's book mentioned above.

23. Since the uncanny effect of a 'double' also belongs to this class, it is interesting to observe what the effect is of suddenly and unexpectedly meeting one's own image. E. Mach has related two such observations in his *Analyse der Empfindungen* (1900, p. 3). On the first occasion he started violently as soon as he realized that the face before him was his own. The second time he formed a very unfavourable opinion about the supposed stranger who got into the omnibus, and thought, 'What a shabby-looking school-master that is getting in now.' I can supply a

similar experience. I was sitting alone in my *wagon-lit* compartment when a more than usually violent jerk of the train swung back the door of the adjoining washing-cabinet, and an elderly gentleman in a dressing-gown and a travelling cap came in. I assumed that he had been about to leave the washing-cabinet which divides the two compartments, and had taken the wrong direction and come into my compartment by mistake. Jumping up with the intention of putting him right, I at once realized to my dismay that the intruder was nothing but my own reflection in the looking-glass of the open door. I can still recollect that I thoroughly disliked his appearance. Instead, therefore, of being terrified by our doubles, both Mach and I simply failed to recognize them as such. Is it not possible, though, that our dislike of them was a vestigial trace of that older reaction which feels the double to be something uncanny?